Soviet-American Rivalry in the Middle East

Edited by J. C. Hurewitz

Published for
The Academy of Political Science
Columbia University
by

FREDERICK A. PRAEGER, *Publishers*
New York • Washington • London

FREDERICK A. PRAEGER, *Publishers*
111 Fourth Avenue, New York, N.Y. 10003, U.S.A.
5, Cromwell Place, London S.W.7, England

Published in the United States of America in 1969
by Frederick A. Praeger, Inc., Publishers

Library of Congress Catalog Card Number: 78-76866

Material in this book appeared in *Proceedings of The Academy of Political Science*, Vol. XXIX, No. 3. It had previously been presented at a conference held at Columbia University, December 13–14, 1968, and financed by a grant from The Ford Foundation.

Printed in the United States of America

Contents

Prefatory Note

No area of the world today presents such a great challenge to peace as does the Middle East. Age-old tensions among the nations there are made more acute by the rivalry of the Soviet Union and the United States.

The purpose of this volume is to outline the scope of Soviet-American rivalry in the Middle East, to set forth the problems the two nations face in their rivalry, to measure its impact upon the region, and to assess the results of alternative policies that these two powers may pursue in the decade ahead. The Academy takes no official position on these matters, but an objective discussion of the problems and the alternatives may help in deciding upon a sound course of action for the United States.

Professor J. C. Hurewitz was the director of the conference at Columbia University on December 13-14, 1968, at which some of the material presented here was discussed. He was also the editor of this volume. The Academy is deeply indebted to him for his imaginative programing, stimulating leadership, and careful attention to detail. The Academy was indeed fortunate to obtain his services for this undertaking.

The authors of the chapters in this volume are affiliated with various universities, research organizations, and government agencies. The views they express, however, are their own and do not necessarily reflect the position of the institutions with which they are associated.

The Academy also wishes to express its appreciation to the presiding officers and commentators for each of the conference sessions. The chairmen of the first day were: Colonel Amos A. Jordan, United States Military Academy, and Mr. Willard Thorp, Council on Foreign Relations; for the second day: Dr. Frederick H. Burkhardt, American Council of Learned Societies, and Dr. Joseph E. Johnson, Carnegie Endowment for International Peace. The commentators were Adam Yarmolinsky, Harvard Law School; Warner R. Schilling, Columbia University; Peter G. Franck, Syracuse University; Marvin Zonis, University of Chicago; Raymond A. Hare, Middle East Institute, Washington, D.C.; and Elie Kedourie, London School of Economics.

The Academy is grateful to The Ford Foundation for providing the financial support that made the conference and this volume possible, and to the Columbia Graduate School of Business, which generously made available the conference rooms.

ROBERT H. CONNERY
President

Origins of the Rivalry

J. C. HUREWITZ

The United States and the Soviet Union in the late 1960s seemed to be moving on a collision course in the heart of the Middle East. There the two superpowers became entrapped on opposing sides in interlocking regional disputes that almost defied rational analysis. The Arab states and Israel were starting the third decade of their irrepressible quarrel, ostensibly over Israel's right to existence, while the Arab states were tangled in their own irrepressible quarrels, ostensibly over differing political systems. In this highly charged zone, the superpowers were engaged after the mid-1950s in rivalry for prestige, position, and influence. In competing for favors, there was a danger that each superpower might become committed to upholding the security and integrity of opposing states and regimes.

In the Arab-Israel zone the Soviet Union was pursuing the diplomacy of polarization. In the hope of enlarging its own influence and destroying American influence in the Arab world, Russia proclaimed itself the patron and protector of the Arab cause in the dispute with Israel and advertised the United States as the patron and protector of Israel. The Russians made no bones about their endorsement of Arab claims. They did this by propaganda and, at the United Nations Security Council, by resort to the veto of all proposed resolutions favoring Israel and by the insistence on removing references of censure of the Arab states. While upholding Israel's right to existence with an implied guarantee of its survival, the United States countered with the diplomacy of antipolarization. The United States attempted to straddle the Arab-Israel issue and to cultivate the friendship of Arab states, especially those regimes which the military had not yet overturned.

The diplomacy of polarization proved versatile in the confusing interplay of politics even within the Arab area as such, where doctrinal divisions were taking shape. In the inter-Arab contest, the Soviet Union championed the military republics which Moscow hailed as the "progressive" Arab states, as contrasted with the "conservative" Arab states that became American protégés. The Arab military republicans were political radicals in the sense that they had seized power from civilians and from time to time called for the "liberation" of the remaining Arab regimes, which they labeled "reactionary" and "tools of Western imperialism." Though political radicals and sometimes socialists, the Arab military rulers were not necessarily progressive. None of the military republics, moreover, could point to solid achievement in social and economic reform, not even the United Arab Republic (UAR), as Egypt has been known since 1958. The UAR in the 1960s introduced the most wide-ranging socialist program in the Arab world. After prospering in the opening years, with the generous material support of both superpowers, the program began to falter after 1965, following the Egyptian alienation of the United States and the suspension of American aid.

In the rising competition over the Arab area, reactive diplomacy made the United States a consequential polarizer. The United States prodded the so-called conservative Arab regimes into launching welfare programs, and because of the continuity of the planning and the relative stability of the regimes, economic opportunities were expanded and social standards raised. This was as true of oil-dry states like Jordan (before June 1967) and Tunisia as of oil-soaked kingdoms like Saudi Arabia, Libya, and Kuwayt. But most of their leaders lacked popular appeal and seemed to be losing ground steadily in the Arab world at large.

The Russians, therefore, seemed to be gaining ground in the Arab world at the close of the 1960s. According to some observers, the Six Day War of June 1967 nearly accomplished the purpose of dislodging the United States from its positions of influence in the Arab countries. At the start of 1969, more than a year and a half later, the Arab military republics had not yet restored diplomatic relations with the United States, and American prestige among the other Arab states did not rise again to the prewar level.

Still, the Six Day War also dramatically illustrated that the superpowers had lost control—if it was ever theirs to exercise—over their clients, for Russia no less than the United States opposed open hostilities at the time. Yet the superpowers became captives of the arms races in the Arab-Israel zone, the most frenzied in the nonindustrial world. Starting immediately after the Arab defeat, the Soviet Union rearmed Egypt, partly by expensive airlift, at a probable cost to the Soviet treasury of no less than $500 million. Since the Egyptian economy could hardly finance the imports, even on an extended, interest-free installment plan, Russia apparently persuaded 'Abd al-Nasir to repay, in part, in political coin. The Soviet Mediterranean fleet was given storage and repair facilities, or the equivalent of naval base rights, at Alexandria and Port Sa'id; and Soviet pilots were allowed to fly Soviet-made planes with Egyptian markings on Soviet missions in the Mediterranean, representing the equivalent in Egypt of air-base rights.

Continuing its role as balancer in the entangling arms races in the Arab-Israel zone—between Egypt and Israel, between the Arab states and Israel, and among the Arab states between the Soviet-supplied "progressives" and the Western-supplied "conservatives"—the United States made good Jordan's losses after the 1967 war. Although the United States acted more tardily and less generously than the Soviet Union, the American intention to keep the Hashimi monarchy alive and to dissuade Jordan from becoming a Soviet military client could hardly escape notice. The United States also agreed at the end of 1968 to sell Israel F-4 Phantom jets, with delivery scheduled to begin a year later, thus enabling Israel to preserve its superiority in airpower among its neighbors.

In these bewildering, split-level arms races the suppliers were as deeply engaged as were the clients. The United States, particularly after the spring of 1967, openly favored the introduction of supplier restraints on arms transfers; but the Soviet Union rejected American overtures. The Russian delegate insisted on striking out of the resolution that the Security Council adopted in November 1967 a provision for restricting arms exports to the Arab states and Israel. No mention of arms control was made even in the

Soviet proposal for an Arab-Israel settlement, submitted to the United States, Britain, and France at the end of 1968.

The United States and the Soviet Union, it was often contended, did not want a military confrontation in the Middle East, and so none need ever take place. The superpowers eluded such a confrontation in the Suez crisis of 1956 and again in 1967. But now the Russians were losing flexibility in relations with their Arab arms clients; and by the rules of the superpower game in the Arab-Israel zone, the Americans were also likely to lose flexibility among their clients. Nor could the United States simply withdraw from the contest without destroying its influence altogether. If it is true, as Charles Yost has argued, "that no government plotted or intended to start a war in the Middle East in the spring of 1967,"[1] what would happen if such an unwanted war broke out again? Would the superpowers be able to stand aside?

Soviet-American rivalry in the Middle East reached beyond Israel and the Arab East. In the frontier zone comprising the non-Arab Muslim states (Turkey, Iran, Afghanistan, and Pakistan), Russia began challenging Western influence immediately after World War II, when Stalin was frustrated from seizing the Turkish Straits and dismembering Iran. Superpower tension in the zone remained high following the creation, on American and British initiative, of the Baghdad Pact in 1955 and its conversion four years later into the Central Treaty Organization (CENTO). Each of three regional members of CENTO (Turkey, Iran, and Pakistan) concluded a bilateral alliance with the United States. The competition after 1962 took a more benign form, as Moscow attempted to lure its non-Arab Muslim neighbors into "normalizing" their relations with the Soviet Union and into ending their alliances with the United States.

In North Africa, or the Maghrib (Libya, Tunisia, Algeria, and Morocco), at the western end of the Middle East, the Soviet-American contest was slowest to appear. The Russians gained an entering wedge in 1963 when Algeria signed its first arms contract with the Soviet Union. By 1968 the three former French dependencies were caught in their own arms race, minuscule and leisurely by Arab-

---

[1] Charles Yost, "The Arab-Israeli War: How it Began," *Foreign Affairs*, XLVI (January 1968), 319.

Israel standards but nonetheless disconcerting in North Africa, where the United States became Tunisia's arms provider, and both superpowers, arms purveyors to Morocco.

In many ways, even more serious than the arms-supplying contest in the Arab-Israel zone and in North Africa was the naval contest in the Mediterranean, a not wholly unrelated phenomenon. By establishing a continuous naval presence in the Mediterranean in the mid-1960s, the Soviet Union began to change the superpower military balance in the region. With the impending British disengagement from the Persian Gulf before the end of 1971, the Soviet-American rivalry was threatening to spread east of Suez.

II

Soviet-American rivalry in the Middle East, a postwar development, is still gathering momentum. It grew out of the wartime breakdown of the Soviet-sponsored buffer in the frontier zone and the progressive decline, after 1945, of British and French influence throughout the region.

The struggle began in the frontier zone as early as 1945, even before the last shot was fired in World War II. At that time Turkey, as a formal ally, was receiving military and economic aid from Britain, while Iran was still occupied by Russian and British troops. Of the three buffers, only Afghanistan upheld its neutrality throughout the war. Instead of trying to restore the buffers, Stalin in 1945 denounced the treaty of neutrality and nonaggression with Turkey and demanded joint Russian-Turkish management of the straits and the surrender of three provinces in the northeast adjacent to Soviet Armenia. With Red Army units still in Iran, he promoted the secession of Azarbayjan and Kurdistan in the northwest. Stalin's heavy-handed diplomacy deprived Russia of an opportunity to update the 1936 Montreux Convention, which regulated the use of the straits, and forced Russia to withdraw its troops from Iran with immense embarrassment, in the full international glare of the Security Council. It also drove Turkey, and later Iran, into intimate relations with the United States.

By the time that Nikita Khrushchev framed his strategy of peaceful coexistence, the two Muslim states along with Pakistan were already allied to the West. For differing reasons in the early 1960s, each Muslim ally of the United States became dissatisfied with American policies. As their friendship with the United States weakened, they responded variably to Soviet gestures of cooperation.

The overtures came after a prior period of experimentation with peaceful coexistence in Afghanistan. The informal accommodation there could be attributed, after the start of the Soviet military aid program in 1956, largely to the Afghan refusal to terminate the American educational mission that had been advising the government since 1952. The appearance of the Soviet military mission, however, touched off a lively superpower contest in economic aid. On the insistence of the Afghan government, the superpowers cooperated informally, often against their expressed wishes or intuitive inclinations. The most visible product of the friendly Soviet-American contest was the basic highway system that the superpowers built in the land-locked kingdom.

The experience in Afghanistan inured the superpowers to informal coordination of aid-giving and enabled Afghanistan's neighbors in the frontier zone to recognize the benefits of cultivating both superpowers. Pakistan became the first CENTO member to court the Soviet Union because of disillusionment over the military aid that the United States began giving India late in 1962, during its border war with China. The alliance with the United States virtually ended, however, only after the Indo-Pakistan war of 1965, when the United States suspended the export of arms to the subcontinent. In many respects, by the late 1960s, arms sales to Pakistan had become a Russian problem. Pakistan was trying to procure from the Soviet Union sophisticated weapons which the Indian government did not wish to see going to an adversary. Impelled to choose between the two, the Kremlin apparently acquiesced in the Indian demand, inducing Pakistan to fall back again on Communist China and to appeal to France.

Loss of confidence in the American commitment also spread to Iran, which established the firmest foundations in the frontier zone for expanding trade with the Soviet Union, based principally on the exchange of natural gas, a hitherto wasted resource, for capital goods. In 1967, for the first time, the shahdom also bought armored troop carriers and trucks from Russia. The purchase of nonsensitive weaponry was designed, some observers believed, as much to persuade the United States to sell Iran sophisticated items like Phantom jets as to open new channels for contingency procurement, if the United States were to withhold future exports for whatever reason.

Turkey remained the most cautious of the three. Despite unhappiness over its continuing high dependence on the United States and the West and the growing uncertainty of the American alliance, Turkey explored "normalization" with the Soviet Union only tentatively. Manifestly unwilling to weaken its ties with the United States, the Turkish government seemed to ignore the increasingly vocal protests by Turkish socialists against the American alliance.

The relaxed Soviet-American rivalry in the frontier zone in the late 1960s was essentially a projection of the limited détente in direct superpower relations, as enshrined in the nuclear test ban treaty, the arrangements for the hot line between Moscow and Washington, and the negotiation of the nuclear nonproliferation treaty. It was also a projection of the limited East-West accommodation in Europe. The Soviet Union seemed to be wedded once again to the notion of reconverting the frontier zone into a buffer, which had served the Russians well in the interwar years by keeping the great powers at a distance from a vulnerable boundary. If the reestablishment of a buffer were indeed the Soviet objective, the invasion of Czechoslovakia in August 1968 and the later enunciation of the Brezhnev Doctrine, which stipulated that any state may enter the Communist fraternity but none may leave it, set the cause back. Fear of Soviet motives was aroused among the Turks and the Iranians, possibly also the Afghans and the Pakistanis, and certainly the Americans and their European allies.

III

South of the frontier zone in Asia and stretching westward across North Africa, most of the Middle East countries in 1945 still fell under British and French rule. Saudi Arabia and Yemen, the only sovereign states in that part of the Middle East before then, were traditional monarchies whose political and diplomatic horizons were essentially limited to the Arabian Peninsula. Otherwise, from Morocco to Iraq, the Arab territories in an unbroken belt had been engulfed in the preceding century by the British and French empires. The European imperial systems in the Middle East, however, were seriously undermined after 1939, although Britain and France emerged from World War II determined to cling to their possessions.

The French imperial presence in the Arab East, it is true, barely survived the war. Lebanon and Syria became fully sovereign by 1946, when France finally withdrew its troops. But that retirement simply hardened France's desire to stay in North Africa. Britain, too, was slow to give up its dependencies, which—Libya apart—were located in the Arab East. The Arab League, which Britain helped create in 1945 in the expectation of enlarging its influence in the Arab world, turned immediately into an agency for promoting Arab political emancipation. Palestine became a test case. The Arab nationalists attributed to the machinations of the West—especially the United States but also Britain, the former mandatory power—and original sponsor of the Jewish National Home—the Arab failure to prevent the establishment of Israel. Britain's neutral position at the United Nations, between the inscription of the Palestine issue on the agenda of the General Assembly in the spring of 1947 and the negotiation two years later of the armistice system under the auspices of the Security Council, did not slow the pace of melting British prestige in the Arab world.

In the first postwar decade, Soviet-American rivalry in the Arab-Israel zone and in North Africa took place on the sidelines. Russia supported every move that would hasten the European imperial withdrawal and that would exclude any American presence. The United States endorsed the principle of national self-determination; yet it did not wish to weaken the position of its major allies, so as to procure access to British and French military bases and related facilities in time of need for the protection of common interests. A primary aim of American diplomacy, after the creation of NATO in 1949, was to find a formula for bringing its allies and itself into partnership with the newly sovereign states in matters of defense, and thereby contain the spread of Russian influence into the region.

In the pursuit of these aims, the United States favored collective measures. This invariably included the referral to the United Nations of disputes precipitated by the Arab struggles for independence in British and French imperial possessions. In the General Assembly and the Security Council, the superpowers upheld the principle of political freedom for dependent Arab territories. But the Soviet Union urged the immediate grant of sovereignty with or without imperial consent, while the United States advocated the grant of sovereignty on agreed terms only. By contrast with its position

at the United Nations, where the United States support of independence movements annoyed its allies, within the Arab Middle East
the United States accepted the leadership of Britain and France,
framing with them joint policies for regional security and economic
development. As early as May 1950, for instance, the three powers
issued a statement outlining a program for the Arab-Israel zone.
The Tripartite Declaration called for joint allied management of arms
exports to the area, based on estimated needs for internal security
and external defense; expressed vigorous opposition to the forcible
change of boundaries or armistice lines; and encouraged local participation in a Western-sponsored collective defense system for the
region, offering the prospect of generous supplies of modern arms as
an inducement. The United States, however, refused bids altogether
from states that were still locked in dispute with Britain and France,
preferring instead that the latter continue as the major suppliers
to their former political wards.

After earlier failures to bring the Western and Middle East states
into a single defense system, Britain and the United States finally
created the Baghdad Pact in 1955 under their exclusive patronage,
but only at a steep political cost. France was omitted largely because
its two allies regarded its North African policies as a liability in
negotiating with the Arabs. And because of its omission, France lost
resolve to work together with its allies on Middle East problems. The
inclusion of Iraq as a founding member outraged Egypt, which saw
in the pact an Anglo-American plot to promote the Hashimi monarchy as a rival leader in the Arab world. The inclusion of Pakistan
incensed Afghanistan, to say nothing of India. But, above all, the
creation of a Western alliance system, smack against Russia, infuriated
the Kremlin, which denounced the pact as a poor disguise for building
American military bases at its back doorstep.

Up to then the United States and its allies had assumed that
the Soviet Union would not offer modern arms to non-Communist states in the Middle East, and that even if it did, there would
be no Middle East takers. The formation of the Baghdad Pact gave
Russia its opportunity to prove the Western assumptions wrong. In
the Arab Middle East, the Soviet Union could trade on its psychological advantages, since, unlike the states in the frontier zone, no
Arab state touched Russian borders and none had ever experienced
Russian imperialism. The Soviet search for Arab friendship began

soon after the death of Stalin in 1953 with the Russian espousal at the United Nations of Arab claims in the dispute with Israel. The United States had been trying through its strategy of containment to commit the Arab states to the Western side. The obvious reply was noncommitment, on which, the Soviet Union insisted, its strategy of peaceful coexistence rested. In winning Egypt as a client on these terms in 1955, the Soviet Union destroyed the West's monopoly of the modern weapons market in the Middle East. In the year that followed, three other states—Syria and Yemen in the Arab-Israel zone and Afghanistan in the frontier zone—became Russian military clients. Thus, in the second postwar decade, the cold war strategies, shaped by the dominant members of the two major coalitions, became competitive in the Arab Middle East.

The Soviet policies aroused deep anxiety in the West. As a rival arms purveyor to Arab states, the Soviet Union catered to neutralism in the cold war. No longer was the Kremlin insisting that material aid could be given only to "progressive" regimes; the Russians even acquiesced in the suppression of local Communist parties and the arrest of their leaders. The scope of Russian diplomatic action was suddenly widened, as the number of independent Arab states multiplied. By the end of 1955, there were twelve sovereign states in the Middle East, as compared with only five a decade earlier, and six of the seven new states were situated in the Arab-Israel zone. Four more were added in the first four months of 1956, two apiece in the Arab-Israel zone and in North Africa. Until then, despite the quickening of disimperialism, the United States mediation between its imperial allies and the Arab nationalists, and its willingness—indeed eagerness—to play a subsidiary role had helped keep the Anglo-French system alive.

The Suez crisis late in 1956 marked the turning point. The United States' humiliation of Britain and France in compelling them to abandon their plans for the forcible seizure of the canal abruptly terminated the Anglo-French system. That act also brought to an end the collective responsibility of the three Western powers for the defense of common interests in the Arab-Israel zone. The United States almost inadvertently had assumed the role of primary defender of the Western cause in the region. Soviet-Western rivalry in the Arab-Israel zone had thus been transformed into Soviet-American rivalry. Despite the competition, it looked at first as if the United States was imposing a pax Americana on the region. The Eisenhower Doctrine of 1957, in stating that American armed forces would defend the sovereignty and territorial integrity of any Middle East country "requesting such aid against overt armed aggression from any nation controlled by International Communism," was in essence reaffirming as an exclusively American, if also limited, guarantee what had formerly been a tripartite one. But the American intervention in Lebanon in 1958, even in the absence of a probable threat from international Communism, in effect enlarged the range of the voluntary American obligation to restore peace anywhere in the Middle East. Neither the Soviet Union nor any of its Arab arms clients seemed prepared, until the start of the third postwar decade, to challenge the United States' self-proclaimed role as primary peacekeeper in the Middle East. In 1963, for instance, when Egypt seemed on the verge of widening the war in Yemen by attacking Saudi Arabia, the assignment on Saudi invitation of a small United States Air Force unit for temporary duty in the kingdom inhibited an adventurist Egyptian policy.

Despite differences in style, Soviet military aid policies in the Middle East were just as pragmatic as American policies, to which they were at the outset reactive. Soviet military aid to Afghanistan was designed not to arouse the enmity of the allies of the West in the frontier zone, but to persuade them that even the procurement of weapons from the Soviet Union need not be feared. And Russia seemed wholly unperturbed by its sponsorship of a program to modernize a prenationalist, traditional Muslim monarchy. In Egypt and Syria, as later also in Iraq, Algeria, and even Yemen, on the other hand, the Soviet Union hardly disguised its approval of efforts by its clients to overthrow neighboring Arab regimes that continued procuring weapons from the West. Into client Arab states the Soviet Union poured lavish amounts of modern arms, stirring up restiveness in the region and attempting to undermine American influence and prestige. The policy netted growing returns. Once the Soviet Union acquired an exclusive arms account in the Arab Middle East, it did not later lose the account—at least through 1968.

What is more, after the Soviet policy took hold in the Arab states, American policies became reactive, as the United States devised ways of keeping the Western clients satisfied. The United States, in effect, served as arms balancer, even though at first it preferred in most cases to have its allies sell the equipment. Thus until 1965, Jordan bought weapons from Britain with American funds, furnished, starting in 1957, as annual grants for budgetary support. In this period, France, Britain, and West Germany became the primary suppliers for Israel. Only in the mid-1960s did the United States become a direct major supplier, continuing its balancing role even after the Six Day War.

The rising levels of weaponry, in quantity and quality, tended to compound the tensions in the Arab-Israel zone. Each side in the interlocking arms races sought security by trying to change the local military balance in its favor. The suppliers which sought political influence through arms exports soon discovered that such influence was evanescent. Moreover, the contestants' resort to war in 1967 also threatened to lead to supplier confrontation. Clearly by the end of the 1960s the superpowers were taking progressively greater risks in failing to modify their competitive arms policies.

The Soviet Union, it should be noted, accepted payment for its arms in barter and in local currency. Soviet economic aid, primarily in the form of credits, was also repayable in barter and in local currency. As a cumulative consequence of these practices, the pattern of external trade of certain client states was redirected from heavy dependence on the West to even heavier dependence on the Soviet bloc. Indeed, the Egyptian economy in the late 1960s was becoming virtually subordinate to the Soviet economy. American economic aid was often grant aid, and even when it was not, as under the Public Law 480 sale of agricultural surplus, the American accumulation of local currency was used to stimulate local development projects or to encourage closer cultural ties with the United States.

IV

Strictly speaking, Soviet-American naval rivalry in the Middle East west of Suez was a phenomenon of the late 1960s, for only then did Russia establish a permanent naval presence in the Mediterranean. Russia had tried earlier to keep a handful of submarines in the Mediterranean, only to abandon the experiment after three years when Albania in 1961 withdrew berthing privileges at Valona, after Albania aligned itself with Communist China in the sharpening Sino-Soviet quarrel. The Soviet Union resumed the experiment at the start of 1963. In retrospect, it seems undeniable that the

Soviet security planners had decided to deploy in the Mediterranean a substantial and versatile force, as the ships became available and the mode of maintenance was worked out, in manifest emulation of the United States to consolidate Russia's role as a superpower and in manifest security interest to compete more effectively with its superpower rival in the Mediterranean and the Middle East.

The United States by 1963 had amassed the foremost fighting machine in the Mediterranean. The Sixth Fleet consisted of two task forces, each built around an attack aircraft carrier, a cruiser, several destroyers and submarines, amphibious assault ships, minesweepers, and logistic and operational support ships. The combat ships were equipped with guided missiles, and some with nuclear warheads, including IRBMs on the Polaris submarines that occasionally joined the fleet. Attached to the Sixth Fleet were marine battalions and, in a crisis, the commander could summon reinforcement from American garrisons in Europe. All three branches of the armed forces had taken part in the Lebanese landing of 1958, with infantry flown in from Germany. The vessels of the fleet practiced underway replenishment and repair, and the flagship divided its command time between sea and anchorage. The fleet headquarters at anchor were located, not in any existing or former British or French dependency, but at Villefranche (France) and after 1966, at Gaeta (Italy). A roving base, the fleet projected American naval and air power across the Mediterranean and the Middle East.

The jurisdiction of the Sixth Fleet, even after 1956, was limited essentially to the Mediterranean. East of Suez, the primary responsibility for defense of Western interests fell on the British Command with headquarters at Aden. With modest land, sea, and air forces strung along the southern and eastern coasts of the Arabian Peninsula, Aden became in the late 1950s Britain's principal base in southwest Asia. The United States maintained only a small naval squadron in the Persian Gulf, stationed on the Bahrayn Archipelago, still under British rule.

As the central element in the Western security system in the Mediterranean, the Sixth Fleet had substantially replaced British and French bases west of Suez after 1956. Although the United States deliberately refused land-based facilities that might invite nationalist agitation, it did not shun them altogether. On joining NATO in 1952, Turkey shared its military installations with the

United States and its NATO allies. Under the agreements, Turkey permitted the erection of an elaborate air-defense system almost within breathing distance of Russia; and farther east, a replica was installed at Peshawar, Pakistan. At the end of the 1950s, Turkey also authorized the United States to fix fifteen Jupiter or intermediate-range ballistic missiles to pads within reach of major Soviet targets. President John F. Kennedy ordered the removal of the missiles early in 1963, when Polaris submarines were becoming available for regular duty with the Sixth Fleet. The United States Strategic Air Command (SAC) had procured bases in Saudi Arabia, Libya, and Morocco to enable American long-range bombers—in the period before IRBMs and ICBMs—to deliver nuclear weapons to primary Soviet targets, in case of retaliatory need against nuclear attack by Russia. Use of the fields in Morocco and Libya, rented to the United States by France and Britain, was continued after independence by the successor states. Because of sensitive relations over the Arab-Israel dispute, the Dhahran field in Saudi Arabia never fulfilled the original American hope of becoming a fully developed SAC facility, remaining available only for transit and support activities.

As a force in the Mediterranean, the Sixth Fleet had a dual mission: deterrence of the Soviet Union and support for American diplomacy in the Middle East. For its strategic mission, the fleet maintained close liaison with NATO, through its naval headquarters in Naples. The diplomatic mission grew almost imperceptibly, as Britain and France progressively disengaged themselves from their former dependencies in the Middle East, until the end of 1956 when the United States found itself transformed suddenly into the primary guardian of Western interests in the region.

The Cuban crisis of October 1962, it is generally assumed, persuaded the security planners in Moscow that a Soviet fleet continuously deployed in the Mediterranean would reinforce Soviet diplomacy. The creation and growth of that fleet in the first half-dozen years was impressive. From a level of some twenty vessels, reached by the end of 1966, the size of the force was enlarged to thirty by the eve of the war in June 1967 and then by half as much again immediately after it. The Soviet Mediterranean fleet, which ranged between thirty-five and fifty-five vessels in 1968, included submarines, surface combat ships (guided-missile frigates, destroyers, landing craft, and for the first time even a helicopter carrier), electronic trawlers, and logistical support ships (tenders, oilers, and tugs). The Soviet naval force copied the American practice of refueling, replenishment, and repair at sea. It selected as anchorages more than a half-dozen protected bays in international waters near islands and the mainland right across the Mediterranean. These anchorages were retained even after June 1967, when Russia procured base privileges at Alexandria, Port Sa'id, and Latakiyah. Soviet units also paid courtesy calls at the ports of Algeria and Yugoslavia. Soviet ships even visited Malta for naval repairs on a commercial basis, since the dockyards at Valetta, idle after the closure of Suez, welcomed new sources of revenue.

Time and again after 1956 the Soviet Union publicly warned the United States that it would not abide American military and political paramountcy in the Middle East, so close to Russia. Accordingly, the Kremlin seemed to proceed from its premise of the desirability of clearing the vicinity of all competitive military capability to the logical conclusion that it had to neutralize the Sixth Fleet, or surpass it, or drive it out of the Mediterranean altogether. Russian arms export policies toward the Arab states, in part, aimed at weakening the Sixth Fleet by blocking its accessibility to important Arab coastal countries. The steady enlargement of the number of Soviet Arab clients led in most instances to the reduction of Western, particularly American, influence in these states. From all, the United States was totally barred after the Six Day War. At the same time, Soviet naval- and air-base rights in Egypt and Syria, and potentially also in Algeria, were intended to bolster Soviet military capability in the Middle East.

The Sixth Fleet, despite the Soviet gains, was far from neutralized. Nevertheless the military balance was changing. No longer was the Mediterranean a Western naval monopoly. The Soviet Mediterranean fleet was capable of interposing itself between a friendly Arab state and the Sixth Fleet or even of experimenting with intervention in such a state by local invitation. But such actions also courted military confrontation with the United States. More than that, the Soviet-American naval rivalry seemed on the verge of thrusting eastward, soon after the reopening of the Suez Canal. Indeed, it might already have begun, for Britain retired from Aden late in 1967, and soon thereafter announced its impending retirement from the Persian Gulf before the end of 1971.

V

The essays in this book seek to examine major aspects of postwar Soviet-American rivalry in the Middle East. For the purposes of analysis, the papers investigate four types of competition. In the section devoted to the superpower struggle for military supremacy, the interest lies mostly in an evaluation of the regional consequences of the flow of massive quantities of modern arms, coming increasingly from the superpowers and going largely to states that are tortured by regional disputes. Also considered in this section is the brisk naval competition between the United States and the Soviet Union, which has already transformed the naval profile of the Mediterranean from one that was predominantly British and French to one that has become predominantly American and Russian. The obvious problems for the 1970s are how to induce supplier action, with client consent, on curtailing arms exports to the Middle East and how to reduce the naval contest in the Mediterranean and prevent its spread east of Suez.

The papers on economic subjects explore the changing patterns of superpower aid and trade in the Middle East, particularly after 1955 when Russia first entered the regional competition. Arms transfers furnished one means of promoting bilateral commerce between Russia and selected Middle East states, since payment for the arms was arranged through barter agreements. On the American side, there was little direct interest in trade with the Middle East, and although American-owned companies dominated its oil production, only a small portion of the crude oil actually reached American markets. Based chiefly on easy credit, Soviet aid took the form mostly of export of capital goods and of such commodities as grain to Egypt that assured high political returns. Aid from the United States, though on a far bigger scale in the past than from all other extraregional countries combined, appears to be phasing out. The implications for the Middle East states, and for the United States influence in the region, of the possible disappearance of American economic aid in the 1970s are explored. Also assessed is the significance of heavy dependence by Egypt and other Arab states on trade with Russia.

The cultural contest receives separate treatment. Although the "slow" or educational media, in theory and under American law, have been independent, they have nevertheless in practice been placed overseas under the management of the "fast" or information-al media specialists. This equivocal condition, despite the clear intent, has in effect made the American export cultural program similar to the Soviet program, which has always been managed by the Communist party and tailored to its ideological line. The future conduct of amicable cultural rivalry between the superpowers in the Middle East is examined in the light of the repeated insistence by Soviet spokesmen that there can be no ideological peaceful coexistence. Still, there are lessons to be learned from the experience after 1956 in Afghanistan, where American educational missions have been working side by side, so to speak, with Soviet military missions.

The quest for stability is the theme of the essays on the political-diplomatic relationship between the superpowers in the Middle East. Political multipolarity combined with military and economic bipolarity obviously makes for unstable diplomacy. The problem is further compounded, because the Middle East seems to be vital to neither superpower. The question that must always be asked is: To what extent is each behaving simply as a superpower, and to what extent is each motivated by a national interest such as security, prestige, protection of economic investment, or cultural leadership? The advantages that the superpowers might expect to gain from a limited détente which by definition would fall short of erecting a multipolar system are explored. A limited détente might of course help stabilize superpower politics, while unstabilizing regional politics. But above all, attention is given to ways of bringing the bipolar military and economic capabilities of the superpowers into phase with the multipolar, political realities of the industrial world, so as to help create a stable international and regional system for the Middle East.

Struggle for Military Supremacy

Strategy and Arms Levels, 1945-1967

GEOFFREY KEMP

The purpose of this chapter is to outline the important factors that have influenced the supply of and demand for arms since 1945 in the various regions defined in this book as the Middle East. In particular, the strategic and political factors that have caused local countries to seek arms, and the policies of the United States and the Soviet Union toward arms supplies will be examined in the hope of clarifying the intricate and often oversimplified relationships between arms supplies and cold war strategies in the Middle East.

Many countries in the Middle East did not exist as sovereign states in 1945. The postwar years witnessed a remarkable redistribution of military and political power throughout the area. The most significant factor was de-colonization. Not only did de-colonization create new states in its wake, but also, new conflicts, varying in intensity from the India-Pakistan wars and the Palestine dispute to the recent troubles in South Yemen and in Sudan. The Soviet Union and the United States have both shown concern over the years lest either side be drawn into a local Middle East conflict and thereby forced to confront each other on opposite sides.

It is important to appreciate that the cold war policies of the great powers have exacerbated existing local conflicts, which in turn have led to greater pressures for armaments.

Another point worth stressing has been the relative weakness of Soviet military power in this area, especially in the period 1945-1967. The Soviet Union has had no overt defense treaty with any of the countries in the Middle East since 1945. Balanced against this, the United States has had bilateral defense treaties with Turkey, Iran, Pakistan, and military-base agreements with Morocco, Libya, and Saudi Arabia. Britain has had treaties and base rights in many Middle East countries over the years. The Soviet Union has never fought a major war in the area, and until recently had virtually no capacity to intervene speedily with military force in the area beyond Turkey, Iran, and Afghanistan.

Arms Levels in the Middle East

The Middle East is the most highly armed area in the nonindustrial world, as a consideration of the raw statistics of military equipment reveals. The gross figures are impressive; since 1945, at least 2,700 jet combat aircraft have been delivered by the industrial powers to the countries in the area; at least 4,000 tanks have been transferred, along with hundreds of thousands of mortars and artillery pieces, and literally millions of small arms. Very few warships have found their way into local inventories, but this could change in the next decade, especially in terms of smaller missile-firing and patrol boats.

Before 1955, Britain supplied arms to eight countries in the area, including Egypt, Iraq, Israel, and Pakistan, and had military bases in several other countries. The United States supplied arms to three countries: Iran, Pakistan, and Turkey; France supplied arms to Israel. In 1955, the Soviet Union joined the ranks of major donors, and by 1967 was supplying ten countries; the United States was supplying nine; Britain, at least twelve; France, six; and Communist China, one. However, by 1967, the United States and the Soviet Union were responsible for most of the bulk deliveries, especially to the countries with the largest armed forces: Algeria, Egypt, Iran, Iraq, Israel, and Pakistan. The exception was France, which until late 1967, was the sole supplier of combat aircraft to Israel.

The aggregate totals of weapons delivered to the area neither reflect the total number of weapons in operational service at any given time, nor do they reflect the respective capabilities of the recipients to wage war. Many weapons were destroyed in the India-Pakistan wars of 1948 and 1965, the Arab-Israel wars of 1948, 1956, and 1967, the Yemen, Iraqi and Sudanese civil wars, the Algerian-Morocco conflict of 1963, and other, smaller, skirmishes. Further, weapons have had to be replaced because of obsolescence and attrition.

To understand the pattern of weapons acquisitions, it is necessary to examine the inputs over time, and try to separate weapons transfers due to normal replacement, those due to losses in warfare, and those that represent a net increase in respective force levels.

There is not space here to present a detailed, quantitative analysis of arms transfers to the Middle East since 1945. However, sufficient study has already been done on the subject to suggest that the most significant factors influencing overall force levels over the past twenty years have been the build-up of armed forces in Turkey, Iran, and Pakistan by the United States as part of its forward-defense strategy, the large inputs of arms into Egypt, Iraq, Syria, and Algeria between 1956 and 1967 by the Soviet Union, and the continued weapons procurement policies of Israel. These eight recipient countries have accounted for well over 90 per cent of the major weapons delivered to the twenty Middle East countries.

More interesting, but less understood, are some of the qualitative features of these arms transfers. Arms transfers to the big-five recipients, Turkey, Pakistan, Egypt, Israel, and Iran, have included some of the most sophisticated weapons available to any country in the world. For instance, Iran is currently receiving F-4 Phantoms from the United States; Israel will start receiving this aircraft late in 1969. The F-4 is a fourth-generation Mach-2, multipurpose, jet combat aircraft. It has excellent performance characteristics and unlike most modern Soviet aircraft, has been well tested in battle (Vietnam). To give some idea of the advanced qualities of the Phantom, major powers such as Britain, West Germany, and Japan have recently placed large orders for it, and it has still to enter service with their armed forces. Similarly, the French Mirage IIIs, in service in Israel and Pakistan, are by any accounts excellent systems and are still to be found on the front line in the air forces of France, Switzerland, and Australia. The Soviet Union has transferred some of its latest support fighters to Egypt, including the Su-7, many interceptors that are in service with its own forces (the MIG-21), and hundreds of modern T-54 and T-55 tanks. Britain has sold Mach-2 interceptors (the Lightning) to Saudi Arabia and Kuwayt, and has recently negotiated agreements for the supply of advanced surface-to-air missile systems to Libya and Iran.

Only in the field of surface-to-surface missiles and warships has the qualitative pace of the arms build-up in the Middle East fallen

TABLE 1

Changing Pattern of Suppliers to Major Middle East Countries
1945-1954 (in Roman) and 1955-1968 (in Italics)

(Figures in parentheses indicate approximate number delivered when known.)

Recipient	Jet Aircraft	Tanks	Warships
Algeria*	—	—	—
	USSR (200)	USSR	USSR
Egypt	GB (100)	GB, US	GB (7)
	USSR (800+)	USSR (1,200)	USSR (15), GB (1)
Iran	—	US	GB (1)
	US (200)	US	GB (3)
Iraq	GB (30)	GB, US	GB (7)
	USSR (200)	USSR (500+)	USSR
Israel	GB (20), FR (12)	GB, FR	GB (2)
	FR (400), US (40)	US (350), GB (100+), FR (100+)	GB (4)
Jordan	GB (20)	GB	—
	GB (20), US (5)	US (200), GB (200)	—
Morocco*	—	—	—
	USSR (20), US (20), FR (20)	USSR, FR	GB (1)
Pakistan	GB (20)	US	GB (3)
	US (200+), China (50)	US, China	GB (7), US (1)
Saudi Arabia**	—	—	—
	GB (30), US (20)	US, FR	—
Syria	GB (20)	GB	—
	USSR (250)	USSR (500)	USSR
Turkey	US	US	US
	US (500+)	US (600+)	US (20+)

*Not independent in 1954.
**Received no major weapons during 1945-1954.

Notes

Jet aircraft figures include jet combat aircraft and armed jet trainers, acquired by purchase, grant, or licensed production.

Tanks include light, medium, and heavy tank designations only.

Warships include aircraft carriers, cruisers, destroyers, escorts, submarines, and missile-firing patrol boats.

Source: *Arms to Developing Countries 1945-65* and *The Military Balance 1965-68*,
Institute for Strategic Studies.

behind developments in Europe, the United States, and the Soviet Union. So far, the United States and the Soviet Union have shown marked reluctance to give their clients advanced conventional offensive missiles. Egypt's much talked of surface-to-surface missile program has not been supported by the Soviet Union, but has been developed by engineers recruited on the open market in Western Europe. Only Israel has cooperated with a major government, France, for the development of a surface-to-surface missile, the MD-626, although the delivery of the finished product to Israel remains in doubt, owing to the ambivalence of French arms export policies.

Although a great many advanced weapons have entered the inventories of Middle East powers, it would be wrong to assume that the recipients, with the exception of Israel and possibly Turkey and Pakistan, have, or have had, the capability to use them effectively in sustained combat operations. The Arab-Israel war of 1967 indicated that mere possession of sophisticated weaponry is not enough to win wars. The India-Pakistan war of 1965 demonstrated a different lesson; although some less developed countries may be competent at operating advanced weapons, they are still very dependent upon outside sources for those crucial elements in all military operations, spare parts, and major servicing (the exception would be India).

Not mentioned so far, but very important in most conflicts, are small arms (rifles, machine guns, mortars, and grenades). These weapons have long durability, are very easy to obtain and to hide, and have great effectiveness in battle. The market for small arms is huge; at least twenty industrial powers outside the Middle East manufacture and export them to various regions in the world. Israel and Egypt have their own ordnance factories, and most criminal organizations in the Middle East conduct a lucrative trade smuggling small arms and ammunition from conflict to conflict.

Factors Influencing Demand for Arms

Unless there had been a high level of demand for armaments in the Middle East since 1945, the high levels of supply would not have been possible. It is therefore important to look at the demand market before discussing the role of suppliers. The factors that have influenced the demand for arms in the Middle East have varied from zone to zone. Each country has had different perceptions regarding the role of the armed forces in its search for security; each has had different foreign policy goals and relations with local and external powers, quite apart from varying amounts of political and economic resources with which to barter for or buy arms. Nevertheless, three broad reasons for seeking arms have been evident: internal security, external military contingencies, and prestige. In many cases all three reasons have contributed towards demand in a particular country. Prestige plays a very important part in Arab politics, and the need to "show the flag" on National Parade Day has often resulted in the transfer of more advanced systems than have been suitable for a country's existing security commitments and technical base.

In order to indicate some of the less general factors which influenced strategic planning and arms procurement, it is necessary to make brief reference to the security problems of the major groupings of countries within this vast region.

Morocco and Algeria used arms against each other in 1963 over Morocco's irredentist claims to parts of Algeria's southwestern borderlands. Since 1963, both countries have increased their weapons inventories as a result of French, United States, and Soviet assistance to Morocco, and Soviet assistance to Algeria. However, the rate of acquisition of modern weapons, especially jet aircraft and tanks, by Algeria has increased substantially since June 1967. Algeria's growing reputation as a "revolutionary" power has caused concern in Morocco, Tunisia, and Libya. The three moderate Maghribi countries with their strong links with the West have sought to redress the nominal military balance in Algeria's (and Egypt's) favor by seeking further political and military support in the West. Libya's recent agreement with Britain for a $200 million air-defense system has to be seen in terms of the inter-Arab rather than the Arab-Israel military context.

Egypt, Syria, Iraq, Jordan, and Israel form the nucleus of the Arab-Israel conflict. In addition to their confrontation with Israel, the Arab countries have had to concern themselves with other military contingencies over the past twenty years. Though Israel's military power is presently the most important factor influencing strategic planning and weapons requirements in Egypt, Iraq was a serious rival as late as 1958. Between 1956 and 1967, Egypt's relations with Saudi Arabia steadily deteriorated, owing to their respective support for the republicans and royalists in the Yemen civil war. In this conflict Egypt deployed more than 60,000 troops in

Yemen, and diverted combat units and logistics resources that could have been used to bolster her capabilities against Israel. Over 50,000 Egyptian troops were still in Yemen at the time of the June 1967 war. Syria and Iraq have both had to earmark large numbers of their armed forces to keep order in the home capital. The instability of successive Syrian governments and the continuing Kurdish insurgency in Iraq must be seen as factors influencing demand for military equipment. In addition, Iraq has made claims against Kuwayt and Iran, and in 1961 precipitated a major crisis which caused the British to deploy troops in Kuwayt.

Israel is a case by itself. Israel's small size, urban society, its advanced industrial base, and the recent history of the Jewish people, have persuaded Israel planners to rely upon the use of overwhelming and effective military force to secure the two most important ob-

TABLE 2

Military Force Levels, Defense Expenditures, and GNP in the
Major Middle East Countries, September 1968

	Estimated GNP, 1967 (billions)	Defense Expenditures, 1968-1969 (millions)	Percentage of GNP, 1967	Army	Navy	Air Force
				(Total strength in thousands)		
Maghrib						
Algeria	$ 2.6	$173	4.9	55.0	1.5	2.0
Morocco	2.8	150	3.6	50.0	1.0	3.0
Frontier						
Iran	7.0	495*	5.5	200.0	6.0	15.0
Pakistan	13.1	514*	3.6	300.0	9.0	15.0
Turkey	10.1	472*	4.6	425.0	39.0	50.0
Arab-Israel						
Egypt	5.1	690	12.7	180.0	12.0	15.0
Iraq	2.2	252	10.3	70.0	2.0	10.0
Israel	3.6	628*	13.8	29.0**	3.0**	8.0**
Jordan	0.5	81	12.8	53.0	.25	1.75
Saudi Arabia	2.4	321	11.9	30.0	1.0	5.0
Syria	1.05	137	11.9	50.0	1.5	9.0

* Sum budgeted for defense.
**When fully mobilized: Army, 275,000; Navy, 6,000; Air Force, 14,000.

Note
Force levels are not inclusive and do not represent "in commission" systems. This is particularly true of the reformed forces of Algeria, Egypt, Jordan, and Syria.
Source: *The Military Balance 1968-69*, Institute for Strategic Studies.

jectives of its military strategy: first, to deter the Arabs from using force as a means of solving the Palestine problem; second, given that this deterrence fails, to ensure that Israel can win the ensuing war with the minimum number of Israel casualties. These objectives are very different from those of the Arab states, who can afford much larger losses in battle and still feel confident of winning the long-term conflict. Israel cannot afford a pyrrhic victory; casualties in the tens of thousands would seriously undermine the future security of the state of Israel. For this reason, and others, Israel has consistently placed emphasis upon a high level of sophisticated armaments to secure her objectives. Until such time as there can be a guaranteed peace between Israel and the Arab states, no Israel leader can conceive of giving up the quest for military superiority based upon highly trained manpower and advanced weapons systems.

Given these asymmetric strategic perceptions, Israel has always attempted to keep ahead of the Arab countries in qualitative terms. Her highly educated population has so far ensured her superiority in terms of trained military manpower, and her strong lobby in Western Europe and the United States has so far ensured her the weapons.

Although the three forward-defense countries—Turkey, Iran, and Pakistan—have been members of Western military alliances since the mid-1950s and have had bilateral defense treaties with the United States, it would be wrong to assume that defense planning in these countries, especially Iran and Pakistan, has been solely preoccupied with the Soviet "threat." The value of the alliances to the local powers, especially CENTO, has been measured in economic rather than military terms.

Being a member of NATO, as well as CENTO, Turkey has had more formal links with the United States than Iran or Pakistan, and has played a more active role in inter-allied military cooperation. This can partly be explained by the NATO command structure which does not exist in CENTO. The levels of United States arms supplied to Turkey have been very high. United States military assistance during the period 1950-1966 has been valued at $2.3 billion. With over half a million men under arms and over 500 combat aircraft now in service, Turkey has remained the most strongly armed country in the Middle East since 1945.

Though Turkish defense planners have focused primarily upon the NATO contingency plan, the dispute with Greece over Cyprus nearly led to fighting in 1964 and 1967. Consequently the relative levels of United States arms supply to Greece and Turkey for NATO purposes are watched suspiciously in Athens and Istanbul.

The danger that aid recipients will not use military-assistance grants for the purposes stipulated by the donor has particular relevance to United States arms policy toward Iran and Pakistan. Iran's armed forces, like Turkey's, have been modernized and strengthened almost entirely with United States assistance, which amounted to $670 million between 1950-1966. The Shah of Iran was prepared to accept United States aid in large quantities after the fall of Dr. Muhammad Musaddiq in 1953. The supply of United States equipment was further accelerated in 1958, after the coup d'etat in Iraq, which overthrew the Hashimi monarchy, and led to Iraq's withdrawal from CENTO. The Shah's reason for accepting United States aid (both military and economic) was simple: first, there was a genuine fear of the Soviet Union, because of the Azarbayjan crisis of 1946, and the historic Russian desire for an outlet to the Indian Ocean. Second, the Shah's internal support depended upon his ability to ensure the loyalty of the army. For this reason, he had to see that the pay and weapons of the army were improved. Iran also has had to consider the vulnerability of its vital oil facilities and the sea routes in the Persian Gulf to possible hostile action by local Arab powers. It would be wrong to suggest that the oil installations could be literally defended by military force—they are far too vulnerable for that—but Iran's ability to strike back at a potential aggressor with offensive air, land, and sea power has made some sense in military terms. The eventual British withdrawal from the Gulf has already led to an increase in Iranian procurement of naval forces. As an oil-rich state, Iran has gradually received less military assistance from the United States, and now has to pay for most of its purchases on a long-term credit basis.

Pakistan, too, has been prepared to accept large inputs of United States military equipment over the years, for reasons that have not been directly related to Soviet or Chinese "aggression." The primary concern of Pakistani and Indian defense planners in the 1950s and early 1960s was the threat posed by each other's armed forces. Pakistan was quite prepared to modernize its armed forces with United States help, under the guise of the CENTO and SEATO alliances, knowing full well that its main enemy was India.

The lessons of the Pakistani and Iranian experiences are clear. Factors influencing demand in aid-recipient countries often have little to do with the reasons given by the United States for supplying the equipment.

Not mentioned so far are the many smaller countries, including Afghanistan, Sudan, and South Yemen. Until 1967, the armed forces of these countries existed primarily for internal security purposes. However, one area where this phenomenon is already under change is the Persian Gulf littoral, where not just Iran, Iraq, and Saudi Arabia are improving their armed forces, but also the Trucial States, Bahrayn, Kuwayt, and South Yemen. The evolution of force levels in that area, has, in the past, always been a function of inter-Arab rather than great power quarrels. Saudi Arabia's major reequipment program in 1965 was undertaken with an Egyptian threat in mind.

Factors Influencing the Supply of Weapons Since 1945

In the early and mid-1950s, when the two mainstays of United States strategic policy were the military alliance systems and the nuclear deterrent, Middle East real estate was of great significance to United States defense planners. The purpose of creating a military-alliance system including Turkey, Iran, and Pakistan (and until 1958, Iraq) along the northern tier of the Middle East was threefold: first, to improve the capabilities of the local armed forces to hopefully assist in the containment of the Soviet Union, should it ever decide to march south (this went under the guise of "collective self-defense"); second, to provide some measure of internal stability for the regimes in the alliance, by the provision of economic and military assistance; and third, to provide the United States with bases in Turkey, which were then essential to ensure the effectiveness of the nuclear deterrent built around B-47 medium bombers and Jupiter missiles which had insufficient range to reach the Soviet heartland from the continental United States.

The use of United States military aid to support non-Communist powers and secure base rights was not restricted to the forward-defense areas: Iraq, Morocco, Lebanon, Libya, Jordan, Saudi Arabia, and Tunisia have all received amounts of United States military assistance, although not all contained United States military bases.

However, contrary to popular belief, the United States has not pursued a particularly aggressive military-assistance program in those areas of the Middle East that did not fall into the forward-defense category. In 1950, the United States, Britain, and France signed a Tripartite Declaration, which was designed, among other things, to prevent an arms race among the major local powers in the Middle East, in particular Egypt, Iraq, and Israel. One result of the Western policy on arms supplies was to persuade Prime Minister Gamal 'Abd al-Nasir of Egypt in 1955 that only the Soviet Union would provide him the arms he needed to challenge Iraq for the political leadership of the Arab world. Thus one contributing factor to the 1955 Egyptian-Soviet arms deal was Western *restraint* on arms supplies. Similarly, the United States-British arms embargo toward India and Pakistan after the 1965 war persuaded both local powers that they could no longer rely on the major Western suppliers in times of crisis. As a result, both diversified their sources; Pakistan turned to Communist China for some aircraft, and India purchased more Soviet equipment. The United States was reluctant to become a primary arms supplier to Israel, and it was not until 1963 that a major United States-Israel agreement was signed for Hawk air defense missiles. It must be admitted, though, that prior to 1963, the primary United States support to Israel had been symbolized by the awesome presence of the United States Sixth Fleet in the Mediterranean, then completely unchallenged by the Soviet Union.

The evidence of the past twenty-eight years in the Middle East suggests that United States arms transfers made free of charge, or on very generous credit terms, have given the United States some influence with the recipient though not always as much as it hoped for. For instance, there is no doubt that the United States policy of supporting the shah of Iran has been successful so far. The shah remains on the throne of Iran and loyal to the West. But United States policy has not prevented the Soviet Union from making considerable inroads in Iran such as the 1967 arms agreement with Iran for armored troop carriers and trucks.

The United States has also had to bear in mind the trade-offs which occur among itself, the recipient of its arms, and a third country, which may be friendly toward the United States, but hostile towards the arms recipient. The Middle East provides several illuminating examples of this phenomenon, the "domino effect" of arms transfers. Up to 1965, the United States supplies to Pakistan were part payment for United States base rights in the country and were, according to official United States policy, to be used in the event of an attack on Pakistan by a major Communist power. As suggested earlier, Pakistan's number-one enemy in the area was India. Throughout the 1950s and early 1960s India complained to the United States that Pakistan would violate the supposed United States restrictions on the use of its equipment, and fight India with United States arms. After the Chinese invasion of India in 1962, the United States gave small quantities of military aid to India, and in turn, incurred the wrath of Pakistan. The war of 1965 confirmed the worst fears of both sides; Pakistan *did* use its United States equipment against India. The United States responded by cutting off aid to both India and Pakistan.

The Soviet Union's first major breakthrough into the Western monopoly of arms supplies to the Middle East came with the 1955 Egyptian deal mentioned earlier. From both a military and political standpoint, this was an extremely significant watershed. In military terms, it had serious implications for Israel and France (Egypt was used as a base to smuggle arms to the Algerian insurgents). In political terms, the deal represented a major change in Soviet foreign policy, demonstrating the Soviet Union's resolve to become embroiled in the affairs of the non-Communist Middle East. After the initial deal with Egypt in 1955, the Soviet Union rapidly extended its military equipment programs to other countries in the area, Syria (in 1955), Afghanistan and Yemen (1956), Iraq (1958), Morocco (1961), Algeria (1962), Cyprus (1964), South Yemen and Sudan (1967), and probably Pakistan in 1969.

It was relatively easy for the Soviet Union to obtain a bridgehead in the Middle East in the mid-1950s, symbolized by arms supplies. Not only had the West tried to exploit its monopolistic position by refusing to supply more than nominal amounts of arms to the local powers, but the West committed two further errors as seen from the Arab perspective: it sided with Iraq against Egypt, and persuaded Iraq to join the nefarious Baghdad Pact; and it openly supported Israel. In doing so, the West failed, in part, to recognize the power, significance, and the essentially non-Communist nature of Arab nationalism.

It has been suggested that the Soviet Union has displayed a more provocative and irresponsible policy toward arms supplies to the Middle East than the United States; the supply of Tu-16 medium bombers, Il-28 light bombers, and the Styx ship-to-shore missiles to Egypt and Syria are usually quoted in this context. However, it must be remembered that though the United States may not so far have supplied such large quantities of weapons to the countries participating in the Arab-Israel dispute, France has supplied Israel with light bombers and missiles, and the United States itself has used territory in the Middle East for what has been construed as provocative acts both against the Middle East countries themselves and the Soviet Union. The deployment of nuclear missiles in Turkey, the U-2 flights over the Soviet Union from Pakistan and Turkey, and even the Lebanon landings of 1958 can all be cited in this context.

There is evidence to suggest that the Soviet policy on military assistance to the Arab countries in the Middle East was based, at least up to June 1967, on political expediency rather than a wish to develop effective military forces in recipient countries. It is difficult to avoid the conclusion that Soviet arms-transfer policies to the Arab countries have primarily been motivated by a desire to win overwhelming influence in several "progressive" states, which, for one reason or another, had abandoned significant links with the West (Egypt, Algeria, Iraq, and Syria). This influence has been achieved by supplying large quantities of modern arms, but until late June 1967, very little support and training facilities. In short, it has not been Soviet policy to provide its clients with what, in Western terms, would be considered a totally satisfactory military capability. Soviet policy has also aimed to win influence in several conservative countries which still retain strong links with the West (Iran, Morocco, and Pakistan) by supplying token amounts of arms. Only since the war of June 1967 does the Soviet Union seem to have adopted a more rigorous United States style of military assistance.

However, the Soviet Union appears on occasion to have oversupplied arms, especially small arms, to its clients—particularly Egypt and Algeria. This has led to talk of a Soviet "warehouse" policy. Egypt has been used as a base for funneling arms to support "progressive" wars in Africa and Asia (Yemen, Algeria, and Congo), but also civil wars, such as Nigeria. (It is Soviet and Czech supplied Egyptian aircraft and bombs together with British small arms that are being used against Biafra.) It has also been suggested that the present high level of Soviet arms transfers to Algeria should not be viewed as an attempt to build up the Algerian forces—they could never absorb these amounts of equipment—but to store weapons, especially aircraft and tanks to be used by Egypt in a future war with Israel.

It is not easy to make a direct comparison between the United States and Soviet arms supply policies to the Middle East in the context of the cold war, since neither power has competed with the other for the major role of supplier in the five highest armed countries. The Soviet Union replaced Britain and France as major supplier to Egypt, Syria, and Iraq after 1955. The United States never served as a major supplier to any of these Arab states. Since 1955 both suppliers have attempted to win influence with arms without becoming overcommitted politically to the regimes in the Maghrib area. However, only the Soviet Union has attempted the tricky game of supplying both Morocco and Algeria.

In the central Arab countries (Egypt, Syria, and Iraq), the Soviet Union has shown far more willingness to be the sole supplier, and thereby run risks of involvement in times of crisis (or equally run the risk of criticism for noninvolvement in times of crisis). The United States, however, has been a cautious supplier to Israel, Jordan, and Saudi Arabia, and has encouraged Britain and France to continue to play an active role in these countries with respect to the supply of military equipment. As for the forward-defense areas of Iran and Pakistan, the Soviet Union has only recently attempted to use arms supplies as bait for better political and economic relations. In 1967, the shah of Iran signed the agreement with the Soviet Union for $100 million worth of army equipment. Similarly, there have been the reports that Pakistan will sign a limited agreement with the Soviet Union for arms. Neither of these developments is startling. Iran has long wished to sever *some* of its close links with the United States, while, of course, remaining on the best of terms and keeping the defense treaty, and wants to do so all the more now that Britain has decided to leave the Persian Gulf. Pakistan ceased to have strong links with the United States after 1965, and from that time has sought to diversify her arms supplies by turning to Communist China, France, and occasionally Iran as well as the United States and the Soviet Union.

Since 1956, the primary purpose of British and French arms sales to the Middle East has been commercial. The oil-rich countries, Israel and Pakistan, have provided a welcome market for hard-pressed

European arms manufacturers. In the past two years, Britain has secured orders worth over $500 million from Iran, Saudi Arabia, Libya, and Kuwayt. France has had lucrative contracts with Israel, Lebanon, and Pakistan.

Both countries have attempted to relate their political objectives in the area to their commercial arms sales. France's decision in June 1967 to embargo the Mirage-V sale to Israel can be seen as an attempt to win more influence, both commercial and political, in Arab countries, and force the United States to assume the responsibility of being prime supplier of arms to Israel. Britain has consistently emphasized the defensive qualities of the major weapons it has supplied to the area—interceptors, surface-to-air missiles, anti-tank missiles—though this argument does not stand up under careful analysis since it is not possible to treat the performance characteristics of one weapons system in isolation from other systems in the inventory. If surface-to-air missiles "protect" an airfield containing offensive strike aircraft, they play a crucial role in the conduct of offensive operations.

Conclusion

The patterns of arms transfers to the Middle East since 1945 have varied in quantity and quality from region to region. The United States has remained the predominant supplier to Turkey and Iran. Since 1955 the Soviet Union has been responsible for the big build-up of forces in Egypt, Iraq, and Syria; Britain, France, and the United States have shared the task of maintaining high numbers of weapons in Israel. If the Soviet Union decides to supply Pakistan with arms, that country will have received equipment from five great powers in the past decade.

The entangling relationship between arms supplies and local conflicts is one of the most significant features of the transfer patterns. Arms originally supplied to one country for the specific purposes of internal security or alliance contingencies have often caused nervous neighbors to seek for some reciprocity to offset the possibility that the arms could be used against them rather than designated third parties. The "domino" effect of arms transfers can be discerned in the Maghrib, the Arab-Israel conflict, and the India-Pakistan conflict.

Although the quantity and quality of arms found in the Middle

East has been extremely high, none of the local powers have had the capacity to produce any significant number of advanced weapons systems. Israel, Egypt, Pakistan, and Turkey have all developed a small armaments industry and servicing facilities, but for the next decade it is highly improbable that any power will be self-sufficient in weapons production. For this reason the external powers, especially the United States and Soviet Union, will have to continue to weigh the risks of supplying arms to their clients against the possibility that to deny them arms will make it easier for the other, or a third party, to win influence by assuming the role.

The evidence of the past twenty years neither confirms nor rejects the thesis that there is a strong correlation between competitive arms supplies under the rubric of the cold war to a conflict region and the likelihood of an outbreak of hostilities. The two most serious conflicts, India-Pakistan and Arab-Israel, have both been fueled by a wide number of donors. The United States and Britain have supplied arms to both parties in these disputes. Nor is it possible to generalize about the degree of political influence purchased from arms supplies. However, the evidence would suggest a negative correlation; to cut off arms supplies to a recipient that faces well-armed adversaries loses the original donor considerable influence in the short run.

Arms Transfers and Arms Control

LINCOLN P. BLOOMFIELD
AMELIA C. LEISS

The Middle East is a huge, complex area, stretching from the Atlantic Ocean to the borders of Burma. It has been the scene of five major interstate wars in the past five years, and at least five of the countries in the area have been engaged in civil wars in this same period (see Figure 1). Nor are the prospects bright for peace in the coming decade. Precise predictions would be presumptuous, but Figure 2 suggests a not unreasonable clustering of conflict groupings that have some probability of degenerating into hostilities over the next ten years.

The volatility of the area is obvious. It is into this inflammable situation that the great powers, in their search for influence, bases, and markets, have intruded their own competition and rivalries. The supply of arms is a major means for external states to manipulate developments in the area to their own advantage—or so they customarily believe.

Let it be said at the outset that the issues that divide the states in this area and that lead to their wars are local issues, not having their genesis in the quarrels of the arms suppliers. Indeed, it was the existence of local rivalries and animosities that created the opportunity for external states to meddle in local affairs. It was the presence of so many local conflict situations that helped to ensure that the supply of

This paper is based in part on research conducted under a contract with the U. S. Arms Control and Disarmament Agency, but the judgments expressed are those of the authors and do not necessarily reflect the views of that agency.

arms—a commodity for which there was high local demand and that was not available locally—would be an outstanding feature of that external involvement.

FIGURE 1
Conflicts in the Middle East That Have Led to Hostilities*
in the Past Five Years

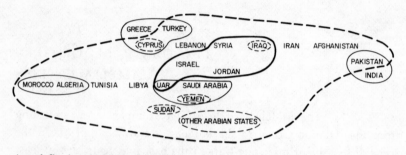

Area defined as the Middle East — — — — — — —
Circles around individual states indicate civil wars.
*Pro forma declarations of war that did not involve commitment of troops are not included in hostilities.

FIGURE 2
Conflict Patterns in the Middle East with Potential for Hostilities
in the Next Decade

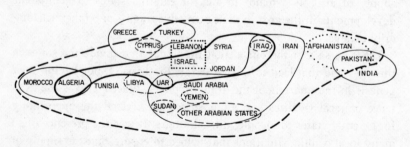

Area defined as the Middle East — — — — — — —
Circles around individual states indicate civil wars.

But if externally supplied arms are not in any real sense the basic cause of local warfare in the Middle East, it is equally true that all the local wars, internal and interstate, that have taken place there in the past five or ten years have been fought with these same arms. The current patterns of supply of major weapons systems to the countries in the area are depicted in Figure 3.

It might be supposed that in these local conflicts, against the back·ground of the cold war, the Soviet Union supplies one side and the West the other. One of the most extraordinary things about the Middle East situation is that "it ain't necessarily so." Table 1 makes it

FIGURE 3

Current Patterns of Supply of Major Armament Systems

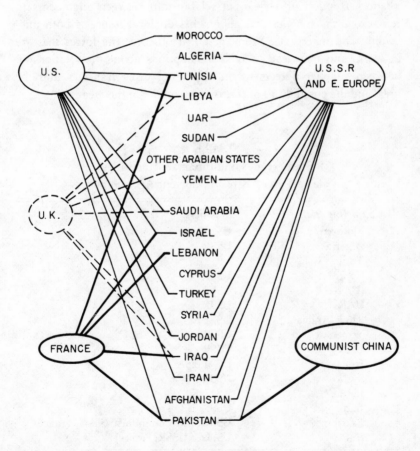

plain that there is no perfect or even good match between the pattern of arms-supply and partners in conflict. In one of the wars, Soviet equipment constituted a major part of the inventories of the opposing sides. In three, United States equipment was employed by both sides. The neat picture that is frequently drawn of an alignment of United States clients versus Soviet clients breaks down still further upon examination of possible conflict patterns in the future (see Table 2). Here one sees an even more complex mixture of Soviet-client allied with United States-client versus Soviet-client allied with United States-client.

The chief point that emerges from even this very cursory treatment of arms and conflicts is that here, as in many other ways in this region, common impressions may be very wrong. Clearly the simplistic perception of a clear-cut relationship between alignments in terms of arms-supplier and alignments on local issues is both misleading and inaccurate. Worst of all, it obscures the forces that are at work, and may lead to false assumptions about the relationship between supplier agreement on regulating arms transfers into the area, and the possibilities of controlling conflict in the area.

TABLE 1

States Engaged in Interstate Hostilities
in the Past Five Years and Current Arms Suppliers

	Conflicting States	Suppliers
1.	Morocco	US, USSR
	Algeria	USSR
2.	Turkey	US
	Cyprus	USSR
	(Greece	US)
3.	UAR	USSR
	Saudi Arabia	US, UK
	Yemen	USSR
4.	UAR	USSR
	Israel	US, France
	Syria	USSR
	Jordan	US, UK
	Iraq	USSR, UK, France
5.	Pakistan	US, USSR, Communist China, France
	(India	US, UK, USSR, France)

I

If oversimplified pictures are often drawn of "good guy" Western-supplied states versus "bad guy" Soviet-supplied states, a further distortion that frequently occurs in characterizing an arms acquisition process is to label it an "arms race" and delude oneself into thinking that one has adequately described the situation or contributed to its analysis.

The term "arms race" is most often used in a pejorative sense, to connote a negative judgment on a particular competitive arms acqui-

TABLE 2

States Likely to Engage in Interstate
Hostilities in the Coming Decade and
Current Arms Suppliers

	Conflicting States	Suppliers
1.	Morocco	US, USSR
	Algeria	USSR
2.	Libya	US, UK
	UAR	USSR
3.	Algeria	USSR
	Israel	US, France
	UAR	USSR
	Jordan	US, France
	Syria	USSR
	Iraq	USSR, UK, France
4.	Greece	US
	Cyprus	USSR
	Turkey	US
5.	Pakistan	US, USSR, Communist China, France
	India	US, USSR, UK, France
6.	UAR	USSR
	Sudan	USSR, UK
	Saudi Arabia	US, UK
	Yemen	USSR
	Other Arabian States	UK
	Iraq	USSR, UK, France
	Iran	US, USSR
7.	Afghanistan	USSR
	Pakistan	US, USSR, Communist China, France
8.	Lebanon	France
	Israel	US, France

sition process that, in the view of the person making the judgment, is dangerous, wasteful, irrational, or irrelevant to the "real" needs of the country or countries involved. The phrase "arms race" is thus intended not to describe an objective reality, but to underscore the negative consequences of a process as viewed from the speaker's perspective. The section that follows will describe the various arms acquisition processes in ways that may be more analytically useful.

All arms acquisitions are, in some sense, competitive; that is, they are calculated in terms of: (1) a vague criterion as to what states "ought to have"; (2) measurement against specific states, although not necessarily in a conflict situation; and (3) measurement against specific adversary states in an existing or potential conflict situation. While all arms acquisitions are competitive, however, not all are designed to change the relative power of the states in a region or between specific competing pairs of states.

If one were to try to place the various elements that characterize the arms acquisition process on a scale of "least" to "most" dangerous, they might cluster as follows:

Least Dangerous	*Most Dangerous*
Competitive with vague standards or with specific nonadversary states	Competitive with specific adversary or potential adversary states
Designed to maintain the existing power hierarchy	Designed to change the existing power hierarchy
Consistent with normal "style"	Departures from normal "style"
Consistent with normal rate	Departures from normal rate

Two elements are missing from the above—expenditures and qualitative types of acquisitions. Any sharp rise in expenditures should alert one to the possibility of some departure from past acquisition "style." But the meaning of such rises may be something quite different. These departures from a normal curve for a given country may be explained by such things as pay raises for the military and the like. Furthermore, declines in expenditures are not inconsistent with efforts to improve one's relative power—witness the "more bang for the buck" doctrine. Furthermore, arms acquisitions consistent with the "least dangerous" pattern suggested above can be as costly or even more costly than those in the "most dangerous."

Qualitative distinctions among various acquisitions are hard to make on a globally valid basis. What is militarily significant in some parts of the world is not necessarily relevant in others. That which in the local context is militarily most significant of all and relatively cheap—in some cases trucks, fuel supplies, ammunition, or long-range communication equipment—may be easily overlooked.

Nevertheless, there are some qualitative distinctions that are genuinely relevant in deciding on the meaning of a given acquisition.

Imitative acquisitions. Among nonadversaries, the acquisition of identical new weapon systems should lead one to suspect that prestige is the basis of the process. Among adversaries, on the other hand, it is equally likely to reflect the operation of a deterrent philosophy.

Offsetting acquisitions. Among assumed nonadversaries, the acquisition of an offsetting system (e.g., anti-aircraft systems or interceptor aircraft as a reaction to a bomber acquisition) may well be more destabilizing than the imitative acquisitions. This is so because it implies a conscious comparing of military capabilities. Among adversaries, on the other hand, such offsetting acquisitions may well signal the end to whatever stiff arms competition has preceded it, particularly competition featuring offensive weapons.

Generational jumps. As long as acquisitions among competing states are roughly within the same generation of weaponry, the momentum of the competitive process is likely to be less.

This should not be credited with giving a precision to the problem that is not warranted. This is particularly so since, whatever the intentions of one state, they may be misperceived by other states in the area, whether adversaries or not. Military planners are invariably a supremely cautious lot, probably rightly so, who feel they must plan for the worst possible contingency rather than hope for the best. If one is suspicious of what one's neighbor's future designs may be, one must prepare against the day when he may turn his capabilities in one's direction. And, of course, one credits him with extraordinary luck. This penchant for assuming the worst plays particular havoc in areas such as the one examined here, with shifting alignments depending on which conflict situation is considered.

If one wants to restore some useful meaning to the term "arms races" it should be confined to referring to the *acquisition of arms by adversary states that are intended to alter the relative power relationship between or among them.* They are characterized by *departures from past habits and patterns of acquisition, and efforts to shorten the time between a decision to acquire and the actual acquisition.* Sharp rises in military expenditures that cannot be explained in nonequipment terms should also alert one to the possible commencement of an arms race, if adversaries react to them.

If this definition of the expression can be accepted, then only the relationship between Israel and Egypt seems to combine the elements that qualify for the description of "arms race"—attempts by one side to alter the existing balance and determination by the other to prevent it, generational jumps in weaponry, foreshortened time between each successive acquisition, and so forth.

II

The United States has pursued three objectives in its decisions on arms transfers to countries in the area. The first is to seek, by a policy of "maintaining balance," to prevent any anti-status-quo state in the region from becoming sufficiently strong to challenge successfully the existing regional order. This policy is sometimes equated with efforts to deter war by making the status-quo powers sufficiently strong to repel any challenges, and thus, in theory, dissuading the challenger from the effort. If such deterrence is the aim, the policy has been a notable failure—as the number of recent wars in the region attests. Pakistan has fought India; Jordan has fought Israel and vice versa; Saudi Arabia has been in conflict with Egypt and Yemen; and Morocco with Algeria. In the most critical conflict of all, between Israel and its neighbors, the policy of deterrence through balance is bound to continue to fail as long as Israel, unable to withstand the casualties that a sustained defensive effort would entail, equates successful deterrence with the capacity for preemption, i.e., a "first-strike capability."

A second theme of United States arms policy has been an attempt to ensure, by the types and quantities of arms supplied, and most particularly by controlling the supply of spare parts and other requirements such as fuel and ammunition, that wars are limited in intensity and of short duration. Among the states in the Middle East, only in Pakistan, in its 1965 war with India, can one say with some confidence that the policy has clearly worked. Morocco's war with Algeria was brief, but attrition of equipment does not appear to have been the reason. The brevity of the Arab-Israel war of June 1967 was clearly unrelated to the number of spare parts and other expendables that were available on either side. In any event, in circumstances such as those represented by many of the conflicts in the Middle East— where the "sides" are coalitions and where each coalition and many individual states have multiple arms suppliers—such bilateral control devices will be difficult to call into effective operation. Nevertheless, even if such imperfect "control" as this policy represents is insufficient to prevent wars from breaking out, it profoundly affects the nature of the warfare that can occur.

The third aspect of United States arms transfer policy in the Middle East is a function of the desire of the United States to insulate itself from the consequences of the conjunction of local conflicts and United States arms—to ensure, in other words, that it is not drawn into the conflicts directly, and particularly that a clash with the Soviet Union is not precipitated by other people's quarrels. The success of this policy to date is self-evident. The degree to which it will continue to succeed depends in large measure on developments being considered in other parts of this volume, notably on the degree to which the existence of both a United States and a Soviet fleet in the Mediterranean enmeshes both superpowers still further in events they can only imperfectly control. The point to be made here is that, even before Vietnam increased United States sensitivity to direct commitment of United States forces in the Middle East or elsewhere, this government was loath to engage itself so deeply in the Middle East that it could not remain aloof at periods of hostility, coupled at times with strong public and private pressure on client and non-client alike to bring the fighting to an early end.

The same motivation probably helps to explain why the United States did not look with disfavor on France's assuming the role of Israel's major pre-June 1967 supplier and why, until recently, a large portion of Jordan's requirements were met from British equipment supplied with partial United States subsidy. Indeed, one can argue that the reason the United States has sought to maintain a "balance" in the Middle East that has consistently kept Israel the strongest military power is precisely in order to avoid the one contingency most likely to lead to a direct United States involvement—that is, the threatened overrunning of Israel by its Arab neighbors, whether supplied by the Soviet Union, Britain, or the United States.

What can be said of Soviet objectives? Surely on the last two, the Russians have shown themselves very much of the same mind as the

United States. When, for example, the June 1967 war broke out the Russians moved with alacrity to assure the United States of their intention to remain aloof. Soviet restrictions on supply of spare parts are reportedly at least as severe as those of the United States.

What about Soviet policy on the first objective, the supply of arms to preserve existing military relationships rather than to upset them? On the face of it, particularly given the kind and number of Russian weapons systems supplied to Egypt before and after the 1967 round, there appear to be marked differences between United States and Soviet policies. But great caution needs to be exercised in drawing from an examination of the particular kind of weapons transferred a firm conclusion concerning the intentions of either recipient or donor. The principal reason for caution arises from the fact that the developing world as a whole, including the countries of interest here, is armed with weapons that have become surplus in the stocks of the industrial states by the rapid pace of the latter's armaments program, or that represent part of the production runs required for economic production in the indigenous weapons industries of Western Europe. That is to say, only rarely are arms designed for the developing countries per se; they are designed for the supplier countries' inventories.

In the context of superpower competition in a highly volatile region, this point is of profound significance, however obvious it may appear on reflection. Because Soviet doctrine, tactics, and physical environment are different from those of the United States, the weapons they develop are different. Thus one finds heavy emphasis in Soviet armor on amphibious capability, while in United States armor the emphasis is on air-transportability. Soviet calm-water assault vessels developed for use primarily on inland seas have led to the development of missile patrol boats, whereas the recent United States world role called for ocean navies, relying on air forces to patrol and protect coastal waters. The special requirements and customs involved in Soviet aircraft use have led Moscow to the development of more single-purpose combat air systems. On the other hand, United States doctrine, research and development style, and budgeting practices have led to highly complex multipurpose systems. The list could be extended.

The consequence of all this is that from looking at the arms the Russians supply it is difficult to read the true purpose and intent of the Russians in making the transfers. The same is true for the United

States. Consider one specific case. The existence in the UAR inventory at this particular juncture of amphibious armor of Soviet origin is of great potential military significance, and Israel cannot but take into account the capability it represents. But since all but the heaviest Soviet armor is amphibious, can one be certain that this capability is anything but an incidental effect of Soviet assistance? And if one wishes to read Soviet intentions into the fact that the systems they supplied have given Egypt this capability, what do the same systems imply about Soviet intentions in Algeria or in Afghanistan, where amphibious capability has little of apparent operational value?

Moreover, can one legitimately infer from Soviet arms shipments to Egypt that Moscow positively desires to see Cairo in a position to wage a successful war against Israel? Superficially, the answer is yes. In terms of sheer quantity the Russians have been far more generous than any Western supplier to most of their clients in the area, notably the UAR. In initial deliveries to a client, the Soviet objective appears to be to overwhelm whatever remnants of Western equipment there are, and rapidly establish a position of complete dominance of the training, resupply, spare parts, and related activities.

But this would not explain the magnitude of subsequent shipments, nor the speed with which they arrive. So frequently do the quantity and pace of delivery outstrip local abilities to keep up with, let alone utilize, the materiel that one is forced to the conclusion that the Soviet purpose, if there is a conscious one, is to create a political impression of strength and commitment rather than rapidly to alter established military relationships.

Moreover, since the obvious answer to inadequate local absorptive capacity is for the Russians to bring in their own technicians and military advisers in substantial numbers, one could also conclude that Soviet arms transfers are subsidiary to a strategy of penetration and securing a foothold that resembles a base. Flooding a relatively backward area with more arms than can be handled produces a natural demand for technical assistance, training, and even supervision.

If these capabilities are interpreted in the light of intentions, as they should be,[1] it then needs to be said that many observers do not

---

[1] There is a distinction to be made here. Military planners must, when looking at the inventories of potential adversaries, base their assessments on what the force and weapons can do, not what the leadership of the opposing state says its intentions are.

believe Moscow wants to see a hot war in the Middle East, particularly with Soviet personnel involved. If this is so, the intrusion of substantial quantities of arms must be seen as building a capability that Moscow does not wish to see used or is confident it can halt short of the brink. No other explanation would fit the basic assessment of Soviet intentions, always excepting the possibility of a grave miscalculation in the Kremlin.

One far-out but possible interpretation that struck some in 1967 was that Moscow is actually better off, in its penetration and influence policy in the Middle East, if the Arab states lose rather than win their wars with Israel. A frustrated and needy loser offers far more foothold opportunities than a confident victor freed from threat.

A final point about the asymmetries between patterns of Soviet and United States inventories is that they create a series of thresholds of decision that are not immediately obvious. By this is meant that there are qualitative distinctions that can be detected and that can be used to define plateaus on which the qualitative aspects of an "arms race" may be arrested. Nuclear versus conventional weapons is an example of a threshold that is generally accepted as of great significance, even though in real military terms the smallest nuclear weapons would be virtually interchangeable with conventional ones. There may be less dramatic thresholds in the conventional field.

Thus one consideration that should have weighed heavily in the minds of United States decision-makers in assessing Israel's urgent, recent requests for F-4 jet fighter-bombers is that there is no aircraft in the Soviet inventory that is comparable to it in range, payload, or general performance and versatility. This is not to say that Soviet planes are not as good as United States planes, just that they are different. It can be predicted that the Soviet Union will have difficulty in responding effectively to their clients' certain appeals for systems to match the F-4, and the temptation may be great to react with systems of a different and more provocative character—in this case, missiles.

Much more careful examination of Soviet-American asymmetries needs to be undertaken before too many conclusions can be drawn. But the evidence to date suggests that, if and when the United States and the Soviet Union are prepared to observe mutual restraint on their arms shipments to areas such as the Middle East, these asymmetries will create both problems and opportunities. Problems because it is more difficult to persuade one's self and others that an agreement is "equal" if it is not symmetrical. Opportunities because, if this can nonetheless be done, it may avoid substituting a quantitative race for a qualitative one.

III

From this background of indigenous conflicts and flow of arms into the region from external suppliers, one may turn to speculation. What can be anticipated for the 1970s if the cold war continues between the superpowers as at present; if it thaws into something resembling a limited détente; or if, *mirabile dictu*, a generalized détente develops between the superpowers?

If things continue as at present in Soviet-American relations, several general lines of policy and action may be envisaged in the decade ahead. The deep-rooted Russian drive for a leading position in the Middle East will continue. While some parts of the region are doubtless more important to Moscow than others, the catholic (read Muslim) definition of Middle East followed here is not too broad for the continued Soviet efforts one can foresee to penetrate and influence developments. This is happening in the Maghrib and the Palestine area, no less than in the locus of traditional Russian aspirations, i.e., "the area South of Batum and Baku in the general direction of the Persian Gulf" in the words of Molotov to Ribbentrop in 1940. The Russian dagger pointing downward through Turkey, Iraq, and Iran to the Persian Gulf still represents Moscow's shortest avenue to the traditionally coveted warm water ports giving on open ocean space. But the flanking movement southwest to North Africa and Palestine not only provides alternative routes to the Indian Ocean via Suez and the Red Sea, but also gives Moscow a continuing bullish position in the regional influence market. This is unlikely to change even if the most worrisome ideological competitor in that market in the 1970s becomes Peking rather than an inward-turning Washington or an impoverished London. In her role as exporter of capital, technical knowhow, and culture, Russia will continue to flow southward, at least as long as Chinese pressures on her eastern flanks do not require a major *recul*.

In the face of this probable policy, and given the likely continuation in the entire region of gross underdevelopment in terms of industry and technological skill for at least another decade, arms exports from Moscow to at least ten Middle East clients will continue as a major expression of Soviet policy. Arms will be a principal agency of policy not because Moscow wants war on her southern flanks, but for two other reasons. Arms will reflect the demands of clients from Casablanca eastward to Dacca. They will also serve the unfolding Soviet strategic concepts of mobility and flexible response, by placing Soviet outposts of varying depth on waterways and land peninsulas from the eastern Atlantic through the Mediterranean, Red Sea, and Persian Gulf to the Arabian Sea, Bay of Bengal, and Indian Ocean. No tsar in his wildest dreams could count on such an empire of influence and, potentially, control.

United States policy will confront continuing choices, some of them familiar, some possibly new. One can envisage continuation through the decade of the indigenous "pairings" in the region as a whole—Algeria vs. Morocco; the UAR vs. Saudi Arabia and Jordan; Saudi Arabia vs. South Yemen; the India-Pakistan conflict; and above all the Arab-Israel War, now 21 years old, potentially as durable as warfare of the late Middle Ages. In a cold war environment Washington will continue to see itself as a potential "balancer" in some of these, favoring Morocco and the Arabian Muslims because they represent a status quo, and Israel because of a deep ethnic and sentimental preference.

But notice a preference for India or Pakistan is excluded here. The 1965 war was an eye-opener for the United States, pitting against each other two countries friendly to us, each employing arms supplied by Washington or Paris or London. It is no longer so easy as it was before 1965 for American planners to calculate the relative costs and benefits of arms shipments to India or Pakistan in terms of any given American interest, whether "deterring" Russia, keeping a friendly country out of the Peking influence sphere, encouraging a nonsocialist country vs. one that is socialist, or preventing outbreak of hostilities in local conflict in which we feel relatively impartial.

The same development of American "neutralism" may happen with respect to some other pairs. Morocco has seemed to Washington more like an American "friend" than has Algeria. But Morocco now receives Soviet tanks. What outcome of an Algerian-Moroccan conflict will Washington prefer if Morocco becomes a postmonarchical, semisocialist state, friendlier than before to Moscow and Peking, and expressing greater solidarity with Cairo in the holy war against

Zionism? Could not the same question be asked with respect to traditional American support of the monarchs of Iran and Libya?

Under such circumstances, United States interests should be recalculated. Such reassessment could conceivably lead the United States to decide, for the first time in some years, that it does not particularly care about the outcome of a given conflict in that particular area, unless the Soviet Union were one of the parties. America would no longer try to strengthen one country against another by supplying arms for that purpose.

This does *not*, however, mean the United States would necessarily be indifferent to the outbreak of *violence*, particularly if there is a chance that it might spread. Of course, if hostilities could be localized and insulated, the United States may be relatively indifferent even as to that. But the nature of America's historic position is such as to make it automatically concerned whenever peace and order are threatened. The implication of this is that even if the United States does not feel impelled to choose sides, it will continue to have a strong interest in minimizing international violence.

A switch to a primarily conflict-preventing or controlling policy in the Middle East as a whole would entail, first of all, far greater American efforts to secure agreement among suppliers of arms to exclude sophisticated weaponry, or cut down on numbers and types. One would imagine that in a continued period of tension such agreements would be easiest to reach with Britain, perhaps next easiest to reach with post-Gaullist France, hard indeed to reach with Moscow, and virtually impossible to reach with Peking, with the exception of a Middle East nuclear-free zone.

Failing externally imposed arms-limitation agreements, another avenue of policy would be for the United States to become a more universal balancer. In the same way that the Soviet Union with a remarkable lack of fastidiousness covers its bets by spreading arms to such ideological pariahs of Communism as Morocco, Iran, and Afghanistan, the United States might consider using arms exports to radical regimes on generous terms, both to offset potential miscalculation by their neighbors and as articles of commerce. (The United States has done this with Yugoslavia, with rather fair results.)

Israel will doubtless remain the exception to any such policy shifts. There is little or no chance of the United States' adopting a totally impartial policy between the sides, except for the support given to shaky allies of Egypt such as Jordan and Saudi Arabia. The only foreseeable condition under which the United States would be likely to refuse Israel's pleas for arms would be if Moscow ceased, for whatever reason, to supply the UAR, Syria, Iraq, Yemen, *et al*. Even then, the local arms competitions might continue if post-Gaullist France remains intractable to arms-control schemes, whether for reasons of profit or politico-cultural *hubris* (or if de Gaulle actually does live forever). In that case even a reduction of Soviet activism in the region, expressed through arms-supply policies, might find Paris moving into the market regardless of American-British pleas for solidarity in carrying out externally imposed arms controls. A United States conflict-minimizing policy would then have to act through its arms shipments to balance incremental increase in offensive capabilities courtesy of Paris. This possibility is both real and full of potential danger, as demonstrated by the reported recent quiet substitution of French for German technicians in the Egyptian missile developmental program and, with a fine display of even-handedness, its concurrent collaboration with Israel missile efforts.

In sum, assuming continuation of the cold war, one can envisage a determined Soviet drive for regional influence primarily through supply of arms, however inappropriate some of those arms may be to the operational needs of the countries concerned (see above). One can predict increased United States efforts to negotiate restraints on the supply of arms to the region as a whole, particularly to the conflict-prone Palestine and Indo-Pakistani areas. Failing that, one may envisage United States consideration of a *conflict control strategy*. Such a strategy would use arms transfers for the prime and explicit purpose of preventing, containing, and terminating local conflict, rather than for upholding a particular regime preferred by the United States —always with the unique exception of Israel.

IV

The second scenario postulates a "limited détente" between the superpowers. This presumably means an incremental increase in Soviet-American agreements on specific issues in contention; increased, but still restricted, cooperation to maintain international peace and security; *and* a continued adversary relationship on other important matters. Otherwise the détente would of course not be limited.

The logic of such a scenario must be derived from further expected

Soviet movement toward a status quo position in the world, its growing concern for international stability accompanied by further erosion of its revolution-promoting ideology. Under such circumstances it would of course be natural for Moscow to be more receptive than it is in the late 1960s to United States proposals for mutual restraints in the competitive, and in some cases noncompetitive, arms supplies to conflict-prone portions of the Middle East.

An American-Soviet agreement, whether explicit or tacit, to stop pumping offensive arms into the Middle East would have a number of portentous consequences. It would bespeak the probability of important mutual action by both in the event of unwanted violence, and of a common front against troublemakers and destabilizers such as Peking or Havana. But it is not at all certain that it would have a decisive effect on the continuing potential for violence in the Middle East.

As suggested above, of the chief present suppliers, France and China would offer potential difficulties even if the two giants were in accord. There is of course no reason in theory why inducements could not be used to persuade France to abstain from arming the area. There is no inherent obstacle to the use of strong coercive measures such as blockade, threats, and even the use of force, to restrain China. The obstacles to such bilateral enforcement action are formidable, and obvious, although perhaps they would be more acceptable to other countries if United States-Soviet agreement took the form of a multilateral arrangement through the United Nations. This would be very difficult to achieve if the states in the region objected to being thus dealt with by others.

This last point underscores the inherent irony of such a scenario. To the extent that Moscow and Washington cooperate in this matter, they will appear to be ganging up both on recipients in the Middle East and on suppliers in Europe. To that extent it is likely that, politically speaking, Europe would be even more inclined to independent action: to the same extent Peking would undoubtedly feel itself to be even more isolated, and act even more neurotically than at present.

There are more optimistic versions of this picture. One is that American-Soviet cooperation to increase stability in the Middle East would profoundly and favorably influence other suppliers, both in Western and Eastern Europe, to follow suit. The most optimistic version would have all the states of the region cooperating in a multi-lateral agreement to limit arms to those needed for defensive and internal security purposes only. One would have to place a somewhat higher probability on the version that sees American-Soviet agreement as accompanied by bitter resentment on the part of their client states, and by efforts on the part of other supplier states to capture these arms markets as sources of revenue, influence, or both.

V

The third scenario does not differ very much from the second: its principal feature is a deepened détente between Washington and Moscow—but not necessarily one with China. Again, it could have consequences far-reaching in nature, particularly if a general détente comes to resemble an entente. It would doubtless connote an end to the dangerous rivalry for position in the developing regions, as well as a settlement in Central Europe. *A fortiori*, it would without doubt entail explicit understandings as to the levels and types of arms, weapons systems, and military assistance to be furnished to recipient countries.

But unless it were accompanied by a number of other things, it could still suffer from the same disabilities as the limited détente when it came to enforcing on third parties the desires of the two superpartners. Those disabilities have already been outlined.

The "other things" accompanying a general détente that *would* make a difference to the arms flow problem would be: universally agreed general and complete disarmament, universally agreed regional arms limitations, and settlement of the Arab-Israel conflict. An Arab-Israel settlement would so reduce the demands for arms that the problem would assume a very different cast. General and complete disarmament *without* such a settlement would not be likely to affect the politics or even military aspects of the Middle East arms situation until relatively far along in the process. An indigenous regional self-denying ordinance is unthinkable without settlement of the Arab-Israel conflict.

The Sixth Fleet and
American Diplomacy

J. C. WYLIE

Three thumbnail sketches of incidents in which American naval forces were, or might have been, involved in the Middle East should help clarify the contribution of the Sixth Fleet to American diplomacy. The three incidents were these: the 1956 Suez crisis, the 1958 civil war in Lebanon, and the 1967 Six Day War. Each incident was different. In each, the political context and United States political aims differed, and the military response to the political aims was adjusted to suit the circumstances.

In 1956, the French and the British were concerned about the nationalization of the Suez Canal Company, and Israel was disturbed by Egyptian activities in the Sinai. And so the three countries laid on military action against Egypt. This took place in late October, about ten days before the United States national elections, and policy guidance to the United States military was rather more general than that available in the current decade. The United States aims were three: (1) to be alert and ready in case the situation expanded into a major conflict; (2) to protect and evacuate United States citizens from Egypt and the other active countries of the Middle East; and (3) to avoid becoming involved locally, but to try and restrain the actions of those already involved on both sides.

The ships on the West Coast moved toward the central Pacific; those previously in Hawaiian waters moved toward the Asian littoral; the Seventh Fleet, already in the western Pacific, moved south, some of it into the South China Sea and some of it, including its amphibious forces, on through the Indian Ocean into the Arabian Sea within reach of the Red Sea and the Persian Gulf. In the Atlantic, the forces on the East Coast moved south of the Azores where they could reach either the West Coast of Europe or into the Mediterranean. At the same time, inside the Mediterranean, the Sixth Fleet sailed eastward.

This took care of item one, to be ready in case the situation expanded. What the Navy did was to close in on Suez, from both sides, from all around the world. This produced rather garish newspaper headlines, charging "rocket rattling" and the like and inviting countercharges. But a major stabilizing element in the international situation at this time was that, except for the ships in the eastern Mediterranean, no one knew where the American fleets were. It was known only that they had left their usual operating areas.

As to the second of the general aims, the evacuation of United States citizens, the Navy, in effect, placed itself at the disposal of the State Department. This is normal. The Navy and the Foreign Service have always worked closely together. Both keep tabs on United States citizens overseas at all times, and in this instance the United States Embassy in Rome, under Ambassador Claire Booth Luce, was the regional coordinator for the other embassies and consular offices and the miltary. The amphibious forces lifted two thousand United States citizens out of Alexandria after the State Department had arranged some exciting motor convoys from Cairo; other ships and aircraft lifted two thousand more out of Israel and adjacent countries.

The third aim was to try and restrain the actions of those already involved at the scene. The Sixth Fleet Commander took his main force, the carriers, cruisers, and destroyers, and operated idly midway between Suez and Cyprus. He kept his destroyer screens out and his combat air patrols up. But he took no action, even though he was obviously ready and everyone, on both sides, knew he was ready. This did tend to exert a stabilizing influence, enough so that President Eisenhower could successfully urge that other nations stay out, and that all four combatant nations stand down.

The second incident, the civil war in Lebanon in 1958, was somewhat different. In that case, there was stress within a single country; the head of state, President Kamil Sham'un, asked for United States help; Ambassador Robert McClintock relayed the request to Washington; and the Sixth Fleet responded. One component of the Sixth

Fleet was then, and still is, marines embarked in amphibious assault shipping. As requested by the President of Lebanon, these forces were landed. Their landing was covered by the ships and aircraft of the Sixth Fleet in case anything went awry. The Commander in Chief of the United States Naval Forces in the Eastern Atlantic and Mediterranean sailed his flagship into Bayrut. Some United States Army forces were later brought down from Western Europe. And the United States Ambassador, the United States Naval Commander in Chief, President Sham'un, and the Lebanese Commanding General, Fuad Shihab, who later became President, managed to work out arrangements whereby internal differences were adjusted and stability was reestablished in Lebanon. The point to be made here is that a friendly country was in trouble, it asked for help, help was given, and stability was restored. When that came about, United States forces were withdrawn.

There were interesting sidelights in the Lebanese incident. The political problem in Lebanon was associated with the proposal to change the Lebanese Constitution to permit a second term for President Sham'un; his earlier request for United States assistance; the United States clarification of the terms under which it would assist, which did not include the internal constitutional issue; the overthrow of Nuri Sa'id in Iraq, which threw the whole Middle East into turmoil; the specific request for help which was then authorized by President Eisenhower; the coordination with the British help to Jordan; the rapid response in less than twenty-four hours; the two literally last-minute requests by the Ambassador, one to defer the landing and the other to send "marines with tanks" to guard President Sham'un; and the dilemma facing the officers making the landing at the airport, who knew, when apparently the Ambassador did not, that President Eisenhower was making a statement at 3:00 p.m. Lebanon time that the landings were being made over the beaches beside the airport. There were a few acerbic comments from the diplomatic and military participants—not unusual when strong men meet, because no man can always see clearly through other men's eyes. The United States Naval Institute *Proceedings* of October 1962 contains articles by both Ambassador McClintock and marine Colonel Hadd, who was on the beach that afternoon. A reading of both should help clarify the problems.

The third incident was the use of United States naval forces before and during the Six Day War in the spring of 1967. The Egyptians mobilized in mid-May, and the Israelis, of course, followed suit almost at once. There ensued a two-week period in which both sides rearranged their force dispositions and traded verbal blows. In that period the United States did some rearranging of it own and what it did and why may shed light on the use of the naval forces.

The main portion of the Sixth Fleet was in the western half of the Mediterranean when the crisis broke. At first, as might be expected, there was a move eastward, but with three important restrictions. The naval command estimated, correctly as it turned out, that the United States policy would be to stand aloof from military involvement if possible, to play the United States military role in as low a key as possible in order to give the greatest scope for diplomatic maneuver, but to be ready and on hand.

The first restriction placed on fleet movement was that no scheduled visit in any Mediterranean port was to be interrupted or shortened. The ships already at sea moved eastward, but no ship left port ahead of schedule. Recent political terminology gives much importance to "signals." The fact that the ships remained in port was a clear signal that the United States was not rushing headlong into the affair. The signal was clearly understood by allies of the United States and by others. Newspapers all over Europe reported this at once. As the ships left port on the previously announced schedules, they quietly sailed eastward, with one exception.

The second restriction had to do with the amphibious forces. Those ships with their embarked marines were in Naples. They stayed there, as scheduled, until about the third week in May, and then put to sea. Their location, with nearly two thousand combat marines embarked, was of considerable interest to many nations, and so, to reinforce the United States attitude of no military involvement, the amphibious forces put into port in Malta as soon as they left Naples. This put them where everyone could see them and know exactly where they were—a thousand miles away from the southeast corner of the Mediterranean. This signal, too, was promptly received and noted.

The third restriction related to the sailing of the main body of the Sixth Fleet. As an indicator of the United States' attitude, the forces did not sail all the way to the coasts of Egypt or Israel. A line was drawn roughly from the bulge of Libya to the eastern end of

Crete, and the Sixth Fleet operated generally west of this line, south of Crete. They were well over three hundred miles from Suez and at least two hundred miles from Egypt's western desert. Since many newsmen (not always the most tractable of men), were on board, and since the Russian ships were with ours south of Crete, American whereabouts and actions, or lack of action, were known to all interested parties. This signal, too, was received and understood. An anecdote that originated in the United Nations bears repeating. The Egyptians charged that United States naval aircraft were involved in the initial air strike on Egypt. This was publicly rejected by the United States as untrue. The rest of the story is that later, informally in the United Nations lounge, a United States official told an Egyptian official that if he did not believe us to ask the Russians, for they were with our ships and knew that no strikes were flown against anyone.

Thus the move to readiness in the Arab-Israel mobilization period had three careful signals built into it: no premature departures from scheduled port visits; the deliberate and visible retention of the amphibious forces in the central Mediterranean; and the purposeful retention of American forces south of Crete and well clear of the prospective scene of action.

Two other naval moves illustrate how naval forces are able, quietly, to support national policy. One has to do with destroyers and the other with an aircraft carrier. At the time this mobilization took place in mid-May, the carrier *Intrepid* was on her way from the east coast of the United States to the South China Sea, as part of the forces off Vietnam. She had been routed by way of Suez and was just entering the Mediterranean past Gibraltar when the mobilization took place. Normally, in cases of this sort, transiting ships automatically come under command of the flag officers in the waters through which they pass. *Intrepid* would normally have come under the Sixth Fleet Commander while in the Mediterranean. In this case, the Navy did not want to give the impression that the Sixth Fleet was being reinforced. So *Intrepid* did not report to the Sixth Fleet Commander; she remained a separate unit directly under the Commander in Chief, Naval Forces, Europe, in London. The request for Suez transit clearance went to Egypt, not from the Sixth Fleet but from London. There were a few days' delay, and *Intrepid* stayed well clear of the ships of the Sixth Fleet, off the coast of Libya (also observed by ships of other nations), until clearance was granted. She made her southbound transit of the canal and went on a thousand miles down the Red Sea and then eastward through the Arabian Sea and the Indian Ocean. This deliberate refusal to reinforce the fleet in the Mediterranean was also duly noted.

One other redistribution of forces is worth mentioning. The United States normally has a small naval force, a small flagship and two destroyers, patrolling east of Suez in the Arabian Sea, the Persian Gulf, and the Red Sea. The two destroyers in this force were normally supplied from the Sixth Fleet, for tours of two or three months, and they normally relieved one another at Port Suez at the south end of the canal. A destroyer exchange had been scheduled for about the third week in May. The southbound destroyer, going to the force east of Suez, made her canal transit on schedule. But the naval command in London suggested to the force commander that he might want to delay the transit of the ship returning to the Mediterranean until the situation became more clear. He did so, and the result was that, when the canal was closed and the fighting started, his force, south and east of Suez, had been increased by 50 per cent. He had a third destroyer under command in his waters.

It has been necessary to go into some detail to make the point here. While it is a highly effective combatant force, the Sixth Fleet is also a most sensitive and responsive diplomatic tool. It functions as one of several tools of national policy. It is a most pliable tool. The Navy is closely tied in organizationally with the other elements of armed strength, the Army and the Air Force. But by the nature of a Navy, its special capabilities and limitations, it is particularly close to the diplomats of the State Department, the prime executors of foreign policy. The Navy likes to think that it understands them and that they understand it, and that they always work closely together toward the common aim of the United States. In the Navy, and particularly in the Sixth Fleet, the nation has a uniquely useful and versatile tool which can be applied overtly or covertly, directly or indirectly, actively or passively, but almost always effectively, in whatever may at any moment be the national interest.

The Changing Military Balance

LAURENCE W. MARTIN

For the Western powers of Europe, the Middle East has long been chiefly important as an east-west route to Asia, while for Russia it has been an obvious but frustratingly obstructed north-south path to southern Asia, the Indian Ocean, and Africa. Thus, for the West in recent years, the main strategic task has been securing the east-west route, denying the north-south one to Russia, and maintaining control over the reserves of oil that have latterly been discovered within the area itself. In very modern times the eastern Mediterranean has taken on the added aspect of southern flank to NATO.

The Middle East is a declining asset to the West in its traditional role of line of communication, for the Europeans have gradually shed their military commitments east of Suez and are increasingly acquiring economically alternative routes for trade and oil, while the United States has always taken a different way to its heavy responsibilities in Asia. For Russia, however, as a power of rising capability and ambition, the Middle East must take on increasing interest as a way to break out finally from its long encirclement.

From the military point of view, the Middle East is, of course, more than a blank space within which the great powers can deploy their forces and strike a balance. It is an area of great indigenous turbulence, marked by frequent hostilities and a continuous arms race which the great powers manipulate to their best ability in the service of their local and general interests, and in which their own armed forces have often played a direct and conspicuous part: Britain and France at Suez, America in Lebanon, and, after the war of June 1967, Russia. Most actual hostilities have so far concerned the Arab-Israel question, but the Mahgrib and the Gulf hold obvious potential for conflict, while on the northern side of the Mediterranean, not only the Greek-Turkish situation but also probable future political up-heavals in Iberia may well produce explosions to disturb the Middle East proper. The United States, which might on many counts regard itself as remote from Middle East affairs, is inextricably involved in the local military balance by its concern for the survival of Israel. This interest would presumably survive even the achievement of a *modus vivendi* with the Soviet Union.

I

The central geostrategic feature of the Middle East, the Mediter-ranean Sea, has for long been an area dominated by a single power—for decades, Great Britain, and then during the cold war, the United States. The most conspicuous strategic change in the last few years has been the well-publicized entry of Soviet naval power. The prom-inence of this development should not, however, be allowed to ob-scure the increasing intrusion of Soviet air forces into Middle East airspace and their association, like the naval deployments, with widespread programs of military assistance and instruction involv-ing the dissemination of spare parts and technical expertise ap-propriate to Russian military systems. Even such a small country as Somalia, capable of commanding important waters, is said to have received one hundred Soviet aircraft and to have large numbers of pilots in training in the Soviet Union. All of this must be thought of in association with a substantial development of a long-range Russian airlift.

Russia's naval investment in the Mediterranean is substantial. After an abortive beginning with the establishment of a submarine base at Valona, Albania, in 1958, the deployment of Russian naval forces operating independent of local bases recommenced in the early sixties and has now become a permanent feature of the Mediter-ranean. The pattern has been of a deployment in the summer, falling back in the subsequent winter only to rise again the next summer to greater proportions than in the previous year. The Arab-Israel war of

1967 produced an extraordinary increase which did not subsequently subside to the normal extent in the winter.

Thus in the winter of 1966-1967 there were one cruiser, three destroyers, four submarines, and five auxiliaries. By May 1967 there were nine destroyers; during the June war, strength rose to two cruisers—submarine depot-ships, fifteen destroyers, twelve submarines, and fifteen auxiliaries, together with the novel introduction of a few small landing ships. The winter reduction of 1967-1968 still left a cruiser, a depot-ship, ten destroyers, and ten submarines; and the summer of 1968 saw an increase to over forty ships, including the brief appearance of the new helicopter carrier, *Moskva*. It is widely expected that the combatant component and proportion of the Russian force will rise as numbers of new missile destroyers, helicopter carriers, and submarines come off the Russian production lines. This Mediterranean deployment, of course, forms part of a general expansion and improvement of the Russian navy.

If the modified adversary relationship that has characterized the last few years of the cold war persists, it seems probable that the motives that have occasioned the Russian naval penetration of the Mediterranean will ensure that it remains a permanent and very likely a growing feature of the strategic scene. What those motives are must, of course, be divined chiefly by speculation. There are compelling strategic reasons for the Russians to expand their navy: defense against Western strategic attack, establishment of a reciprocal offensive nuclear threat to the West, and the general support of Russian diplomacy. Given such an expansion of capacity, geography alone would lead to the appearance of Russian naval power in an area at once contiguous to their homeland and convenient, at least in peacetime, as a route to more distant places. To this expansion and extension the service interests of the Russian Navy as well as the national policy of the Soviet Union doubtless contribute.

From the West it is natural to assess the Russian intrusion as an attempt to outflank NATO and threaten its soft underside. The Reyjavik meeting of NATO Ministers in June 1968 saw the problem in this light and undertook measures of reinforcement to Western forces that since have steadily, if modestly, materialized. Yet it would be easy to exaggerate Soviet naval forces as a strictly military threat to NATO. Given the vast expansion and diversification of strategic nuclear forces, the Mediterranean is no longer a vital area for either mounting or countering a threat to the homeland of Russia. In the event of total nuclear war, the Russian squadrons, still vastly inferior to the Sixth Fleet, without taking account of other NATO fleets in the Mediterranean, would presumably launch a suicide attack on the American carriers, which retain a residual nuclear strike capacity. They could also attempt to deal with any Polaris submarines which the Western nuclear powers had chosen to leave in this strategically unsuitable but politically symbolic shallow sea.

In any direct conflict between NATO and the Warsaw Pact nations that falls short of strategic nuclear war, the Soviet fleet would not much change the strategic picture. It might attack the carriers from which air support was given to the southern flank, but it would have a poor chance of success with conventional weapons. The decisive strategic feature of the southern flank is the preponderance of Communist forces on land, with the consequence that the NATO powers would probably be speedily overrun in a campaign to which naval power would be only marginally relevant. During this process the Russian fleet would almost certainly be quickly destroyed. For if the Russian force poses a theoretical threat to Western communications, its own are much more hopelessly exposed in any open hostilities.

Insofar as the Russian naval penetration has any coherent motive other than mere emulation of the United States, its purpose must therefore be limited and political. Although it is easier to imagine that the goal of such a limited policy must lie chiefly in the Arab lands and those beyond, the political effects on NATO itself may not be negligible. For the local members of NATO, particularly Greece and Turkey, are divided among themselves, one symptom of which is the fragmented and divided command structure of NATO in the area. Moreover, these countries stand virtually alone on their fronts, without the reassuring and deterrent presence of multilateral forces to ensure that aggression against one of them inevitably involves other friendly powers. The Soviet Mediterranean squadrons serve to create a sense of encirclement and isolation, but more important perhaps has been the creeping atmosphere of détente among the leading nations of NATO—prior to Czechoslovakia at least—and the adoption of a strategy of "flexible response," all of which has bred uncertainty as to whether the central allies would really regard an attack on the flank as a *casus belli*. Thus in Turkey as in Iran there have been moves toward reinsurance with Russia, which a change of regime might duplicate in Greece. The relatively mild Western diplomatic reaction to the Czech coup contributed to this movement, and, paradoxically, subsequent moves toward a consolidation of military organization and effort among the Western European powers—the European "caucus," for example—reinforce the tendency. For no one believes that Turkey would be a welcome member of an emergent European Defense Community.

In this respect, Russian policy must be delicately poised, for if Soviet naval presence and other military infiltrations of the Middle East increase the sense of exposure and isolation on NATO's southern flank, too vigorous and menacing an appearance might reinvigorate the central allies' attention to the area and drive the local members to reaffirm their need of the alliance. In this partially lies the justification for Western measures of reinforcement, the strictly strategic reasons for which seem less than compelling.

II

The pace and complexion of Russian policy will very probably be more decisively determined by developments in what they must surely regard as the more open and profitable arenas of the Arab world and the Indian Ocean. Expansion of Russia's own capability for distant operations and her resources for military assistance, the retreat of the final European power, Great Britain, from east of Suez, the distraction of the United States to Southeast Asia and her recent appearance of disillusionment with the support of overseas positions by military means, must all combine to make the prospects of increasing Soviet influence in the Arab world and around the Indian Ocean beyond seem tempting.

Here, as on the southern flank of NATO, one must distinguish between war and peace in assessing prospects. In war there is as yet no Russian presence that the Western allies could not take care of, though the balance in the Indian Ocean and the Gulf could change rapidly if the Canal were reopened. But unless recent developments in Central Europe and the Mediterranean, coupled with the approach of strategic nuclear parity, portend a complete revolution in the place of overt force in Soviet foreign policy, it is probable that Russia intends its military commitment to be a limited one that would fall short of confrontations likely to entail hostilities with the United

States. Moreover, it must be recognized that in many military situations that might arise in the Middle East, naval force deprived of aviation would not be particularly useful.

For a policy of prestige and diplomatic influence, however, naval force has many advantages to which the rapidly increasing number of formal Russian port visits in the Mediterranean, Gulf, Indian Ocean, and Red Sea testify. In several Mediterranean ports such as Latakia, in Syria, and Port Said and Alexandria, in Egypt, the Russian naval presence is now almost permanent, and considerable efforts are being made with Russian financial and technical help to improve port facilities in many places commanding the narrow passages around Arabia. Such aid is associated with assistance to local armed forces, including the dissemination of small but potent naval systems like the famous Komar boats. Economic aid, military assistance, and the acquisition of facilities for a Russian military presence coexist in an interconnected cycle of growing influence and potential control. Justifiably or not, Russian strategists must see a hope that their gradual diplomatic and military pressure upon the Arab states and the shakier NATO allies will ultimately result in the virtual exclusion of Western forces from all the ports, airfields, and airspace of the region.

Two crucial questions about the Soviet military penetration of the Middle East are what effect it may have on the behavior of the local powers and whether the Russian forces will themselves undertake interventions. Precedent suggests that the Soviet Union would be very reluctant to commit its own forces and flag in situations likely to lead to hostilities, particularly if there were any prospect of collision with the West. It is possible, however, that under certain circumstances the capability with which the Russians are providing themselves may become a compulsion. The pervasively dangerous aspect of the new Middle East confrontation is the close association of great-power armed forces with local and highly militarized powers over whom they exercise only partial control. In one possible event, the Russians might find a client regime meeting catastrophic defeat at the hands of a local enemy. Some observers believe Russia would have made a military move in 1967 if Israel had pressed on to Damascus. Certainly it may be far more embarrassing to leave an associate unaided when one's fleet is offshore than when no local means are at one's disposal.

Under other circumstances the time may well come when, in the Mediterranean or perhaps more probably in the Gulf or in Eastern or Southern Africa, the positive advantages to be gained from intervening forcibly in some local, perhaps civil, conflict may seem irresistible. If Russian ships or aircraft could appear first on a troubled scene and thereby impose on the Western powers the onus of deciding upon a counterintervention, with consequent risk of the direct confrontation so earnestly avoided in the East-West struggle, the Soviet Union would have taken a notable step toward parity with the United States in capacity for distant self-assertion. It seems no more than wise to assume that the acquisition of forces for long-range action and their deployment at ever increasing ranges indicate a general inclination toward a more assertive overseas policy, and explicit Soviet statements confirm this. Moreover, it is possible that the use of Soviet forces, under close control, might on occasion seem to be a safer method of intervention than the use of local forces as proxy.

The presence of Soviet armed and perhaps occasionally combatant forces in the Middle East is a factor that local powers will have to take account of in determining their own military policy. Whatever the precise motives of Russian entry into Egyptian ports after the sinking of the *Eilat*, their presence must inevitably have conditioned Israel reprisals—because of its confined maritime nature, it did not preclude them—and it may also have moderated Egyptian policy by extending at least a limited guarantee against further Israel inroads. In the future such guarantees might be used either to inhibit local aggression, by protecting the would-be victim, or to encourage it, by offering the potential aggressor some assurance against reprisal. If great-power intervention of this kind becomes common, however, it may not always have the intended effect. For the probability of intervention will place a premium on rapid, preemptive action to win the day before interference is effective. Middle East terrain, which favors the use of air power, has already encouraged preemptive strategies, and the superpowers have been conspicuously less effective in reversing the results of battle than in bringing hostilities to a halt. It must also be recognized that the economic and diplomatic pressures at the disposal of the great powers are on many occasions likely to prove more serviceable instruments of control and intervention than their military forces.

With two superpowers henceforth present on the local scene, the

Western nations will have new dangers to consider when contemplating the type of intervention they have conducted in the past. For the moment it may well be that they have considerably less enthusiasm than hitherto for enterprises of such a kind. Just as between the great and local powers, however, the presence of a new player in the Middle East military game may either inhibit action or place a premium on rapidity. A power contemplating military intervention will have to weigh the inhibiting presence of his opponent against the possibility that acting first would decisively transfer all those inhibitions onto the shoulders of his adversary. Such a line of thought might encourage adventurousness, but past experience suggests that the superpowers may lean toward caution at least in the volatile eastern Mediterranean. Were this seen to be the case, the ensuing balance of inhibition might give the local powers new latitude to pursue their own quarrels free of interference. When and where the great powers do wish to interpose their power, the growing strength and sophistication of local forces will itself put a premium on speed and will in any case considerably increase the risk of serious losses.

III

For external powers that wish to retain freedom of action and an open line of retreat from impending collision, naval power is ideal. Capable of a conspicuous and persistent presence, it can also discreetly withdraw. Nor does it require permanent bases in the interior of a territory. It is such considerations that make it seem improbable that the active Russian pursuit of access to convenient and adequate facilities for naval support in Middle East and perhaps Indian ports will result in the acquisition of formal bases on the old pattern. Both Russia and the local powers would experience considerable ideological embarrassment if undeniable bases were established, and modern naval forces are in any case increasingly able to operate without such amenities, especially in the absence of major hostilities.

Assuming for the moment that the present trend of Russian policy is not reversed either unilaterally or as the result of some explicit or tacit international understanding, what are the most appropriate responses for the West? Again it is necessary to be clear as to whether we count on peace or war. Clearly the maintenance of a favorable potential balance in the event of war is one of the best ways of averting its outbreak. But in point of fact the balance of combatant strength greatly favors the West so far as naval forces are concerned. The new situation calls for an increase of maritime aerial reconnaissance capability, which NATO is beginning to provide, encouraged, no doubt, by service interests in Italy and Great Britain. Otherwise the naval reinforcements that have been announced would seem to be more relevant to bolstering allied morale and creating a countervailing impression of progress upon local powers than to any anticipated hostilities. For serious combat around the Mediterranean, where the greatest Soviet penetration has so far occurred, air power and land reinforcement would seem to be the more pressing need. A substantial increase of Soviet forces capable of intervention in the Gulf or around the Indian Ocean might call for some revision of this estimate, but this is as yet no more than a prospect, especially while the canal remains closed.

So far as the political impression produced by the new Soviet presence is concerned, the scope for counteraction is limited in principle. Because they are entering for the first time areas in which the Western powers have hitherto been unchallenged, it is inevitable that the result be an impression of Russian growth and relative Western decline. This is a microcosm of the generally more ambitious scale on which Russia has been developing her naval and other capacities to advance her "state interests" the world over. Western countermeasures cannot wholly negate this effort short of preventive war and must therefore be confined to efforts to limit its inroads on Western interests and to avoid dangerous collisions. Because the day when Russia could be excluded by Western sovereign possession of much of the Middle East has passed, these efforts must be made by manipulating the system of states.

A reasonable initial prescription is that Western forces should not be withdrawn or reduced in the absence of some reciprocal Russian action. To make such a reduction would diminish the inhibitions upon Russian exploitation of their forces and go far to confer upon Russia precisely the position of unchallenged dominance of which the West has just been deprived. Such a reduction would also reinforce in local minds the impression of Soviet advance and Western decline. Whether or not Western forces should actually be increased, however, depends upon the extent to which the Russians have set themselves some notion of parity as a goal, for in this case Western

forces would serve merely as a magnet to attract a larger Russian investment. The situation which is fast approaching, in which the
Russian squadron has a nominal equivalence in number of vessels
to the Sixth Fleet but is infinitely inferior in fighting power, might
conceivably be a relationship capable of satisfying Soviet prestige
and Western needs.

The great power balance is itself of limited significance, because
the manipulation of local governments and armed forces will usually
constitute the more potent way of sustaining great power influence.
Thus it may be that diplomatic efforts to resolve local disputes, such
as those between Greece and Turkey, Saudi Arabia and Iran, and to
develop frameworks of local security, as in the Gulf, would do more
to deprive Russian power of opportunities to molest Western interests than simply matching the Soviet investment of forces in
kind. But the maintenance of an adequate Western military presence
is presumably the condition for such diplomatic successes, for only
this can create confidence that aggressive Soviet adventures could
not be matured without fear of counteraction.

It has to be recognized that if Russian military penetration of
the Middle East proceeds unabated, the attempt to build up a unified
response by the NATO powers will not be easy. For the moment the
fortuitous surplus of British naval power, ironically about to withdraw from the more distant part of the threatened zone, has made
possible a show of growing countervailing power in the Mediterranean. It is also conceivable that, especially after de Gaulle, the Soviet presence, coupled with the decline in hopes of accommodation
in Central Europe, may enable the French Navy to make more conspicuous the high degree of cooperation it has never ceased to extend
to its allies. But notions of a standing Mediterranean force or of
highly coordinated politico-military responses are liable to frustration by the sharp divisions of outlook among the Mediterranean
NATO powers, some of which, like Italy, believe that ostentatious
coordination of policy would undermine their considerable hopes of
effectively wooing the Arab states on a national basis.

If the apparent resurgence of the Russian military threat continues, both in Central Europe, as a result of Czechoslovakia, and in
the Middle East, by reason of the naval intrusion, it will remain to
be seen whether this will result in the isolation of the southern flank
as the nations in the center concentrate on their immediate security

and draw Great Britain increasingly into a European defense frame-work or whether the traditional Mediterranean power, Britain, joined perhaps by France and probably motivated chiefly by concern for oil supplies, will reestablish Western European power in the Middle East. The latter prospect is dimmed by the dominant skepticism in Europe as to whether military presence is a necessary or effective way to preserve economic interests. Such hesitance is particularly likely to persist until it becomes apparent how deeply the disillu-sionment of Vietnam has affected America's own readiness to at-tempt military solutions to distant problems.

IV

The difficulties that the Western powers will encounter in devising and executing a strategy for the Middle East should not obscure the pitfalls that lie in Russia's path. On the one hand, an intrusive Rus-sian presence will not always be regarded as an unmixed blessing among Russia's protégés. Czechoslovakia has done nothing to minimize the dangers of close military association with Russia, though the geopolitical circumstances of Middle East countries are very different. The Middle East has not in recent years been an area in which the schemes of outsiders have gone well, and the in-stability that offers Russia her opportunity may also be her undoing. This is the more so as she will be drawn into a series of intractable interstate disputes in which it will be difficult not to alienate some-one. The Soviet Union will have to steer a careful line indeed if her military presence and patronage of some local armed forces is not to drive others to look more anxiously to the West for support. Al-ready she has experienced the difficulty of playing a part on the Indian subcontinent, where there also arises the danger of an in-direct collision with China.

The efforts at moderating local conflicts into which such com-plexity may lead the Soviet Union, as at Tashkent, suggest that Russian presence may sometimes be a stabilizing force. Whether this will justify Western acquiescence in Russian expansion of in-fluence depends partly on the extent to which the Soviet Union uses her access to the Middle East to undermine direct Western economic and political interests and exploits her foothold for further penetra-tions into Afro-Asia. For if it is tempting to derive some comfort from seeing others shoulder the burdens of keeping order in these turbulent areas, we must not forget that such undertakings are the price of global power. Whatever her immediate behavior, there is the danger that an unopposed Russia will become increasingly uninhibited in self-assertion. Moreover, the Middle East is so indigenously turbulent that external powers with interests there have ample opportunity to be drawn into conflicts not of their own making. Above all, the course of acquiescence in complete Soviet control of the local military balance is precluded for America by her relations with Israel.

Is it possible that the spirit of détente will be so reestablished after the dust of Czechoslovakia has settled that the two superpowers will achieve relations of sufficient trust to permit a reduction in suspicion of each other's diplomatic and strategic purposes in the Middle East? The prime objective of those who would achieve some consolidation of détente is an agreement, tacit or explicit, on the main nuclear balance so that the strategic stalemate, on which détente itself depends, may be buttressed and fortified. Such agreements might create conditions for an extension of military limitations and diplomatic *modus vivendi* to other areas of competition. But it is equally conceivable that, with the strategic balance secured, a degree of nuclear parity attained and mutual distaste for major war registered, the Russians would feel safer to push ahead with their plans for expansion by political and conventional military means. A relaxation of the nuclear competition might indeed release economic resources and military energy for employment in more limited adventures. It might also be that Russia would regard a mutual recognition of the nuclear stalemate as conferring a free hand upon her in certain geographical spheres, as she already does in eastern Europe. Her recent penetrations of the Middle East might then in retrospect appear to have been, whether by design or accident, the staking out of a claim to contain all or some of the area within the Soviet sphere.

Alternatively it might be hoped that Russia would be content to withdraw her own armed forces, if America would do likewise. Here there might be a basis for regional arms control. Certainly the naval forces so prominent in the Middle East would lend themselves in some respects to agreed limitations, being readily identifiable and easily deployed to other uses. The obstacles are, however, formidable. Some of America's allies are indigenous to the area and could not withdraw. Russia herself is so close to the Middle East and finds itself so much obliged to use its waters for access to other areas that a complete removal of Soviet naval forces—and perhaps of air forces —seems unattainable. With forces in transit, the opportunities for dispute about agreed force levels are obvious.

A further and decisive obstacle to the complete withdrawal of superpower forces is the role each plays *vis-à-vis* the turbulent local powers. So long as each side retains a residual desire to be able to intervene in local conflicts—and the Arab-Israel dispute argues that this desire must persist—its force levels are not merely determined by those of the other but are related to the requirements of dealing with increasingly strong indigenous powers capable of rapid military coups. Moreover it is far from clear that, in such conditions of turbulence, it would be desirable to remove the potential for quick and crushing intervention, which calls for powerful forces near at hand. At this point the prospects for limiting the military commitment of the great powers become closely dependent upon the chances of controlling the local arms races fed by the programs of military assistance and supply treated elsewhere in this study.

It might be suggested that the requirements of the superpowers in relation to local states could be satisfied by smaller forces than those to which their reciprocal interaction is driving them. Thus there might be a basis for agreed limitations if not for complete withdrawal. This would permit a residual American presence and both presence and rights of transit for Russia. One cannot categorically deny the possibility of such an outcome. But in view of the difficulty encountered in developing all forms of arms control, the special problems already alluded to in this particular case do little to encourage expectation of an early agreement.

The United States might well regard such an arrangement as a defeat, for it would have passed from being the dominant power to one enjoying only equality on a restricted level, by virtue of an agreement that might be taken to imply admission of being the potential loser had the competition continued. Paradoxically, an agreement upon parity would very probably be unacceptable to Russia also, for she is obviously on the make in the area and there is little reason to believe she would accept early termination of a contest she probably entertains high hopes of winning. It is noteworthy that in her demands that the Sixth Fleet should depart, Russia has explicitly based her case on the remoteness of the American force from the territory of the United States. Thus Russia confers upon itself in the Mediterranean a preferred position as a local *vis à vis* a distant interloper. As the whole basis of American security policy since 1945 has rested upon projection of power to meet danger before it is too close to home, it is far from clear that a bargain could be struck. It is possible, perhaps, that some small moderation of competition could be secured by an agreement to exclude strategic nuclear forces from the area. Even this would pose difficulties of definition concerning American carriers and the Soviet vessels armed with long-range tactical nuclear missiles, not to speak of the related shore-based aircraft.

Thus, assuming that an East-West détente on the central nuclear balance embraced a desire to mitigate military competition in the Middle East—as it may not—explicit and overall understandings seem far less likely than an extension of the efforts, ambiguous signs of which have already appeared, for reducing the frictions within a system of interlocked spheres of influence offering both East and West a parallel set of footholds in the region. It would certainly seem quixotic to believe that the present Soviet show of ambition, forwardness and material preparation suggests readiness to undertake complete abstention from the use of military forces as an instrument of policy in the Middle East, or that unilateral abstention by the West would inspire emulation by Russia. Indeed this might be by far the most dangerous course they could take. For it might lure Russia into a series of successful penetrations of the Middle East and nearby Africa which could reawaken cold war anxieties in the United States and thereby produce dangerous confrontations that a more consistent policy of resistance and competition would have averted.

Military Elements in Regional Unrest

I. WILLIAM ZARTMAN

As an international relations problem area, the Middle East is unique. In practice, the uniqueness is found in the persistent, almost doggedly nurtured, inability of neighbors to empathize with and even to understand correctly one another's actions and motivations. It is therefore with temerity that an outsider attempts to analyze, let alone project, these actions.

Perhaps only as an act of academic faith, although with an apparent degree of reliability or "fit" in the recent past, it is assumed here that a neutral, external concept of analysis can be used to form the basis for analysis and projection. The concept used is the international relations system, two forms of which are relevant to understanding the Middle East military response in the seventies. One level is the dominant system, composed of United States-USSR interactions; the other is the subordinate system of the Middle East, complicated by differences in degree of membership. In addition to a core area (the lower Nile and Mashriq or Arab East), there are distant members (the Maghrib or Arab West), a fringe area (the frontier zone) and a thorn (Israel). The thorn is in but not of the system, the distant members are directly but not always immediately involved in intrasystemic interaction, and the fringe area is not even always directly involved. This projection will pay less attention to the fringe area than to the two loci of conflicts within the system itself: inter-Arab and Arab-Israel conflicts.

The purpose here is to examine the behavioral characteristics of the subordinate system in the light of the two conflicts, and then to analyze the nature of relations—with an accent on the military—between the two systems under the suggested patterns of dominant system relations—cold war, limited détente, general détente—and under characteristic patterns of subordinate system relations, as developed below. Attention is focused on two questions: What types of Middle East response to superstate relations and initiatives are likely? What types of Middle East actions are likely to have an impact on superstate relations and initiatives?

I

There are several behavioral characteristics of the two conflicts. The inter-Arab conflict oscillates between Unity of Ranks and Unity of Purpose, the former implying harmony of all Arab states around the lowest common denominator of inaction and the latter implying alliance of a few states based on ideological fervor.

The intensity of the Arab-Israel conflict is dependent on the cyclical intensity of the inter-Arab conflict. During the Unity of Purpose phase, open military conflict is most likely and, even without war, tension is highest. During the Unity of Ranks phase, tensions are lower. It is beyond the scope of this chapter to examine the causes of shifting from one phase to another; suffice it to note that they tend to be internal to Arab states, may be related to Arab-Israel as well as inter-Arab developments, but are at best only indirectly related to extraregional stimuli.

In addition to the ideopolitical rivalry, there is also a continuing geopolitical competition, whose variations from East to West keep it from following either a simple polar, bipolar, or balance-of-power pattern. Egypt is by far the strongest Arab state in the area. To the East, Saudi and Iraqi positions are generally determined by opposition to each other or to Egypt, depending on which state is the greater threat to the third at any given moment. Syria and Jordan are the prey, the issues, and hence also the buffers in this pattern of relations. The result is a modified balance of power—modified because in the time of Unity of Ranks it becomes dormant.

In the Arab West, reactions are not polarized directly about Egypt but about Algeria, which itself is prevented at least by distance from being pressed into the same subpolar relation to Egypt as Iraq and

Saudi Arabia. Relations follow the same Unity-of-Ranks phases as in the rest of the Arab world, but they also have specifically Maghribi Unity-of-Ranks periods, which may or may not coincide with the general Arab phenomenon and which take the form of Maghrib Unity activities. Relations about Algeria do not bear the characteristics of a balance-of-power pattern, since rarely do Morocco and Tunisia coordinate their reactions to Algeria; Tunisia has its own role of mediator that it pursues whenever possible.

In inter-Arab relations as well as in Arab-Israel relations, conflict is as much the coin of cohesion of the system as is cooperation. Whether fighting or collaborating, the states remain important to one another. Even though some outside states—notably the super-states—become more interested in the area, and others—notably ex-imperial states—become less so, they are not able to carve it up, destroy its interacting systemic nature, or replace the primary importance of its members to one another.

In neither conflict is there ever any victor or any end. Cyclical rivalries erupted and subsided between Iraq and Egypt when both were monarchies, when both were radical republics, and when their systems of government differed. Should the whole Arab world turn republican, it is likely that the same cyclical rivalries will break out soon again, either over some new issues or over an interpretation of an old one. Although it may be physically possible to destroy Israel, it is unlikely that Arab states or Palestine refugees will be able to accomplish this end by themselves, and it is considered equally unlikely that an outside ally would be willing to help them accomplish their goal. A fortiori, it is impossible for Israel physically to eliminate its enemies: the only ways are genocide, which is unthinkable, and incorporation, which has its own self-operative limits: Israel cannot incorporate an Arab population of the same size or larger than its own Jewish population. Thus, the conditions are theoretically ripe for the "mental elimination" of the sides qua sides, through reconciliation and peaceful coexistence. Yet the logic of this reconciliation is likely to escape realization for a decade or longer.

The level of power in the Middle East is higher than in many other parts of the third world; that is, Middle East states do have a capacity to change the behavior of other states (in or outside the area) in an intended direction. They have something others want, with which they can gratify or deprive. In regard to external states, this capability is based on the strategic location of the region: its propinquity to Europe, its control of the stopcocks of the Mediterranean, and its position atop the oilkegs of the world. In regard to the states of the region, power is achieved through a full range of instrumentalities, including the manipulation of men, money, and symbols to affect the target state's internal stability. Not all states in the region possess the same capability: if relations fit into polarized patterns, it is because power is polarized or vice versa.

II

The conceptual problems of dealing with power in this study are considerably simplified by the fact that only one aspect—military force—is the direct concern; yet power must not be equated with force alone. A discussion of military aspects of power must keep the other aspects in mind, and must be understood against the political (subsuming economic) background already traced. Such a discussion must also include, in addition to conventional military power, the contemporary higher dimension of nuclear power, and the older "lower" dimension of paramilitary power.

Military force in the Middle East is not an effective element of power against outside states, as much because they are unlikely to invade as because of the local quality of armed forces. It is effective against local states, however, but with a major inhibition: it has generally been considered "un-Arab" to use military force against other Arab states. Armies are reserved for parapolice duties, military coups, and defeats at the hands of Israel. Furthermore, these functions are interrelated, since government abuse of the army's military role, either by tarnishing its image in making it act as a policeman or by not giving it the necessary support and direction in military operations, leads the military to act as an interest group and protect its interests by intervening in politics. In some countries of the Middle East, however, this intervention has become so routine that the army loses its primarily military character (thus enforcing its police role and combat inadequacy, and further increasing its political propensity) and becomes the accepted means of elite succession. Army factions become "parties," and coups became "elections." Syria and Iraq are at this point; Algeria and Egypt could possibly join them.

Armies are useful, moreover, for one other function that involves both local and external states: arms races. The need for arms gives Arab states something to bargain with in dealing with external states, and something to bargain against in dealing with one another and Israel. There is no evidence to show that they have ever bargained conclusively *with* one another or Israel over arms supplies, including local arms control. A constant characteristic can be noted in regard to these arms races: build-up, followed by conflict, followed by replenishment and rebuild-up to comparable manpower levels with increasingly more expensive hardware. Two additional inhibitors can be distinguished in projecting this trend: the limits on the extent to which a developing country's budget can be mortgaged to unproductive arms purchases, and the limits on the rate at which militarily useful manpower can be increased through population growth, education, and industrialization.

In order to conjure up future possibilities of operating in this kind of situation, it is necessary to ascertain whether any of these behavioral characteristics are likely to change, or more manageably, whether there are any causes likely to change these characteristics. In so doing, it is hard to separate projections from assumptions. Under whichever heading one choses, these characteristics are considered unlikely to change in the 1970s. Obviously, a scenario could be drawn for the Final Solution of Israel, or alternatively for the establishment of a Peaceable Kingdom in the Middle East. It might even be possible to imagine the establishment of a Communist regime in some country there. But such alternatives scarcely seem likely. The same may be said of major changes in political geography, such as a new and cohesive United Arab Republic (UAR) or a united Maghrib, or, maybe a bit less improbable, the disappearance of Jordan or a remilitarized Arab-controlled West Bank or Sinai. Impossible or not, one may assume that these changes will not take place by the end of the 1970s. It is not unlikely that changes will occur in the distribution of power in the area, however, even though it is assumed that any such changes will not affect the general pattern of relations in the area or its polarized distribution of power.

In nuclear weapons, it is impossible to make any sound projections without changing the ball game. Israel could produce a few low-yield weapons in the 1970s. Such a development would immediately lead Egypt to make strong appeals to the closest nuclear power for interim aid or guarantees. The actual use of nuclear weapons by either side would be an act of irresponsibility and desperation, growing out of a grim and hopeless confrontation. That situation is considered extraordinary enough to be unlikely but not impossible. The threatened use of nuclear weapons by either state would more probably be part of a bargaining situation than a military situation, although a called bluff could easily produce pressure to make it good. Such nuclear blackmail, in practically any great state configuration, is here assumed to be likely to lead to great state efforts to cool the conflict or at least to keep the bargaining political. Only the rise of a strong military faction in Soviet politics might change the situation.

The "lower" dimension of military power is paramilitary. A national liberation movement in Palestine is already a reality, but its continued existence depends on its continuing success. An Israel response of repression or integration, or both, could deny it the success it needs. The history of liberation gives no examples of success by movements that are doomed by ethnic considerations to remain minorities. Thus, a Palestine liberation movement is less of a threat to Israel than to Jordan, where it can win majority support. A radicalized or even revolutionary Jordan could conceivably launch a crusade against Israel, but such an eventuality could be more easily mastered by Israel than a return match with an Egypt that had learned to handle its arms. Thus the danger of paramilitary forces lies—in the future as in the past—in their role as a potential trigger in both inter-Arab and Arab-Israel conflicts and their relative immunity to external arms control measures, since they can be fed by small arms producers and indirect suppliers, including area ones.

But changes can occur in conventional military power. It is hard to see any major shift in the relative manpower levels of the Arab and Israel armies. Mobilization figures given for the late 1950s and the late 1960s are about the same. Arab states can expand their mobilization more than Israel can, but the quality of recruits is another matter. Thus, the mobilized manpower balance seems relatively constant: Israel somewhat bigger than Egypt; Iraq, Syria, Saudi Arabia, Morocco, and Algeria at similar levels less than half of Egypt; Jordan straining to keep pace at a comparable level. Iran and Turkey can continue to be at or above the Egypt-Israel levels, but are not considered as primary actors here. The relation between men and machines in the Middle East armies was well stated by France's Minister of the Armies in early February 1969. He said,

"Israel has an army and an air force. The Arab states have tanks and planes." Rather than mere manpower it appears that technology and alliances are the two interrelated means of altering military power; armaments figures for the 1950s and the 1960s show a notable increase.

III

Since military power and its use in the Middle East depend primarily on external inputs, a military analysis must first examine the political relations between the dominant and subordinate systems. Theoretically, cold war implies an alliance race, in the broad sense of either an overt attempt to enlist new allies, as in 1949-1955, or at least an attempt to undermine the opponent's close ties with third states, as in 1956-1961. In this situation, a third state has power over members of the dominant system: it has something these members want, namely itself.

Practically, the Soviet Union has developed a substantive interest in the Middle East over the past decade or more. Whether this is because of the oil or because of a need for warm-water ports or because of a newly or renewedly felt manifest destiny is an intriguing and unending argument, which is irrelevant to the basic fact. The fact is that this interest, in a cold war situation, leads Russia away from past efforts at merely disruptive activities within a Western preserve and toward a new effort to achieve firm commitments. Thus, Syria and Iraq with their unstable revolutionary traditions are less appropriate foci of attention. Far more logical, considering the current nature of the Soviet government itself, are the radical technocracies of Egypt and Algeria, and perhaps by the 1970s, Sudan. The technocratic focus also goes hand in hand with current attention to the military establishments in these two countries, and also leads away from the need for a party-based Communist take-over. It is assumed here that in no Middle East state will the local Communist party be the major governmental force at any time during the period.

In the inter-Arab conflict, these characteristics correspond to a Unity of Purpose phase, pushing Jordan and Saudi Arabia, and Morocco and Tunisia, closer to the West as a political ally and military supplier. In such periods, pressure on Israel tends to increase, couched not only in terms of Arabist slogans but in ideological slogans in line with current trends, with Israel seen as a "have," a neobourgeois society, a capitalist state, and a colonialist beach-head. However, the danger of the pro-Western Arab states being lumped with Israel may work to reduce either their pro-Westernness or, paradoxically, the pressure on Israel as such pressure is diverted to the pro-Western Arabs.

There is an inhibitor on this escalating process, however, and that is the great state awareness of the dangers of World War III. It is clearly a time of brinkmanship, when incidents increase but the consciousness of their potential end product also grows clear. Such incidents can be many. Arms races in the Arab West and the Arab East, as well as between Arabs and Israel, are likely. They are likely too to focus not only on tanks and artillery, but on jet fighters, missiles, and on at least rumors of atomic weapons, although the inhibiting factor can be considered to work most strongly in the area of nuclear proliferation. Probably missiles are the most dangerous, since their impersonality reduces the elements of skill and nerve so necessary in jet warfare.

Another likely incident is great state intervention. A likely case would be a 1958-Lebanon-type intervention by the Soviet Union in Syria, the UAR, or Algeria to protect a friendly government at its invitation. It is even conceivable that close maneuvers, with or without shooting, could occur between Soviet and American ships, possibly in the eastern Mediterranean. Russia cannot take over the Mediterranean, nor is it likely to cut the basin in half with a twentieth-century Lepanto: it can only "cohabit" the sea along with American and Italian and French ships. The competing fleets would then be psychological inhibitors, since even in a new cold war, both sides would think twice before taking an action in which the other might interfere. Not only Suez but also the Lebanese and Cypriot crises would have been complicated by a Soviet fleet's presence.

A related element is the Suez Canal: Israel would be hard-pressed to fire on clearing crews if they were Russian. Yet if the canal were opened to Russian naval ships, psychological means of exerting pressure and tangible means of extending aid in East Africa, Yemen and South Yemen, the Gulf of 'Aqabah, and even the Persian Gulf and the Indian Ocean would be available. All this would take place under conditions of vulnerability and overextension for Soviet supply lines, but this inhibitor is less comforting than it appears: American supply lines too could become vulnerable and overextended. Such a major Soviet drive would increase the sense of insecurity of West-leaning states like Spain, Morocco, Tunisia, and Turkey; in any case, short of war "overextension" and "vulnerability" have less meaning than "psychological inhibitions" and "encouragement."

It is hard to tell how the world would get out of this phase. It would depend on developments within the dominant system and with the superstates. What is important is that the detail confirms the principle: in many of these incidents, the subordinate system members, and hence the system itself, have causative effects, and hence power, over the dominant system and its members.

There is another potential inhibiting factor, however, that comes from the subordinate system itself. The postwar evolution of inter-Arab relations has been toward asserting the system's autonomy and removing dominating foreign influence. There is no guarantee that this trend will continue. But to the extent that it does and the superstates' awareness of nuclear danger is paralleled by local awareness of the dangers of external dominance, the region's own sense of identity and its desire to control its own destiny—a characteristic of developing foreign policy—can help the cold war from reaching its logical extremes. This inhibitor would work best in a Unity of Ranks phase, when the pressures for outside allies are lowest.

IV

The third worldwide configuration is taken out of order, since a description of it allows a clearer understanding of the intermediate case of limited détente. Under general détente, the subordinate system's power over the dominant system is greatly reduced, although two types of relations between the two systems are possible. General détente implies a Great Coalition, again in the broad sense of either a formal agreement (truly the Peaceable Kingdom!) or merely tacit cooperation. For the Great Coalition to remain, its members must feel a common interest in reducing tensions that threaten it. However, the loss of small state power over the dominant system does not necessarily imply the reverse, the rise of great state power over the subordinate system. The Great Coalition might merely agree to treat the region as a ghetto, free to fight its own fights, police its own beat, tend its own local stores, and revel in its autonomous identity, as in Africa today. Only when conflict threatens to get out of hand and imperil the détente would the dominant system impose itself. In either case, great power interest shifts from the subordinate to the dominant system.

Yet the scenario looks too simple. There is no need for the great states to obtain acquiescence for arms control measures: they only have to apply them. There is no need for the great states to obtain agreement in a peace-keeping operation: they only have to implement it. For as long as this power configuration obtains, certain actions are possible, but when these actions become impossible, the power configuration changes.

The one area where fruitful attention can be focused is regional military power and its use. The original assumptions have stated that cyclical inter-Arab and Palestine conflicts will continue, whatever the dominant system patterns. Furthermore, even if inhibitions to nuclear proliferation are enforced by great state cooperation, paramilitary and conventional military power is still available to local states. For positive arms-control measures to find an open ear in the region, as contrasted with negative arms-control measures imposed from outside, the cyclical conflicts would have to be at their low point; and since it has been posited that the Palestine conflict is dependent on the inter-Arab conflict, a phase of Unity of Ranks would have to obtain.

This precondition too is almost definitional. For regional agreement to be obtained, a disposition toward common action, or toward common military inaction, would have to pre-exist. Yet from that point, a number of measures could take shape within or from outside the region. A denuclearization treaty might provide a start, particularly since it would automatically involve Israel as well as Arab participation. Among measures involving outside efforts, the refugee problem could provide an initial point of attack; although this would appear to be a socio-political problem, it is actually profoundly military, since the refugees provide manpower and motivation for the liberation armies. Conceivably at a time of Unity of Ranks, an approach might be for massive outside capital joined with Israel, Kuwayti, and Libyan assistance to settle refugees, with compensation, in reclaimed lands and new cities, perhaps in southwestern Jordan or northern Sinai and in Israel for the few who so wish.

There appears to be one totally different way in which the Great Coalition might favor regional arms control. It has already been pointed out that general détente in the dominant system need not imply détente in dominant-subordinate system relations—indeed, almost inevitably to the contrary. It is at least theoretically conceivable that Great Coalition dominance over the area might become so offensive to both sides in both conflicts of the region (Palestine and inter-Arab) that the states of the region might react against the great states by cooperating among themselves. Such a notion is not fantastic: it is merely premature for the 1970s.

V

Between the domination or autonomy of the general détente and the brinkmanship of the cold war lies the limited détente. The years from 1963 to the present seem typical of this type of configuration. They were characterized by mixed cooperation and conflict among the greats, and nuclear proliferation among two or three second-rate states with polycentric tendencies. It is hard to imagine a true multipolar system in tomorrow's world, but the nuclear capability plus the polycentrism afforded by their second-rate status allows increased opportunities to countries like France and China. In this situation, the Middle East has different possibilities for maneuvering than under either of the other two configurations. Lines are not as sharply drawn as in the previous cases; chances of external political and limited military support are increased, but the chances of either firm alliances or cooperative control from above are diminished. All of the polycentric states, with the possible exception of China, which may continue to be debilitated by internal unrest for some time, would tend to hover between friendly relations with some states and a policy of disruption toward those too friendly with another side. In a period of polycentrism, a weak state can be opposed to both of the two great states and still be able to find a strong ally.

Arms control under these conditions is nearly impossible, and many of the inhibitors of the other two configurations are absent. Even if the two great powers agree temporarily on embargo, there is always France or Germany or Britain or Italy or Czechoslovakia, and the more the United States and the Soviet Union agree under these conditions, the more the secondary states are willing to capitalize on this ostensible joint world domination to further their own fortunes. These fortunes are real, not merely opportunistic: Europe needs Middle East goodwill and oil, in a way that the United States and the Soviet Union do not. Since the atmosphere is deceptively relaxed, however, the inhibiting fear of escalation and cataclysm characteristic of the cold war is absent, along with the firm cooperation and control that would be found under general détente. The world is back in the 1965 arms race among Israel, Egypt, Saudi Arabia, Lebanon, Libya, and Jordan, and among the United States, the Soviet Union, France, and West Germany, a sequel to which was the 1967 war. As long as alternative suppliers are available to the region and uncontrollable by the great powers, arms control is likely to be ineffective as well as resented by suppliers and supplied.

Arms control and peacekeeping measures depend on prior or concomitant agreement among the external states, in the absence of self-control by the regional states. The history of the Tripartite Declaration (1950) provides ample evidence. So does the United Nations Emergency Force, which could have been maintained at the time when it was really needed only through concerted backing by all great and secondary states. Now discredited, the potentially useful United Nations interposition forces can once more be a useful inhibitor to Middle East conflict only if the great states will commit themselves to making it a tripwire for their own concerted diplomatic pressures—tantamount to guaranteeing the territorial inviolability and passage rights of Israel, the Arab states, and one another.

Limited détente looms as the most unstable of the three periods. It is the time of false hopes, unclear rules, abrupt comeuppances, and needed lessons. Every Middle East war has occurred in a period of relaxed bipolar tensions relative to the previous period. But limited détente is also the path that leads from cold war to general détente. It might therefore be suggested that, if limited détente is not a stable pattern of relations but a transition and a direction, it is the period when the Middle East can contribute to furthering great state harmony. Arab states and Israel can cool their own conflicts and arrange their own arms control agreements, thereby removing not only a danger of local war but also a snare that could pull the great states, and themselves, back into cold war. To do so would be a real exercise of power by the small states over the great powers and an impressive move by the states of the region to control their own destinies. Given their currently demonstrated goals and tactics, it is doubtful that they will seize the opportunity.

The conclusions are clear, if unencouraging. In none of the three scenarios examined does there appear to be any local interest in strengthening initiatives to reduce tensions, either within the region or as a contribution to the elimination of the cold war. In some ways, even to Western "rationality," this should not be surprising. Small states generally get what they want by borrowing power from bigger states. They also improve their position by banding together. In the Middle East, banding together means an intensification of either the inter-Arab or the Arab-Israel conflicts. All this is more likely to occur, of course, at times of Unity of Purpose than Unity of Ranks. But even here the chances for optimism are not clear, for Unity of Ranks has in the past been used more as a breathing spell than as a time for constructive tension-reducing accomplishments. If Middle East initiatives toward the reduction of tensions can be expected to be weak, their reactions to outside attempts to reduce tensions may be stronger but no more constructive. If the great states were ever to agree on the reduction of naval strength in the Mediterranean or on a new version of the Tripartite Declaration controlling arms imports into the region, they would have to contend with pressure from insistent and offended states which would argue persuasively that their margin of security was being eroded by time, and their national interest was in danger. Unanswered, such arguments could eventually turn—as they have in the past—into threats "to go elsewhere" and into local attempts to restore just enough rivalry among outside powers to produce the needed arms. In the wings, secondary states on the northern side of the sea, which are and for centuries have been more authentic Mediterranean powers than the superstates, would be waiting to further their own interests. Arms control in this situation is a job for St. Michael and other iron-clad angels. Conflict containment and conflict management appears to be the better part of valor.

Economic Competition in the 1970s

Declining American Involvement

GARDNER PATTERSON

Only a small part of the present interests of the United States in the Middle East are economic, in the narrow sense of that term. American private direct investment in the area seems to be well under $3 billion, of which a little over $2 billion is in the petroleum industry.[1] These figures can be put in perspective by comparing them with a total foreign direct investment of some $59 billion and a worldwide total of about $17 billion in petroleum. The $2 billion or so in petroleum understates the economic significance of this investment, however, because perhaps at least twice as much again of United States investment in ships and in refining, distributing, and marketing facilities in Western Europe is devoted in large part to handling oil imports from the Middle East. Still, these are relatively small amounts for the United States, although huge for particular countries and companies. United States merchandise exports to the area are currently running at from $2 to $2.5 billion per year and imports are at a rate of from, say, $1 to $1.25 billion per year. Comparable figures for trade with Canada, for example, are about $7 billion in each direction. The United States also directly and indirectly now earns in the neighborhood of $1 billion a year from its role in the drilling, plus the transportation, refining, dis-

[1] The "Middle East" as defined here differs in its geographic coverage from that of any of the regions for which most economic data are assembled and so only rough estimates have been used. The investment data are as of the end of 1967.

tribution, and sale of Middle East oil to West European consumers.[2] America has an economic interest in the right of overflights for its commercial (and military) aircraft, it earns and spends some on tourism and various other services, but these amounts are small. The United States direct economic stake in the area is modest. Perhaps its greatest economic interest is a derived one: its interest in Western Europe and that area's dependence on Middle East oil.

America's major direct interests there are political, military, and cultural, including a humanitarian concern for poor people and a wish for the survival and growth of democracy and economic liberalism, aspects explored in other chapters. America is currently trying to further the noneconomic interests by the use of such economic instruments as development loans, technical assistance, P.L. 480 help, and military-equipment grants and loans. These are dissimilar, and it is both difficult and dangerous to make a quantitative estimate of their value, but they seem to be running, currently, at something between $0.75 and $1 billion dollars per year. How are these economic interests likely to change in the coming decade?

I

Whether the next decade witnesses a continuation of the cold war in more or less its present form, or moves toward a more comprehensive détente, it is likely that American economic involvement—government aid, trade, and new investment—in the area will decline, relatively, from the levels of the past two decades.

There are several reasons why the emphasis in the United States on economic transfers, on *government aid*, whether direct or indirect, is likely to shift, at least in relative terms, toward internal United States problem areas and away from external ones. First is the fact that the Congress, and it would seem much of the articulate public as well, have become disenchanted with foreign aid and what it has accomplished. Not only have the extravagant claims by its supporters failed to be achieved, but it is extremely hard, in the very nature of the phenomena, to trace the benefits, although many who have examined the problems are convinced that they are substantial. The periodic "crises in aid giving" have not only increased in intensity

---

[2] Considerations such as tax laws and the like seem to determine how the companies allocate this amount between the Middle East and Western Europe.

recently in the United States, but there is also much disaffection and disenchantment in Western Europe as well. The result is that competitive pressure on the United States from its friends to do more is reduced. Moreover, after twenty years, foreign aid often is not regarded as an undisguised blessing in the recipient countries, and this in turn tends to increase its unpopularity in the United States. A reading of recent Congressional debates and hearings suggests that if foreign aid of current, to say nothing of larger, dimensions is to be provided, the so-called cold war conflicts will have to become more acute. Moreover, if interest is to be revived, new approaches to the problem of foreign aid are likely to be necessary in the United States.[3] Any new methods, approaches, and techniques for foreign aid of sufficient novelty and substance to have any appreciable effect will take some time to develop, however.

Not only is foreign economic aid suffering from a decline in public and Congressional esteem and support, but as a claimant for American resources in the 1970s it will face a powerful competitor: the urban poor. Surely, one of the most important recent developments in the United States has been recognition that its security is threatened at home as well as abroad. The importance attached by almost all Americans to solving their own urban and social problems is new in kind, not just in amount. It is all too clear that solutions will require huge amounts of aid for housing, education, medical care, job training, and the like. Indeed, much larger amounts of whatever funds can be found will need to be devoted to meeting these newly recognized domestic needs. Particularly important here—and permeating all aspects of American foreign affairs—is that for some years to come the intellectual resources of this nation, especially of the young, will be largely concentrated on domestic rather than international problems. In other words, foreign aid must compete as it has not in recent years for both intellectual and physical resources.

One may safely assume that the gross national product of the United States will continue to increase and that as a consequence the amount of funds that could be devoted to aid to the poor and underdeveloped, whether in this country or abroad, will increase. But it remains that the recognized needs of the lower-income groups in this

---

[3] For a recent and interesting one see A. O. Hirschman and Richard M. Bird, *Foreign Aid—A Critique and Proposal*, Essays in International Finance, July 1968, International Finance Section, Princeton University.

country, *plus* the demands of the nonpoor for such public goods as better parks, less pollution, and the like, are of such huge dimensions that they can easily absorb the growing available public resources.

Finally, in the competition for aid funds the virtual absence of a "constituency" for foreign aid that is meaningful to those responsible for making the decision to provide funds, and the very large constituency for domestic aid, can be expected to make themselves felt.

This bleak prognosis for the amount of United States foreign aid to the Middle East has its parallel in the prospects for American investment and trade in the Middle East. The currently available evidence strongly suggests that the next decade will see the United States entering a period of increased rather than decreased protectionism and smaller rather than larger foreign investments.

Following the implementation of the Kennedy Round, the trade barriers will be down to levels where the welfare cost to the American consumer of the existing barriers on a great number of goods will be small, particularly with respect to the sort of goods that come from other developed countries. It is, therefore, difficult to mount public support and enthusiasm for freer trade, support that is necessary if the government is successfully to resist the constant and pervasive efforts of import-competing producers to erect new barriers, to say nothing of governmental efforts to cut the remaining barriers. Relevant here is the fact that the results of the Kennedy Round are being spread over a five-year period, and so even the more energetic supporters of freer trade find a sufficient reason for sitting still in the interim, while those opposed are given time to mount their offensive against further cuts, and for hacking away at past liberalization.

It is true that the barriers against many—but by no means all—of the imports from many of the developing countries, including several of those in the Middle East as here defined, are still high. Here the consumer welfare costs and inefficiencies in production are large, and a strong case exists for further cuts. Unfortunately, these are often precisely the goods for which further cuts will hurt domestic producers and ones for which institutions and policies have already begun to be developed which make further cuts extremely difficult. It is often the case that, excluding petroleum products, the goods the Middle East countries are eager and able to export in increasing amounts are those in which the input of labor is relatively high and for which the total demand in the United States, as well as in other developed nations, is expanding relatively slowly. Favorite examples are textiles, clothing, footwear, furniture, and many simple machines. These are also goods in which the United States already has well-established industries. Not being "growth" industries, any substantial increase in imports must be absorbed in the form of decreased employment and/or profits in the affected domestic firms. These are precisely the sort of industries for which a strong political case, and often a domestic social one as well, can be made for protection. One might hope that the growing national income of the United States would facilitate a more liberal import policy because it would make it less burdensome for the nation to take care of those who suffer from import competition. Unfortunately, it also makes it easier for the United States to pay the price of the inefficiencies that result from protecting the domestic producers. It is much easier for the rich to tolerate pockets of national inefficiencies than it is for the poor.

This is not all that augurs ill for the exports of developing countries in the coming decade. The past few years has seen the development of institutions making restraints on trade in their goods internationally respectable. The most important of these for the Middle East nations is the recently formalized and internationally sanctioned "market disruption" doctrine. This has come to mean that it is perfectly all right for a rich, developed nation (as well as a poor, undeveloped one) to restrict the imports of goods which would otherwise increase rapidly and create serious adjustment problems for the domestic industry concerned. The existing Arrangement for International Trade in Cotton Textiles—opposition to the implementation of which has found Israel and the United Arab Republic spokesmen giving interchangeable speeches—provides a prototype for nations like the United States restricting imports of goods of the kinds the developing countries themeselves produce efficiently. Current efforts to expand its coverage to wool and man-made fiber textiles are ominous.

For reasons that space does not permit even listing here, there is an increasing economic interdependence in the world. This seems to have been accompanied by a less-rapid growth, perhaps even a decline, in the number of *acceptable* market-type adjustment to disequilibrium. It therefore seems likely that in the future the nations of the world will have to strive for "negotiated" adjustments to the disequilibria that will follow from increased interdependence. Because capital movements have become such an important part of the United

States balance of payments, and because they lend themselves rather quickly and, as these things go, efficiently, to controls, it seems reasonable to expect that the decade ahead will see increased restrictions on such capital movements. The Middle East, especially the oil-dry nations, those in need of foreign capital, cannot expect to escape.

II

Against this gloomy forecast of probable United States foreign economic policies in the 1970s, what can be anticipated about some of the more important specific economic variables in the Middle East on which United States action can have an impact? One may anticipate that most of these matters will be only modestly affected during the next decade by the state of Soviet-American rivalry, so long as that remains within the assumed limits.

The recent closures of the Suez Canal have dealt a serious blow to a major source of foreign-exchange income for the area, and the prospects for the 1970s are not likely to be much affected by whether the cold war continues in more or less its present form or a détente is achieved. This die has already been cast. The two recent closings of the canal have provided a powerful incentive to those who use it to find alternative means of moving their goods. In recent years, roughly three-quarters of the canal traffic tonnage has been of ships transporting petroleum products. Even before the 1967 closing, the economics of tanker construction and transportation had dictated the building and use of vessels of much larger capacity than the present canal could handle. Plans for deepening and widening the ditch to allow tankers of up to 120,000 deadweight tons fully loaded to go through were being made. The capital costs of this would have been very great, but it seemed a wise investment. Since the closing, however, the major American and other Western oil companies have increasingly come to believe that the solution for their problems is the building of gigantic tankers, too large to navigate even the tentatively planned enlarged canal, to say nothing of the present one. These tankers represent very large fixed-cost investments and one can therefore anticipate that when the canal is reopened and smaller tankers create competition, the huge tankers can, and will, respond by lowering prices as necessary to keep a large part—though certainly not all—of the business.

There is another aspect that bodes ill for the canal as a source of future income from United States sources. Twice in recent years it has been closed, each time at a considerable inconvenience to the users. In addition to the monetary costs involved in adjusting to this, a large element of uncertainty has been introduced. American businessmen typically shun uncertainty where possible and are prepared to incur considerable costs, if necessary, to remove it. In other words, the expenses of using the canal are now regarded by the business community as higher than the tolls actually charged. Finally, all users, not just petroleum shippers, have had to find alternative means of moving their goods, and it would be surprising if, as with oil, some of these have not turned out to be more efficient than the canal. The conclusion seems clear. Western Europe, and the American companies that supply it with oil, are likely to be far less interested in the Suez Canal in the future than they have been in the past.

It is perhaps worth noting that reopening the canal may create certain new difficulties and frictions. Now that they have a significant fleet in the Mediterranean, the Russians presumably would welcome this because it would permit that fleet much easier access to India and points east than it presently enjoys. Détente or not, it is not likely that this would be looked upon as a desirable development by the United States or the Western European countries. We may also remember that the closing of the canal has given a big boost to Libyan oil production; it would be expecting too much for Libyans to welcome a move which might mean they had to give up their present role of being almost the biggest oil producer in the region.

An examination of Soviet-American rivalry in the Middle East must anticipate the possibility that the Soviet government will become a Middle East oil producer. Russia and Rumania currently have more than enough crude production to meet all of the Eastern European needs, but assuming only moderate growth in Soviet and Eastern Europe internal demands, to say nothing of Soviet interest in exporting to Japan and Western Europe, it is not difficult to conclude that the USSR might well become interested by the late 1970s in expanding her present minor involvement in Middle East explorations into becoming a major producer. The probabilities of this would be somewhat improved as there was a movement toward a détente because Russia (and the United States as well) would then be under less pressure to develop internal or other "safe" sources.

Should Russia become a Middle East producer, it is quite possible that after a brief period of uncertainty and change the Middle East government and oil company relations would become somewhat more stable than would otherwise be the case. The oil-producing states and the oil companies, including Russia if she were there, are motivated primarily by harsh economic considerations, and theory teaches us that purchase and sale conditions become more stable as the members of buyers and sellers increase; there would seem to be no reason why this should not be operative in the Middle East oil situation. At the same time, an increase in the number of competitive buyers is likely to result in somewhat less favorable terms from the latter's point of view. This would, however, only strengthen a trend that is already present and is very likely to continue, regardless of Russian activity, as a consequence of the expected increase in the demand of Western Europe for Arab oil.

Some observers have expressed concern lest the Soviet Union should be tempted to utilize a position as a Middle East oil producer to accomplish political ends. It might be tempting for them, it has been said, to agree to a higher "take" by the host country, thus forcing the Western oil companies to follow suit and permitting the Russians to claim political credit (and enjoy as a result more influence) with the Middle East states for the increased royalties received from *all* producers. The likelihood of this sort of behavior would seem to be greater under conditions of a continuing cold war than under some sort of détente, but it seems most unlikely in either case. The Middle East states could be expected quickly—say within a month or so—to regard the increased royalties as a proper return to themselves and in no sense aid, from the Russians or anyone else. To the extent they are thankful, the oil-producing governments could not be expected to give the Russians credit for all the increased receipts. Moreover, in view of these probabilities, the policy would have little appeal to the Russians because the economic cost to them of such a move would be real: higher-priced oil. More serious worry has been voiced that Russia as a Middle East oil producer might threaten future oil supplies to Western Europe. This risk would be less as there is a movement toward a more comprehensive détente, but it seems very small even if the cold war continues unabated. It would be serious only if Russia actually displaces Western producers, something the Middle East governments themselves could be expected to resist.

A much more important consequence, for the United States, of Russia's becoming a Middle East oil producer is that it would make it easier for the Russians to make available Siberian oil (where production possibilities are reportedly huge) to Japan. If so, the result could be less dependence by Japan on Middle East oil produced by American companies. The consequences of this on the extensive and complex Japanese-American economic relations, often beset by severe friction these days, fall outside the scope of our present concern, but they could easily dwarf in significance for the United States many of the direct consequences of Russia's becoming a competitor in Middle East oil production.

Glance now at that major area of economic activity that could be quite differently affected by the state of the cold war: allocation of resources to the military. If the United States and the Soviet Union move toward a general détente, it would be reasonable to expect each of them to find less compelling the reasons for providing arms aid to the Middle East states. If, in that situation, the Middle East governments (for reasons of internal or regional concern) should continue to consider it necessary to maintain something like their present level of military effort or preparedness, the drain on their own economic resources—domestic and foreign—would be greatly increased. It is not possible with the information at hand to quantify this increase. Given the cost of modern or semimodern military equipment—whether imported or produced locally—the result could easily be such a burden as to preclude any serious effort at accelerating their economic development. This retarding effect on development is all the more likely because a détente could be expected to weaken the present political motivations in the United States which have so far dictated that the restrictions on capital exports to developing countries should be less severe than those to developed ones, and that has created some support for special concessions (for example, preferences) for goods and services originating in developing nations like those of the Middle East. Moreover, the trend cited earlier toward a less-generous foreign economic aid policy by the United States would almost certainly strengthen as we move toward a general détente. Aid policies then would have to rest more and more on their economic and broad humanitarian justifications. Any reading of Congressional debate and hearings gives ample evidence that the political-military considerations are often more compelling than the others.

Moreover, even if the United States and Russia agree not only to stop arms aid but also to cease all arms sales, it does not follow that the economic cost to the Middle East states of maintaining armed forces would decrease. There are other developed nations that are able and might be willing to sell arms, and it is not beyond belief that a détente between Russia and the United States would be accompanied by growth of interest in Middle East affairs by China, Japan, and Western Europe. The results of this could easily be an increase in turmoil in the area, and so in economic burdens.

It is, fortunately, the task of others to speculate on the effects of a United States-USSR détente on internal peace in the area. It is assumed here that such effects would not be great. If they are, and if they are in the direction of peace, then the economic benefits from the reduction of military outlays could be very great.

The one area where most observers expect movement toward a détente significantly to increase the dollar, and other foreign exchange, earnings of the Middle East is tourism. But even this improvement hinges largely on intra-area peace and stability.

These speculations have ignored the possible effects of a détente on the level of the net foreign exchange expenditures of the United States military establishment.[4] Should these be substantially curtailed, much of the justification for capital-export restrictions, part of the case for foreign-aid cutbacks, but only a minor part of the justification for import restrictions discussed earlier in this chapter would be removed. Such changes would benefit the Middle East area.

Some relief might be expected here—perhaps as much, net, as $1.5 to $2.5 billion in the United States balance of payments on a worldwide basis—if the détente resulted in a very large scale withdrawal of United States forces from foreign posts. There are two reasons why this withdrawal would be necessary if the foreign exchange costs were to be substantially cut. First, there are several "offsets" to the present outlays that would dry up as foreign expenditures declined. Second, the "Buy American" policy has already severely cut the foreign exchange component of the total military expenses. Indeed, it is quite possible that replacing defense expenditures in the federal budget

[4] Total United States military outlays probably will continue at a high level for some years, even if there is a détente, because of the increasing costs of keeping abreast of technological developments in the military field, the need "to get well": to rebuild military inventories and facilities depleted and depreciated as a consequence of recent budget constraints and the Vietnam war.

with others (e.g., public education, urban redevelopment) would *increase* our net foreign exchange expenditures because of the existing exceedingly stringent "Buy American" regulations on defense outlays. It must also be noted that nothing like all of these possible, be they modest, foreign exchange savings are likely to be available to assist the Middle East or other developing countries if for no other reason than that the reduction is assumed to be the consequence of a relaxing of Soviet-United States tensions which would lower the priorities likely to be assigned to assisting the developing nations.

III

The decade of the 1970s seems likely to record greater participation by Eastern Europe, including the Soviet Union, in the trade of the Middle East, and this participation presumably would increase as the giants move toward a comprehensive détente. More trade would reflect both the growing ability of Russia to export relatively simple manufactured goods to developing countries without unduly depriving its own citizens and Russia's increased interest in importing raw materials. Increased trade would be a continuation of a trend of the last several years. Looking at the COMECON as a group, one finds that their share of total world trade has nearly doubled in the past twenty years, rising from just over 5.0 per cent in 1948 to more than 10 per cent in 1966. Moreover, the average annual rate of increase in the COMECON countries' exports to the LDCs during the decade 1955-1966 was nearly 18 per cent, while the comparable figure for their trade with one another was only 9.0 per cent and with the developed countries, 11 per cent. The data for Russia alone were even more impressive, being 27 per cent, 9.0 per cent, and 12 per cent respectively.[5]

Looking ahead to the end of the 1970s, with the possible exception of oil one need not expect any great friction between the United States and Russia to arise from economic competition for *imports* from the Middle East. Expansion of the *exports* of the Soviet group to the Middle East, however, may present the United States some knotty problems. The most important may be simply the increased competition based on greater Russian efficiency in producing some products,

[5] See General Agreement of Tariffs and Trade, *Le Commerce International, 1966,* Geneva 1967, pp. 303-315. The data are to be regarded as approximate for all the well-known reasons. The Russian data reflect recent increases in trade with Cuba.

supported by the understandable desire of the Middle East states to diversify their sources. Such competition may be especially nettlesome, because the methods now used in pricing many Soviet exports are such that it must be expected that complaints of "dumping" and similar "unfair" competitive practices will often be levied against the Russians. Sometimes these charges may indeed be true, but Russia is not a member of the GATT and it does not feel obliged to abide by the rules established there on such matters; nor do any established procedures exist for a quiet, sober, judicial investigation of such charges between the United States and Russia.

The United States has a clumsy defense against injury-causing dumping (selling abroad at lower prices than at home) or export-subsidization practices by foreigners in its own markets in the form of antidumping and countervailing duty procedures. These are not, however, applicable to "unfair" competition faced by the United States in third countries. Should the Middle East countries find their own producers suffering from such competition, they could be expected to invoke similar rules, to the indirect benefit of the United States. It is, in fact, reasonable to expect such protection in United States-Soviet trade competition in Western Europe. But in the case of products for which the Middle East countries have no domestic producers, they could well see it as being in their immediate interest to encourage such practice by the Russians, irritating and "unfair" as it might be to United States exporters.

Assuming the Russians do greatly increase their trade, especially exports, with the Middle East in the coming decade, prudence demands that we assume this will not be in the context of a genuine multilateral trading system but will be within a framework of something like their present state-controlled, bilateral trade arrangements. This must be expected in part because such arrangements are consistent with the nature and degree of central-planning and the economic controls that will surely exist in Russia for several years. Russia's Middle East trading partners also may reasonably be expected to find what they regard as a legitimate interest in controlling the dependence of their exporters on markets the size of which are subject to centralized decision making in the Soviet Union. Besides, they may have a protectionist interest, for both their imports and exports, that can more easily be served by bilaterally negotiated trade-and-payments accords than by nondiscriminatory multilateral arrangements.

This is a milieu in which United States traders have not yet proven themselves adept and one to which the United States government has a long tradition of opposition. It may well be, therefore, that one should anticipate a new source of friction at the government-commercial level and that our traders will find themselves at a competitive disadvantage in vying for the growing Middle East markets for foreign goods during the 1970s. It needs emphasis that for at least several years American competitive disadvantage may be *vis-à-vis* not only the Russian but also the Western European and Japanese exporters to the Middle East. Traders from these countries, permitted and encouraged by their governments, have proven themselves far more agile, energetic, and successful than Americans in capturing markets so organized.

Perhaps this is too pessimistic. Recent negotiations between Poland and the contracting parties to the GATT, which led to Poland's becoming a member of that organization, do provide a clue as to how multilateral relations among an Eastern European state-controlled economy and others might be arranged so that all the parties might be willing to lower their trade barriers and all share in the benefits of more exchanges. The essence of this complex arrangement is that, in return for other countries' lowering barriers—especially tariffs—against its exports, Poland agrees to increase its imports from them as a group by a certain percentage each year. It was also agreed that periodic meetings of all interested parties would be held to see that the free-market economies were reducing their barriers as had been agreed and that Poland was increasing its imports as promised. These meetings also see to it that *each* of the countries that had lowered its barriers to Polish imports benefited in some acceptable way from the increase in Polish total imports or, if not, to negotiate an acceptable adjustment. It is also to be noted, however, that several of the Western European countries refused to make firm commitments to abandon their bilateral trading arrangements as part of the agreement.

It is too early to tell whether this will be a satisfactory arrangement. It has some promise. It does, it must be emphasized, assume continued movement away from autarkic policies by Poland. The scheme thus will provide a more useful guide or clue to ways of organizing enlarged trade between and among the Middle East, Russia, and the United States as the giants move toward a détente.

Soviet Trade and Aid Policies

FRANKLYN D. HOLZMAN

The economics of Soviet trade and aid policies toward the less-developed countries (LDCs), including those in the Middle East, is very much influenced by and can be fully understood only in the context of the centrally planned Soviet economic system. Similarly, the possibility of changing trade and aid policies in the 1970s depends in part on the prospects for change in the character of planning. Therefore, the relevant features of Soviet central planning and their impact on foreign trade and aid mechanisms will be outlined. Then the history of Soviet trade and aid policies with the LDCs, including the Middle East, will be traced. Finally, an attempt will be made to forecast possible changes under the assumptions of cold war and general détente. In particular, there will be an assessment of the possibility that Soviet economic competition in the Middle East may take forms which are more compatible than heretofore with the "liberal" mode of operation that characterizes private enterprise economies.

The Soviet economy is one in which virtually all enterprise, particularly nonagricultural, is owned by the state and run by government-appointed managers. State planners set output, sales, and profit targets and prices for almost all enterprises, determine delivery dates, and tell each enterprise from whom it is to buy a large part of its

The author expresses his appreciation to the National Science Foundation for financial support in preparing this paper.

inputs and to whom it is to ship its products. Since there is, in effect, no real market through which supply and demand can seek an adjustment, this particular chore, which is accomplished anonymously by invisible hands in the West, must be handled explicitly by the planners. This is a laborious process which requires the establishment, for literally thousands of products, of "balances" in which all sources of a commodity are listed on one side and all uses or shipments on the other. If the supply and demand for a product do not balance, or the balance is upset by some unpredicted event, troublesome difficulties are encountered because of the complexity of interindustry relationships. Suppose, for example, that the steel balance shows a million-ton deficit, and it is decided to increase steel output by this amount. That industry will have to be allocated more coal, limestone, machinery, labor, and so forth—upsetting the balances for each of these commodities. Further, in order to produce more coal, limestone, and machinery, it is necessary to have more steel (and machinery, labor, etc.) than the original million extra tons desired; this requires still more coal, limestone, and machinery, and so forth, in an infinite regress.

Another relevant feature of central planning is that in practice it has always been "over-full employment" planning, which means planning for a higher level of economic activity than is possible, given available resources, including labor. As a result, there are always more demands for goods than goods available, sellers' markets are pervasive, inventories are inadequate and badly distributed because of hoarding, planners' balancing problems are aggravated, and there is repressed inflation.

Third, Soviet central planning has always maintained disequilibrium prices, that is, prices which would not equate demand and supply if the economy were "freed," and which do not bear a rational relationship to each other. Soviet accounts do not include proper charges for rent, interest, and profits; the planners have employed large sales taxes and subsidies to manipulate prices for other goals; and prices are rarely adjusted for changes in costs and demands.

What are the consequences of these features of central planning for trade and aid? First, there has been a tendency on the part of Soviet planners to avoid trade. Soviet exports and imports each amount to no more than 3.0 per cent of GNP, less than the percentage for any other nation except possibly China. This is partly explained by the size of the country—large nations tend to be self-sufficient—and by the relative isolation of the Soviet bloc from world trade. Yet some responsibility must be attributed to the central planners' aversion to having to deal with the uncertainties of foreign trade. Irrational pricing contributes its part by making it difficult, often impossible, for the planners to decide what can be profitably traded. A final, but important, contributing factor to the low trade/GNP ratio is Soviet reluctance to become dependent on potential enemies for imports.

Second, foreign trade is in the hands of a state monopoly, and its operation is highly centralized. This appears inevitable, given the centralized nature of all other economic activity and the problems which face the planners in dovetailing imports and exports, especially those which are unplanned, into their commodity balances. The Ministry of Foreign Trade is assisted in its efforts by twenty-five or thirty subministries or combines, each of which administers the exports and/or imports in a particular commodity sector, such as ferrous metals or tourism. The export-producing and import-using domestic Soviet enterprises deal only with combines and have no contact with foreign buyers or sellers.

Third, most foreign trade is conducted under long-term agreements. This is another device to ensure that foreign trade conforms as closely as possibly to the plans of the central planning board.

Fourth, nationalization and centralization of foreign trade operations eliminate the need for tariffs. The planners decide what is and what is not to be imported, and these decisions constitute implicit quotas. The tariffs recently imposed by the Russians are different from Western tariffs in that they do not affect the total amount of any commodity imported, an amount fixed rigidly in the plan, but are designed to discriminate among nations and thereby redistribute the planned imports toward favored suppliers.

Fifth, the "real" cost of Soviet foreign aid is generally much higher than the "real" cost of a comparable amount of aid granted by a capitalist country. Because the Soviet economy is always stretched tight by over-full employment planning, any commodities exported in the form of aid necessarily involve a reduction in consumption, investment, or military expenditures at home. Soviet planners are aware of this fact. Incidentally, this is also true of the 1968 United States economy, with its virtual full employment and rising prices. For most of the past decade, however, much though by no means all of United States foreign aid was financed, in effect, by using otherwise unemployed resources, including labor.

Sixth, the Soviet balance of payments, while usually in balance as a result of controls, undoubtedly would be in deficit if trade were freed. The excess demand created by over-full employment planning and repressed inflation always spills over, where allowed, into higher imports. Further, the prevalence of sellers' markets internally leads domestic enterprises to neglect quality, always important in world markets, and to ignore the possibilities of selling abroad in markets when they have no direct contact, reducing the ability to export.

Finally, Soviet trade is plagued by the twin problems of inconvertibility and bilateralism. These are partly the result of the hidden balance-of-payments pressures just noted. But more important, and unique to the centrally planned economy, is the inconvertibility that results from the central planning. Foreigners are not allowed to come into the Soviet Union and shop around for goods; they are restricted to the few commodities offered by the combines according to the state plan and usually under a long-term agreement. After all, unplanned purchases by foreign importers would disrupt the carefully drawn fabric of the plan. Further, given irrational domestic prices, foreigners might be able to buy commodities at a cost below the real cost of production—heavily subsidized commodities, for example. Thus, the Soviets do not even allow foreigners to hold rubles; and if they did, there would be no takers because of the great uncertainty as to what the money could buy and at what price. As a result of all this, the Soviet bloc nations bilaterally balance trade with one another, and while they do trade with Western nations on a somewhat less restrictive basis, using convertible currencies, they prefer bilateral balancing wherever possible. This has been particularly true of their trade with the LDCs, many of which have a similar predilection because of balance-of-payments pressures.

Soviet Trade and Aid in Nonindustrial Regions

Soviet nonmilitary trade with, and especially aid to, the LDCs on any significant scale date from the mid-fifties. Before that time, exports and imports taken together typically amounted annually to less than $200 million. By 1960, according to official figures, exports to the LDCs totalled $426 million and imports $482 million. By 1966, the corresponding figures were $1,200 million and $862 million.

Between 1955 and 1966, total Soviet trade grew about two-and-one-half-fold, but trade with the LDCs six-fold, and the proportion of LDC trade to the total also increased: exports from 4.0 to 13 per cent, imports from 6.0 to 11 per cent. Trade with nations of the Middle East amounted in 1966 to about one-third (exports) and one-fourth (imports) of total Soviet-LDC trade. More than half of this trade was with Egypt.

There is a strong economic basis for Soviet trade with LDCs. First of all, the USSR is a strong industrial nation and is therefore in a position to export machinery and equipment in exchange for raw materials and foodstuffs. It is probably no coincidence that the upsurge in economic relations between the Soviet bloc and the LDCs in 1955-1956 coincided with a serious raw material shortage in the bloc, one which has not as yet been solved. A second factor is that all these nations have balance-of-payments problems, suffer from currency inconvertibility, and as a result have a strong proclivity to bilateral-balance trading relationships. In addition, the Soviet Union finds nonindustrial nations good trading partners because they are willing to accept manufactured goods, machinery, and equipment that are inferior by Western standards and not acceptable in the markets of the advanced Western nations.

All this is not to deny that the Soviets may desire trade with the LDCs for political reasons. The motivation for the part of trade resulting from aid is primarily political. In addition, the Russians must be conscious of the politically important, dependent relationship that results when a nonindustrial nation becomes accustomed to using Soviet bloc machinery and equipment and to relying on bloc markets for exports. However, with a few significant exceptions, such as India and the UAR, this dependency has so far not been very strong. While LDC trade accounts for roughly 10 per cent of Soviet trade, Soviet trade accounts for only 2.0 per cent of LDC trade.

Economic motivations have ranked much lower in Soviet aid programs to the LDCs. The political motives behind Soviet military aid are obvious. But the political nature of nonmilitary aid also becomes apparent when viewed in the context of the over-full-employed Soviet economy, in which aid extended to other nations automatically cuts back domestic programs. Further, the internal rate of return on capital is generally considered to be very high and, despite a fairly high rate of investment, the Soviet Union has found itself chronically short of capital for undertaking and completing scheduled projects. In these circumstances, the economically rational procedure is to eliminate those projects which use the most capital, take the longest time to "pay off," have the lowest rate of return, and are in nonessential sectors of the economy. Soviet loans to the LDCs fit to a T this description of undesirable projects. Investment in foreign aid each year has been as large as that in almost any internal project. Interest on credits has been low, usually 2.5 to 3.0 per cent. Repayment usually begins a year after project completion (which may take many years) and extends over a period of eight to fifteen years. Finally, repayment is usually in foodstuffs and raw materials which, while useful, are not of high priority to the planners. Thus, it may be inferred that, despite the fact that most Soviet aid is extended in credit rather than as grants and requires repayment with interest, the recipient receives a substantial subsidy. There is evidence that Soviet planners are not unaware of the economic costs of the aid subsidy. In 1958, Premier Khrushchev admitted that "our economic and technical assistance to developing countries is rather disadvantageous to us from the commercial point of view," and a *Pravda* editorial the same year stated that "it would be more advantageous for the Soviet Union to build new plants in [our] country with these funds and to export finished goods."[1]

The Soviet aid program, either in per capita aid or percentage of aid to GNP, has been smaller than those of the major Western nations. From 1954 to 1967, net aid commitments, with repayments subtracted, consisted of some $6.0 billion in economic assistance and perhaps the same sum in military assistance. Economic aid has followed a cyclical course: a gradual buildup over 1955-1957; a big push amounting to an average $600 million per year from 1958 to 1961; a sharp drop to less than $300 million total during 1962-1963; nearly $1 billion per year over the next three years, 1964-1966; and a second sharp drop to $69 million in 1967. The 1962-1963 drop may have been partly a result of the serious slowdowns in Soviet economic growth in that period and related balance-of-payments difficulties dramatized by large emergency imports of grain from the West. Both the 1962-1963 and 1967 drops may also represent an attempt by the Soviet Union to reduce the serious lag

[1] Both citations from United Nations, *The Financing of Economic Development: World Economic Survey, 1965*, part I (New York, 1966), 109.

which has developed, especially following years in which large amounts of aid were extended, between extensions of aid and actual drawings on that aid. At the end of 1967, only about 40 per cent of the aid offered since 1955 had been obligated. The slowness in drawing on aid probably reflects not so much an unwillingness on the part of the Soviet Union to meet its commitments, although this may play a part, as an inability of the LDCs to absorb more aid because of the difficulties in handling the projects in question. Further delays undoubtedly result from haggling over detailed specifications on equipment, costing of successive stages of projects, and other problems of this sort which arise during the implementation of agreements and which are likely to take a longer time to resolve than is usual under the excessively bureaucratic Soviet trade-aid setup. The lag in drawings, combined with the increasing pace of repayments, has led to an anomalous situation: the net outflow of resources to the nonindustrial nations reached a peak of $290 million in 1964, but declined to $155 million in 1966 and $125 million in 1967. Several nations have found it difficult to finance their repayments, even in kind, and delays have had to be granted.

It has been asked if any relationship exists between Soviet aid and Soviet trade with the LDCs. To answer this question, we may begin by calculating what percentage aid disbursements form of total exports to aid recipients—since aid disbursements take the form of exports. Thus, in 1955-1964, Soviet aid disbursements accounted for an estimated 34.9 per cent of total exports to LDCs. That is to say, in the absence of economic aid, Soviet exports to the LDCs could have been as much as one-third less. On the other hand, even without aid, a good proportion of the 34.9 per cent might still have been imported by the LDCs in any case. Information presented by the United Nations suggests that aid has not been very important in the general expansion of trade relationships. The figures show that over the period 1955-1964, Soviet trade with aid recipients grew by 25.3 per cent, whereas trade with all LDCs grew by 20.2 per cent. For most Eastern European nations, however, trade grew faster with all nonindustrial nations than with aid recipients. The relationship between aid and trade is not a strong one when compared, for example, with comparative advantage and the mutual exchange of products that is profitable per se. Perhaps the political character of aid-giving explains the relative unimportance of the aid-trade relationship: that is to say, politics induces substantial aid dealings between nations not particularly complementary in trade.

The Middle East has received a good share of Soviet economic and military aid. Of the $4.0 billion in military aid disbursed by the end of 1965, the UAR received about $1.5 billion, and Iraq and Syria more than $0.5 billion. Since the June 1967 war, the UAR has received enormous additional military assistance. Repayments by the UAR on military aid in the early 1960s were believed to have amounted to some $20 million annually—in recent years even higher—a substantial balance-of-payments burden. Middle East states are also receiving a good share of Soviet economic aid—about 40 per cent of the total. The UAR was the largest single recipient, after India, with credit extensions of close to $1.0 billion by 1966. By the end of 1965, $300 million had been drawn on, amounting to 10 per cent of gross investment and one-fourth of investment in industry, power, and the Aswan Dam. As of 1966, credit extended to other Middle East states was estimated conservatively by Kurt Müller as follows (in $ millions): Afghanistan, 488; Iraq, 181; Iran, 39; Yemen, 40; Syria, 225; Algeria, 228; Ethiopia, 100; Tunisia, 28.

It should be noted that the Soviet approach to aid has been undergoing a gradual change over the past few years. Since the Khrushchev era, the government has become more cautious in aid matters and seems to be attaching more weight to economic criteria. Seldom does the government announce credits until cost surveys have been completed. It now considers more carefully rates of return on the aid investment from the points of view of the USSR and the recipients. Political stability and ability to absorb the aid granted are also important new criteria, it is reported. Further, the Soviet Union appears to be retreating from its previous practice of sending technicians and materials to build complete factories. Instead, the Russians are orienting their credits more and more to imports of machinery and equipment, thereby avoiding or reducing project responsibility as well as the large subsidies that complete factories often entailed. Finally, emphasis on the "commercial" element in aid is testified to by the shift in credit terms from 2.5-3.0 per cent in twelve to fifteen years to 2.5-4.0 per cent in five to ten years.

The Effect of Cold War and Détente on Policies in the 1970s

The volume and composition of Soviet aid in the 1970s to the non-industrial states, including the Middle East, will depend, in part, on the state of Soviet-United States political relationships. Soviet aid, military and economic, has thus far not been on a scale commensurate with the USSR's standing as the world's second greatest industrial power. In comparing Soviet and United States aid in 1963, for example, we find that United States economic aid deliveries amount to 0.8 per cent of GNP and $21.80 per capita, whereas comparable Soviet figures are 0.2 per cent and $2.50. While new Soviet aid commitments were low in 1963, deliveries were at a high level. To be sure, every dollar's worth of aid costs more to the Soviet Union than to the United States. Not only is the USSR a poorer country, it is also always at full employment, so that foreign aid necessarily involves a cutback in domestic expenditures. Furthermore, the country is fighting a declining growth rate. Indeed, the relatively small absolute amount of aid the Soviet Union extends, along with its recent more cautious attitude, attests to its sensitivity regarding possible alternative uses for these funds.[2]

The existence of a cold war or détente also has a complex effect on aid, the net result of which is difficult to predict. On the one hand, intensification of cold war leads to an increase in military expenditures, which in turn requires cutbacks in other expenditures, including consumption, investment, and foreign aid. On the other hand, international tension reduces sensitivity to cuts in domestic consumption and investment and might encourage the sustaining of foreign aid programs in the face of rising military expenditures, particularly if increased aid fitted into the cold war strategy. This may be expected in any part of the third world where United States-USSR tensions find expression. A dramatic illustration is that of recent Soviet military aid to the UAR. The ultimate effect of these extraordinary deliveries may be not only to reduce future economic aid to the UAR, but also, as long as cold war tensions remain unchanged, to reduce economic and military aid to other less-developed

[2] Over the period 1960-1964, Soviet credit commitments to LDCs amounted to almost 2.0 per cent of investment in machinery and equipment. This is still not a large figure but larger than the aid/GNP relationship and more relevant in terms of opportunity costs.

states. Should the locus of tensions shift—to Berlin or to Latin America—the Middle East may expect less of both kinds of aid.

Thus in a situation of general détente, Soviet economic aid is likely to be larger than it otherwise would have been, largely at the expense of military aid. However, should there be fierce political or military competition in any part of the third world, this area may receive a preponderance of the aid to the detriment of other areas.

Another result of a general détente might be a deceleration in the rate of increase in economic aid, as a result of the USSR's growing commercial attitude toward aid, mentioned above, which leads to investing where the economic payoff is likely to be higher. Because of the bilateral character of trade and aid relationships, this might lead the Soviet Union to favor more than before politically stable states, states that have commodities the Soviet Union wants, and states that are likely to have the least serious balance-of-payments problems. Thus, for example, if there is a détente, one might expect Egypt to get relatively less and Iran relatively more aid than before. On the other hand, the importance of economic factors should not be overstated. Political motives will undoubtedly continue to play an important role in the disbursement of aid. And it seems highly probable that the Middle East will continue to be one of the more troubled areas regardless of the state of the cold war in general, thereby qualifying for more than its fair share of aid.

As with aid, the impact of a détente on the volume of trade is difficult to assess because of conflicting effects. In most general terms, a détente will create an impetus to greater trade participation by the USSR. If fear of war is reduced, the USSR will be more willing to depend on outside sources of supply for many commodities that it has always produced for itself, often at relatively high cost and great comparative disadvantage. The introduction into cultivation of 100 million acres of marginal lands in Kazakhstan in the late 1950s in an attempt to be nearly self-sufficient in grain products is a dramatic case in point. For similar reasons, a détente will lead both the Soviet Union and the countries of Eastern Europe to rely less on one another and to look to the rest of the world for sources of supply and for markets. The extent to which these factors will open Soviet markets to the rest of the world, however, should not be overstated. So long as they continue to have inconvertibility and bilateralism and to depend on long-term agreements to plan most of their trade, diversion of trade from previous channels will be limited.

Assuming that a détente is reached and Soviet trade is expanded as well as diverted away from Eastern Europe, what impact, if any, is this likely to have on trade with the Middle East? This will depend largely on the true complementarity between the USSR and the states of the Middle East, that is, on the degree to which the Middle East can supply products which the USSR previously obtained much more expensively either from domestic production or from other Soviet bloc states. It is difficult to envision the commodities that might provide a strong basis for expanded USSR-Middle East trade in the 1970s, especially since much of the expanded Soviet trade with non-Communist states can be expected to be with industrial states. Thus, the Soviet Union might divert some of its imports of machinery, equipment, and manufactured goods from bloc producers to those in Western Europe and Japan.

On the other hand, the USSR has already agreed to import natural gas from Iran and Afghanistan. It might also import oil in large quantities from Iran and other countries in the Middle East, but probably not before the end of the next decade, at the earliest. According to one authoritative study, the USSR is a fairly low-cost oil producer. Furthermore, at the moment the Russians have a surplus of petroleum and export it in large quantities, particularly to Eastern Europe, but also to Western states. This situation will certainly continue to obtain over the next five to seven years.

Over the longer run, the picture is less clear. A large expansion in oil output is planned over the next decade: the output target for 1980 is set at 630 million tons, slightly more than double the present output. However, the Eastern European oil deficit for 1980 is projected at 140 million tons, and some authorities feel that the Soviet bloc as a whole will need at least 730 million tons for domestic use by that date. Second, there is some question whether these projections take into consideration the full possibilities of a really substantial mass-market automobile explosion in the Soviet bloc and its impact on the demand for petroleum. If this materializes, domestic needs may be much greater than planned. Third, Middle East petroleum is, after all, much cheaper to extract than Soviet petroleum, and the recent trend toward development of more rational methods of planning may lead the Russians to want to rely less heavily on expansion of domestic output. Finally, much of southern Russia could be supplied more cheaply from Iraq and Iran and possibly by sea from Middle East ports than from the Second Baku in the Ural-Volga region or from the newly discovered West Siberian fields at Tyumen, because of the high cost of overland transport.

Counteracting these factors is the possibility that Eastern European requirements will be met to a greater extent than before from Middle East rather than Soviet wells. Already, Rumania, Czechoslovakia, and Bulgaria are importing or planning to import petroleum from Iran, and East Germany from Algeria. Petroleum might also be freed for export by the rapid strides the Soviets are making and will probably continue to make in the coming decade in substituting natural gas, of which they have large reserves, for other fuels in a variety of uses, including the heating of apartments.

The net effect of these factors would seem to depend in the final analysis on (1) whether there is cold war or détente in the late 1970s and (2) on balance-of-payments considerations at that time. If there is still a cold war, the Russians would probably be unwilling to rely on imports for so strategic a material as petroleum. Further, under cold war conditions, with military expenditures high, the possibilities of a mass-market automobile explosion are reduced. Given a détente, however, both of these conditions might change.

It seems clear that regardless of what happens, the USSR will continue to be a net exporter of petroleum in the 1970s, though not perhaps in the 1980s, and that trade in petroleum with the Middle East will depend on the possibilities of multilateral trade in petroleum with the Soviet Union, both exporting and importing. At present, the Russians value petroleum exports partly for the convertible foreign exchange they earn. If the balance-of-payments situation does not ease up in the next decade, they would probably be unwilling to buy petroleum with hard currency. Payment in hard currency would convert cheap Middle East oil into an expensive item in real terms. Convertible currency is scarce and at a premium in the Soviet bloc—the ruble is overvalued, relative to dollars and sterling. On the other hand, the Russians might be willing to engage in bilateral arrangements in which they trade manufactured goods and equipment to the Middle East for petroleum.

From the point of view of the Middle East countries, export of petroleum to the Soviet bloc is a bonanza. The oil concessionaires in the Middle East, and especially the National Iranian Oil Company (NIOC), owned by the government of Iran, can put on the market much more petroleum than they can sell in the West without "spoiling the market." Sale to the Eastern bloc by the NIOC, and possibly other government-owned companies, provides a convenient way of disposing of the surplus. This trade would be less profitable to the Middle Easterners, however, if they were forced to barter rather than sell the oil for convertible currency. This point is of greater relevance to strong balance-of-payments, oil-producing countries (and government-owned companies), which have the option of buying machinery anywhere they wish, than it is to the others.

Competitive Styles in Economic Relations

Will a change from cold war to détente affect the competitive style of Soviet economic relationships in the Middle East? What is the possibility that Soviet trade and aid relationships can be made more multilateral? Will the end of the cold war induce the Russians to bid against the West in the LDCs along competitive lines? That is, might markets be captured by lowest-cost producers rather than by governments willing to subsidize? Might aid be repaid in foreign exchange and at going rates of interest rather than in kind or at subsidized rates of interest? To the extent that the imports of goods from the LDCs are controlled, might this be accomplished in the form of either tariffs or explicit quotas rather than hidden behind implicit quotas? One must, of course, be wary of applying to the USSR standards of behavior more utopian than Western practice. Many Western states still use quotas. The European Economic Community, by its discriminatory tariffs, does not allow outsiders equal competition in its markets. However, it can be argued in this case that the outsiders are at least given a visible target to shoot at, and if they are lower cost despite a higher tariff, the market is theirs. Soviet import controls, on the other hand, are always prohibitive. Further, since the UN Conference on Trade and Development in 1964, there has been growing pressure in the West to subsidize the nonindustrial states by better market terms on both trade and aid in ways that depart from the competitive ideal.

Yet a change in climate from cold war to détente is unlikely to have a significant effect on the Soviet competitive style. Soviet trade and aid practices are shaped, as noted above, by the nature of central planning and its many consequences. A détente, by inducing a sharp reduction in military expenditures, could conceivably reduce somewhat the pressures of over-full employment planning.[3] This in turn could reduce balance-of-payments pressures. But would this eliminate inconvertibility and bilateralism? The answer is no: reduction of the balance-of-payments pressures is a necessary but not a sufficient condition for change. It would also be necessary for the Russians to decentralize their economic planning and rationalize their price.

While détente is not likely to alter Soviet planning practices, planning is, in fact, undergoing reform in most Eastern European countries as well as in the USSR. These reforms are the result of general dissatisfaction within the bloc with current rates of economic growth (now much below those of the 1950s), gross misallocations of resources, bilateralism, problems of determining foreign trade efficiency, and many other difficulties believed to be directly or indirectly caused by excessive centralization of planning. The most liberal of the economic reforms in Eastern Europe were those instituted in 1968 by Czechoslovakia (pre-August) and Hungary. By taking a long step in the direction of decentralized planning, both countries hoped to move toward the liberalization of trade, and it was expected that the reforms could be pushed further at a later date. In Hungary, for example, the system of controls and quotas over the distribution of goods between enterprises was eliminated. This involves the abolition of the system of material balances and the reestablishment of a market for intermediate products. The elimination of direct allocation of resources is, of course, a necessary step if trade is to be freed and inconvertibility eliminated, for only under these conditions can foreign buyers and sellers compete in domestic markets.

The abolition of direct controls, while necessary, is not sufficient to ensure the freeing of trade: a number of other conditions must also be satisfied. First, it would be necessary to decentralize price setting and allow prices to become linked, organically, to world prices. If this were not done, firms would often find it profitable to buy or sell goods abroad which involved a loss from the national standpoint.

[3] It is unlikely that over-full employment planning would be substantially mitigated by a reduction in cold war pressures. It seems to be endemic to central planning and is related more to the ambition and optimism of planners regarding what is possible than to outside pressure.

Prices have been substantially rationalized and partly freed in both Czechoslovakia and Hungary. Presumably, more prices are to be decentralized as time goes on. Thus far, however, inflationary pressures, among other things, have prevented further decentralization. Moreover, while prices have been partly freed and rationalized, as yet they have no economic links with world prices. Second, enterprises must be permitted to have direct links with enterprises or state trading boards in other countries, rather than dealing through state-controlled foreign trade combines. Some loosening up along these lines has been planned in both countries, but so far direct negotiations have been the exception rather than the rule. Realistic exchange rates must also be established and maintained. Without such exchange rates, of course, government controls would be necessary to maintain balance in the balance of payments. One could not expect such a step without more drastic reforms and an end to over-full employment planning. It is therefore understandable that neither nation has, as yet, made a move in this direction.

In sum, Czechoslovakia and Hungary, the leading reformers in the Soviet bloc, have not as yet carried their reforms far enough to permit a substantial liberalization of foreign-trade practice. The Soviet reforms have been even more limited. Resources are still for the most part directly allocated by the central planners, although since the Kosygin Reform, first set forth in September 1965, it has been possible for enterprises to freely procure a very limited range of commodities from newly established wholesale warehouses. Much greater decentralization does not appear to be envisaged.

The Soviet price reform of July 1967 appears to have been much more limited in concept than the Czech and Hungarian reforms. Further, the setting of prices remains absolutely centralized and completely divorced from world prices. One may expect that within a short time, whatever rationality was put into the system by the reform will have vanished as a result of changing cost and demand conditions.

In an effort to reduce the isolation of domestic enterprises from foreign trade possibilities, a first step has been taken to have domestic enterprises represented in the management of foreign trade combines. This innovation, if introduced widely, would lead to some expansion of exports and imports. However, without many of the other reforms noted above, it could not lead to a liberalization of trade practices.

What are the prospects for a more liberal domestic reform, and therefore greater trade liberalization, in the USSR? I think the prospects are considerably dimmer than in the other Eastern European nations, for at least three major reasons. First, substantial decentralization of economic decision making is bound to have a major impact on institutions and on internal relationships. Thus, the economic and political power of the bureaucrats will be reduced as many of their major functions wither away. Further, for a complex of reasons, liberalization in the economic sphere is likely to lead to pressures for greater political and intellectual freedom. The interaction between economic freedom and other freedoms has been apparent in Czechoslovakia and Yugoslavia. The Soviet leaders appear sufficiently jealous of their political power so that they are not likely to allow a significant devolution of economic power soon.

Second, foreign trade is a much more intimate part of the economic lives of the smaller bloc nations like Czechoslovakia and Hungary than it is of the USSR. Thus, gains from foreign trade are of much greater importance to these countries, which are more highly motivated to seek wider and more rational trade relationships. Adapting their price structures to world prices is therefore of great importance, as well as relatively easy to accomplish because of the smallness and simplicity of their economies. On the other hand, only 3.0 per cent of the Soviet economy enters foreign trade. The gains from trade are small. To deliberately adjust their whole price structure to world prices to facilitate trade, as suggested by some Soviet economists, must seem to the Soviet leaders like allowing a small tail to wag a big dog. From a political point of view, the adoption of Western prices by the leading Communist power would appear unduly humiliating, even if it made economic sense.

Third, among the glues that bind the bloc together as an economic and political unit are the various institutions such as trade agreements and specialization agreements, which have grown up under COMECON for conducting trade and integrating the separate economies. While these institutions have not been highly successful when judged by economic criteria, they have accomplished their political purpose more effectively. The Soviet Union would be loath to discard this apparatus, and it could not do so without internal economic reforms.

One may conclude, then, that cold war or détente, Soviet

trading relationships are likely to remain largely unaltered over the coming decade. The only development that appears on the horizon at the moment is the production-marketing type of cooperative agreement which Eastern European enterprises have concluded with some Western enterprises. The recent Soviet contract with the Fiat automobile company to supply equipment and technicians for the construction of a complete factory in the USSR suggests that they may be willing to take still another step in emulating Eastern Europe. Cooperative agreements could be used in economic relationships with LDCs. But they are unlikely to be used widely, and this should not necessarily be construed as a step in the direction of liberal trade practices. Unless Soviet internal economic reforms go a lot farther than they have, the use of such agreements must be suspect and each individual agreement judged on its particular provisions and implementation.

Regional Economies in the 1970s

CHARLES ISSAWI

Economists usually begin their statements with *ceteris paribus*, a qualification that often evokes ribaldry from other social scientists. Yet anyone foolish enough to talk about the future must make clear his major assumptions. If things are not going to remain constant, in what direction are they expected to change? Which elements are we considering to remain constant during the period under study (parameters), which do we regard as determined by outside forces (independent variables), and which as changing in response to the independent variables (dependent variables)?

Clearly the various permutations of United States-Soviet-West European relations are, for the purposes of this paper, independent variables. Changes in the Middle East economies induced by such outside forces pertain to dependent variables. But what of the many other, primarily internal, forces that can affect the Middle East economies? Are they to be regarded as parameters—in effect frozen, assumed to be constant, and therefore disregarded? Or should they too be treated as independent variables, which means that *their* probable direction and rate of change must be studied, and the various repercussions on the economy followed up?

Recent Trends and Extrapolations

The easiest way to approach the problem is just to extrapolate recent rates of growth in the major series: population, GNP, industrial output, agricultural production, oil, and so on. This would mean, in effect, treating all other internal factors as parameters—i.e., assuming that they will remain unchanged or that they will change at regular, predictable rates. And perhaps the easiest course is, in this case, the best—at least as a first approximation. Unless one has good reasons to expect drastic changes it is sensible enough to expect recent trends to persist for the next few years—except when one believes that those recent trends were exceptional and unrepresentative.

Now until the war of June 1967—say in the period 1958-1966—the rate of economic growth in the Middle East (but not in North Africa) was high, and compared very favorably with that in other developing regions. It is reasonable to assume that, in the 1970s, the Middle East economies will not grow more rapidly than in the 1960s. This assumption could be invalidated by one of two changes. If foreign investment or aid should increase dramatically, the rate of growth is likely to rise significantly—but this clearly depends on our independent variables, the state of United States-Soviet-West European relations. Or else a revolution may put in power a group fully controlling a country's resources and determined to accelerate growth at any cost. Such régimes can achieve higher rates of growth for a short time and at the cost of severe imbalances which eventually become intolerable and have to be corrected by slowing down the pace—this is what happened in Eastern Europe in 1950-1956 and in China just before and during the Great Leap. But it seems unlikely that the Middle East will see such changes in the next few years.

The other possibility, a deterioration in conditions and a decline in the rate of growth, is more likely. Indeed, in recent years, there have been plenty of examples. In Syria and Iraq, political instability has brought down the rate of growth very considerably. Jordan's rapid expansion in 1960-1966 was abruptly terminated by the June war. The possibility of similar disruptions must be kept in mind when appraising future prospects. So must the possibility, or rather probability, of more regional wars. Nevertheless, as a first approximation, it will be assumed that recent rates of growth will persist during the 1970s, except where there are good reasons for thinking otherwise.

This certainly applies to population growth. There is no reason to doubt that the recent rates of 2.5 to 3.0 per cent per annum will be sustained. It is true that some of the bigger countries—Pakistan, Turkey, the United Arab Republic (UAR), and Tunisia—are implementing birth control programs, which may be expected to become more effective, and to spread to other countries, in the course of the

1970s. But the effect of such measures on the birth rate may be partly offset by the change in age composition, which should raise the proportion of women of child-bearing age. And improved hygiene should appreciably reduce death rates. Table 1 gives United Na-

TABLE 1

Population Estimates, 1950-1960, and Projections up to 1980

(population in thousands)

Region and country	1950	1960	1970	1980
Pakistan	75,040	99,950	134,000	183,000
Iran	16,276	20,182	25,440	33,050
Afghanistan	12,000	14,400	17,600	22,100
Iraq	—	7,000	9,700	13,800
Syria	—	4,682	6,450	9,250
Lebanon	—	1,793	2,350	3,100
Jordan	—	1,695	2,350	3,350
Saudi Arabia	—	6,150	7,450	9,400
Yemen	—	4,500	5,450	6,900
Turkey	20,947	27,818	36,602	48,478
Israel	1,258	2,114	2,615	3,141
UAR	20,448	25,952	34,500	46,750
Sudan	9,750	11,770	14,900	19,250
Morocco	8,876	11,626	16,000	22,400
Algeria	8,753	11,020	14,500	19,500
Tunisia	3,555	4,168	5,125	6,450
Libya	1,195	1,325	1,650	1,850

Source: United Nations, Department of Economic and Social Affairs, *World Population Prospects as Assessed in 1963* (New York, 1966).

tions projections, which are, if anything, too conservative. The figures for Israel may need drastic adjustment, depending on the nature of the final settlement of frontiers and population movements.

It is hardly necessary to recall the numerous difficulties caused by these high rates of growth. The greater part of the increase in income will continue to be absorbed by "vegetative growth." A large share of capital formation will have to consist of housing and social overheads required by the rising population. Rapidly expanding cities will create acute social problems, and so will the presence of millions of restless youths.

However, population growth, large as it is, is unlikely to outrun real income. Table 2 shows that, in recent years, the Middle East

TABLE 2

Annual Rate of Real Growth

Country	Years	GDP[a]	Per Capita	Agriculture	Industry[b]
Pakistan	1960-65	5.3	3.2	2.9	9.6
Iran	1960-65	6.5	3.5	3.0	9.0
Turkey	1960-65	4.6	2.0	1.3	7.1
Iraq	1959-63	[4.4]	[1.1]	—	—
Jordan	1957-65	[8.5]	[5.7]	—	—
UAR	1960-65	[6.0]	[3.3]	—	—
Syria	1953-65	5.0	1.7	4.1	7.4
Sudan	1960-64	4.5	1.6	4.7	8.3
Tunisia	1960-65	5.8	3.8	3.8	5.9
Morocco	1960-65	3.4	0.7	3.5	3.6
Israel	1960-65	10.0	5.7	[10]	[15]

[a]Gross Domestic Product at Factor Cost; Israel at Market Prices.
[b]Mining, manufacturing, gas, electricity and water.

Source: United Nations, *Yearbook of National Account Statistics, 1966* (New York, 1967), 708-715; figures in brackets from other sources.

countries, including Pakistan, have shown a distinct growth in per capita income; the North Africans have not, however, done so well. Although these figures are not above reproach, they can serve as a starting point for tentative forecasts.

The performance of Pakistan since 1965 has been such as to suggest that, barring a major war with India, it should be able to maintain its rate of growth. In particular, improved methods of agriculture are beginning to show results and industry seems to be becoming more efficient and competitive.

One can be even more optimistic for the two frontier zone countries. In the last three years Turkey has raised its rate of growth to over 6.0 per cent, while that of Iran has been nearly 8.0 per cent. Both countries are investing heavily and Iran can look forward to rising oil revenues. Both are just beginning to modernize their agriculture, the output of which can be greatly increased by intensification. And both are rapidly expanding their industry.

Israel's growth has slackened in the last few years, from the 10.0 per cent rate average of 1950-1964 to 8.0 in 1965, 1.0 in 1966, and 2.0 in 1967. Although this recession was partly due to deliberate policy, aimed at making the economy more competitive, it raises some doubt as to whether the previous rates of growth can be regained.

However, it should be noted that Israel's growth in 1968 was very rapid. In the spring Israel introduced a plan for 1968-1971, aiming at an average growth rate of 7.0-9.0 per cent per annum.

As for the Arab countries they can, for the purposes of this paper, be divided into three groups: the sparsely populated oil countries, the heavily populated oil countries, and the nonoil countries. In the first group—Saudi Arabia, Kuwayt, Libya, and the shaykhdoms—oil accounts for the bulk of the GNP, and growth is directly dependent on oil output. Since it is probable that Middle East oil production will continue to expand at some 7.0 to 8.0 per cent per annum, and since the return to the government per barrel of oil is likely to rise slightly, future prospects seem very favorable.

The large oil countries—Iraq and Algeria—occupy an intermediate position. Barring a sudden disruption, their oil production should also continue to grow rapidly. As in the recent past, this should sustain the economies. But the contribution of oil to their economies is far smaller than in the first group and in recent years their overall rates of growth have been low. Should present conditions continue to prevail in agriculture and other sectors, even a rapid expansion of oil output will not suffice to ensure a high rate of increase in GNP.

The third group includes countries with a small oil production, such as the UAR, Syria, Tunisia, and Morocco, but in them as in Sudan, Yemen, South Yemen, Lebanon, and Jordan, which produce no oil, the main impetus has to come from the other sectors. Syria attained a very high rate of advance in the period 1945-1957, but since then it has been hobbled by political instability. Jordan also grew very rapidly until 1967, but the June war dealt it a shattering blow. In Yemen and South Yemen civil war has disrupted the economies. Lebanon and Sudan have shown steady, but rather slow, growth and Morocco has been stagnant since it achieved independence. Tunisia and the UAR expanded quite rapidly in 1960-1965, thanks largely to massive foreign aid, but in both countries the rate of increase has dropped sharply since. Thus, taken as a whole, both the performance and the prospects of this group seem to be less satisfactory than those of the non-Arab countries, or of the Arab oil producers.

This very rapid survey shows that future prospects in the region depend primarily on two factors: oil production and foreign aid. Both of them, in turn, depend on forces outside the region. But before turning to this aspect of the problem, it is advisable to examine in somewhat greater detail the prospects in the three main sectors of the economy: agriculture, industry, and services.

As regards agriculture, Table 3 shows that the Middle East, with a regional rate of growth of 4.0 per cent, has done rather better than the other developing regions or indeed than the world taken as a whole. The performance of North Africa has, however, been very disappointing and output has failed to match population growth. Further analysis shows that, until quite recently, the expansion in Middle East output was achieved by bringing new areas under cultivation, rather than by raising output per acre. Thus between 1948-1952 and 1957-1959, output increased by 47 per cent; this was achieved by extending the cultivated area by 36 per cent and raising yields by 9.0 per cent—in other words, higher yields accounted for one-fifth of the total increase in output. Between 1957-1959 and 1964-1966, however, output rose by 20 per cent, area by 9.0 per cent, and

TABLE 3

Indexes of Agricultural Output

(1952-1956=100)

	1964		1965		1966	
	T	PC	T	PC	T	PC
World	132	109	133	107	138	109
Latin America	136	102	141	103	140	100
Far East[1]	135	109	133	105	135	104
Near East	147	110	146	110	149	109
N.W. Africa	106	85	109	85	86	66
Pakistan	127	100	130	100	128	96
Iran	136	103	146	108	147	105
Turkey	146	110	141	103	158	113
Israel	245	169	255	169	252	164
Iraq	118	88	126	91	127	89
Syria	154	133	151	107	115	79
UAR	141	111	147	112	146	109
Libya	170	121	171	117	174	114
Tunisia	137	115	112	92	95	76
Algeria	82	69	92	75	68	54
Morocco	123	94	129	96	106	76

T: total production   PC: per capita output

[1]—Excluding China

Source: Food and Agricultural Organization, *The State of Food and Agriculture, 1968* (Rome, 1968). Appendix Tables 1A, 1B.

yields by 10 per cent. Higher yields accounted for a little over half the total increase in output. Progress must therefore be achieved mainly by intensification, rather than by extension of cultivation. Such a process is costly, demanding large capital. But once started it can ensure steady growth, at say 3.0 per cent per annum for many years.

The scope for improvement is vividly revealed by an FAO chart listing 52 countries, both advanced and underdeveloped, according to output *per hectare*. Taking the average of these countries as 100, the UAR stood at 1,100 (surpassed only by Taiwan), Israel at nearly 400, Pakistan at 200 and Iran at 100. Turkey, Syria, Iraq, Algeria, Morocco, and Tunisia were, in descending order, below the average. As for output per *active* male, Israel stood at 150 and Turkey at 30; the other countries would probably fall below Turkey.

In recent years the Middle East governments have, at last, realized the need for vigorous promotion of agricultural development, and have taken several steps in that direction. Land reforms in Turkey, the UAR, Pakistan, Tunisia, and Iran have improved the tenure system and removed some of the greatest obstacles to agricultural advance; but in Syria, Iraq, and Algeria their effect has been disruptive. Agricultural credit has been greatly increased, and in several countries it is being more effectively channelled, through cooperatives. Support prices for certain crops have increased farmers' incentives to expand output and sales, and improved rural roads and storage facilities are also helping to increase the amount marketed. At least as important, agricultural productivity is being raised by a wide variety of measures. Many irrigation schemes are being implemented, ranging from such giants as the High Dam in the UAR, al-Rusayris Dam in Sudan, and the Diz Dam in Iran to very small works like tube-wells in Pakistan and improved cisterns in Jordan. Improved seeds and animal breeds are spreading in many countries. The number of tractors in the Middle East increased from 56,000 in 1952-1956 to 108,000 in 1965 and 124,000 in 1966. Still more important is the rise in the use of chemical fertilizers, from 200,000 tons (nutrients content) to 600,000 and 700,000 respectively (not including Pakistan or North Africa); particularly noteworthy has been the rapid increase in Turkey and Iran. In this context it is encouraging to note that the region's fertilizer industries meet nearly half of its total consumption, and that output is scheduled to expand greatly in the next few years, using mainly natural and refinery gas. More generally the Middle East, like other regions, may benefit from the Green Revolution set in motion by American scientists, which has led to spectacular increases in yields of rice, wheat, and other crops.

One last point remains—the possibility of agro-industrial complexes based on nuclear energy. Recent research in the United States has shown that economies of scale in nuclear plants are very great and that power can therefore be supplied at a very low unit cost by large plants. At the same time it has been demonstrated that water requirements for most crops are far lower than was previously believed and that, therefore, water produced as a by-product of nuclear power can irrigate large areas at reasonable costs. Careful calculations have shown that plants producing a wide range of chemicals and crops in desert areas, such as Egypt's Western Desert or the Negev, could be quite profitable. Needless to say, the capital costs of such plants would run in the hundreds of millions of dollars and could be provided only by outside sources.

Little need be said about industry, since the Middle East governments have shown full awareness of the importance of this sector and have, if anything, given it rather more than its share of attention, encouragement, and resources. In recent years some of the larger industrial producers—Israel, the UAR, Pakistan, and Iran—have achieved rates of growth around or exceeding 10 per cent and most of the other countries have not lagged far behind. Such rates compare favorably with those for developing countries, which in 1950-1965 averaged 7.0 per cent, while advanced market economies averaged 5.0 per cent. There is every reason to believe that, given a minimum of outside assistance in the way of capital, technical assistance, and outlets for its manufactures—and assuming that high rates of growth in oil and agriculture continue to expand the internal market—the Middle East can advance at a rate of 7.0 to 8.0 per cent per annum for several years.

Assuming agricultural output to grow at 3.0 per cent and industrial at 7.0 to 8.0 per cent and giving agriculture twice the weight of industry, material production may be expected to increase by 4.0 to 5.0 per cent per annum. It may be taken that services will continue to grow as fast as material production. In other words, GNP may advance at 4.0 to 5.0 per cent, or say 1.5 to 2.0 per cent per capita. In countries where oil plays an important part, such as Iran, these figures may rise to say, 6.0 per cent, or 2.5 to 3.0 per cent per capita. In small states where oil is the main sector the overall rate may be as much as 7.0 per cent, or say 3.0 to 4.0 per cent per capita.

These figures are high, and compare favorably with those attained by the presently advanced countries during their period of development. Maintained for a sufficient length of time they can result in significant increase—thus a 3.0 per cent rate of compound growth will double income in twenty-four years. But for the purposes of this paper it is essential to note that, even if sustained over the next ten years, the economic growth will not stabilize the Middle East. Industrialization will increase, income may rise, levels of living may improve, education will spread, even savings may grow and the economies may meet a larger proportion of their investment needs. But even a rise of a fifth or a quarter in levels of living is likely to fall short of expectations. And since the gap between the Middle East and the more advanced regions is almost sure to go on widening, it would be foolish to believe that the general sense of frustration is likely to diminish. This does not, of course, mean that economic growth is not essential. In its absence things would be truly desperate. But by itself it cannot bring peace. It is a necessary, but not a sufficient, condition.

United States-Soviet-European Relations

In studying the economic relations of the region with the outside world, it will simplify matters to start with the following assumption: the *content* of the flows between it and the rest of the world is determined primarily by economic forces, but their *size* and *direction* largely by political forces. By economic forces is meant, essentially, the relative supply of the factors of production: land, labor, capital, and entrepreneurship or organization. These in turn may be traced to such elements as natural resources, history, past politics, and so on. One may safely say that, in the foreseeable future, the Middle East and North Africa will continue to export oil, cotton, fruits and vegetables, and a few simple manufactured goods, and to provide tourist and transit services. They will go on importing capital equipment, the more elaborate manufactured consumer goods, and many foodstuffs and raw materials. But since the region is only one of several producers or consumers of such goods and services, the size of these flows can be greatly affected by political considerations. And their direction is even more subject to the vagaries of politics. Thus Egypt has, for the last 150 years, been exporting cotton and rice but whereas for long the bulk went to Britain and Western Europe, today it goes mainly to the Soviet bloc. And Iran's principal trading partner was first Britain, then Russia, then Germany, then the United States, and now, once more, Germany. Further study can be made under the headings of oil, trade, capital flows and technical assistance, and services.

The Future of the Oil Industry

Oil is, of course, both the most dynamic sector of the economy of the Middle East and North Africa and the leading export item, accounting for 90 per cent or more of the total foreign exchange earnings of the major producing countries. Over the ten years 1957-1967, production in the Middle East grew at 11 per cent (simple rate) per annum while in North Africa it rose by 32 per cent per annum in the five years 1962-1967.[1] As a result, the revenues of Middle East governments rose from $1,068 million in 1957 to $2,888 million in 1967, while those of Libya rose from $3 million in 1961 to $371 million in 1965 and $625 million in 1968. Algeria's revenues were probably around $300 million in 1967. And to all this must be added the hundreds of millions spent by oil companies for wages and local supplies.

These high rates of growth were achieved thanks to sustained demand by the main customers. Western Europe—which takes a little over half of Middle East oil and almost all North African—increased its consumption in 1962-1967 at 12 per cent per annum (simple rate); Japan—which takes nearly a quarter of Middle East oil—at 20 per cent; and other Eastern Hemisphere countries at over 9.0 per cent. Since Middle East and North African oil are cheaper than any other, and since, out of presently developed reserves, output can be steadily increased at unchanged marginal costs for several decades, the pace of future development will clearly be set by demand. The most recent estimate, made by the EEC Energy Commission, put the anticipated rise in the Common Market's oil consumption at 7.7 per cent in 1967-1970 and at 5.3 to 5.8 per cent in 1970-1980. It may be taken that the rest of Europe will show a similar deceleration— thus the British white paper of November 1967 forecast an increase of only 25 per cent by 1975, or 3 per cent per annum—and

[1] British Petroleum Company, *Statistical Review of the World Oil Industry, 1967* (London, 1968), p. 18. Figures for the first half of 1968 show increases over the first half of 1967 of: Middle East 13 percent, Libya 67 percent and Algeria 14 percent—*Petroleum Press Service* (London) August 1968.

that Japan's consumption will also grow more slowly. "Other Eastern Hemisphere" may be assumed to continue to grow at the present rate. The only anticipated increase may come from Eastern Europe, where several deals for the exchange of Middle East and North African oil against industrial goods have been recently concluded, but the amounts are small. The best estimate puts the anticipated growth in Eastern Europe's oil consumption at about 10 per cent per annum, raising that region's import surplus to around 160 million tons by 1980. Even the assumption that all East Europe's needs are met from Middle East and North African sources would not greatly affect the outcome. Thus it is possible that the growth in overall demand for Middle East oil will slacken to a rate of, say, 7.0 to 8.0 per cent and that for North African to, say, 10-15 per cent.

How would this very tentative extrapolation be affected by the intensification of the cold war? Presumably it would make Western Europe and Japan more nervous about their oil supplies and stimulate the search for alternative sources in Alaska, Australia, West Africa, and elsewhere. Presumably it would also encourage further the search for and use of natural gas, which is expected to meet 11 per cent of Western Europe's energy needs by 1975, compared to 2.0 to 3.0 per cent in the early 1960s. Nuclear energy would be developed more rapidly. In the United States, the cold war could strengthen the feeling that domestic oil should be developed at all costs because Middle East oil, though much cheaper, is unreliable. And the Soviet Union may, for similar reasons, prevent its satellites from buying Middle East oil. There are indications of two schools of thought in the Soviet Union; one seems to be urging the East Europeans to seek raw materials from sources outside the bloc, where they are cheaper. The other seeks, mainly for political and military reasons, to tie the bloc more closely. Presumably the balance of power between the two schools is affected by the state of United States-Soviet relations.

Within the region the effect of such developments may be to increase the squeeze on the companies, and may even lead to some nationalization. The latter may not make such sense, since the consumers have already weathered the two crises of 1956 and 1967, and are now better prepared. But it would be foolish to underestimate the irrationality of any group of men. Nevertheless it can be assumed that an intensified cold war would merely reduce the rate of growth to, say, 6.0 to 7.0 per cent.

The second alternative, a limited détente, would presumably relax such pressures. It might widen the markets for Middle East oil and enable it to compete with other, more expensive, oils. This may raise the rate of growth to, say, 9.0 to 10 per cent.

The third possibility, a fuller détente, would presumably push the process further. The main consumers, Western Europe and Japan, might move closer to the center of the stage, bringing with them new firms with fresh capital and additional outlets. This might further increase the overall share of Middle East and North African oil, at the expense of Venezuelan and Soviet. The latter would also, presumably, be in greater demand at home, since relaxation may lead to greater consumer consumption. In other words, the overall rate of increase may possibly rise to 10 to 12 per cent. The latest Plan revision (in 1967) put the targets for Soviet oil at 345 to 355 million tons in 1970 and 630 million tons in 1980. Soviet consumption in 1980 was estimated by OECD (in 1966) at 613 to 700 million tons. It will thus be seen that, depending on the rate of increase of output and consumption, the USSR will have a *small* export or import surplus, leaving an opening for Middle Eastern oil in Eastern Europe and perhaps in the USSR itself.

This highly impressionistic picture would suggest that, short of war, the state of international politics will affect regional exports of oil only

TABLE 4

Direction of Middle East Trade*

(in millions of dollars)

	Exports		Imports	
	1961	1965	1961	1965
EEC	$1,580	$2,165	$933	$1,372
UK	804	849	563	722
US	324	334	668	954
Japan	457	962	179	318
Soviet bloc	264	441	366	332
Total	$5,083	$6,609	$3,894	$5,094

*Does not include North Africa or Pakistan; the bulk of North African trade is with EEC, followed by the US and UK; Pakistan's trade is mainly with US, EEC, UK, and Japan.

Source: International Monetary Fund and International Bank for Reconstruction and Development, *Direction of Trade, 1961-65.*

quantitatively—the range between the lowest and highest guesses is of the order of two to one.

Increasing Trade with the Soviet Bloc

Oil, the region's main export item, will continue to flow mainly to the non-Communist countries for a long time, but this need not hold for other exports: cotton, rice, tobacco, fruits, vegetables, and simple manufactures. The demand for such goods may be expected to grow more rapidly in the Soviet bloc than in the West, and there is therefore much economic justification (as well as many political causes) for the rising Soviet share in the region's trade. As Table 4 shows, the bloc now accounts for about 7.0 per cent of its trade, and there is every reason to believe that these figures will continue to rise. In some countries, notably UAR and Syria, the Soviet bloc plays a much larger role, accounting for over one-third of total trade. Thus, to take only one example, under the trade agreement of March 2, 1967, Soviet-Iranian trade is scheduled to increase by two and a half times in five years.

The benefits to the region of greater trade with the Soviet bloc are evident: new outlets, giving added safeguards against fluctuating prices in world markets, and a wider choice of supplies of capital goods. The economic dangers of closer ties with the bloc, as distinct from the political, are less obvious but nonetheless real. There is the possibility of exploitation through unfavorable terms of trade, as seems to have happened to several of the Soviet Union's Communist trading partners. There is the virtual certainty of irrational price setting, distortion of channels of trade, and diversion of resources from optimum patterns of allocation. But when all is said, it seems highly probable that Middle East and North African trade with the Soviet bloc will continue to grow, absorbing a steadily rising share of the total. Should the cold war be intensified, the process may accelerate, and conversely during a détente. Deeper involvement of Western Europe may halt or even reverse the trend since, unlike the United States which has little need for Mediterranean products, Western Europe constitutes a huge market for cotton, jute, tobacco, rice, and above all fruits and vegetables. To take only the last item, between 1955-1959 and 1967 Middle East and North African output of citrus doubled, but increasing competition has been met in Western European markets from Spain, Italy, the United States, and South Africa. Clearly prospects depend largely on the preferences granted to the various regions by the Common Market.

Capital and Technical Assistance

Relative to population, the Middle East and North Africa have received more foreign aid than any region in the world. Credits extended by the Sino-Soviet bloc to twelve countries in 1954-1966, inclusive, totalled $4,298 million out of a world total of $8,729 million; a little over two-thirds came from the Soviet Union. The main recipients were: the UAR, $1,636 million; Afghanistan, $605 million; Iran, $376 million; Syria, $363 million; Algeria, $304 million; Pakistan, $294 million; Turkey, $218 million; and Iraq, $190 million. These figures do not include military credits. Figures on actual disbursements, as distinct from credits extended, are not available but it is believed that "to date only about one-third of total communist aid extensions have been implemented" and it seems unlikely that the regional share is much higher—say $1,500 million. No breakdown on the number of bloc technicians is available; in the Middle East it is given as 3,800 and the addition of North Africa, Afghanistan, and Pakistan may raise it to some 5,000, out of a total of 11,730.

United States aid is far larger and has gone to every single country in the region. Between July 1946 and June 1967 economic aid was $11,296 million, of which $5,436 million was in grants and $5,863 million in loans. The main beneficiaries were Pakistan, $3,304 million; Turkey, $2,422 million; Israel, $1,086 million; the UAR, $1,039 million; Iran, $958 million; and Morocco, $587 million. United States investments in the Middle East including Libya, almost wholly in oil, were put at less than $2,200 million at the end of 1966.

To this should be added large sums from Britain and West Germany to the Middle East and from France to North Africa. Loans from the IBRD and grants from the United Nations and the specialized agencies have aggregated hundreds of millions. British investments in oil are probably on the order of $1,200 million.

Clearly, this vast inflow of funds and the still larger one from oil have provided the bulk of investment funds and have been largely responsible for the rapid pace of economic development in the region during the last few years. Their interruption, or sharp diminution, would be disastrous. Is such an outcome to be expected if the cold war is intensified? Or conversely in case of détente? Here perhaps the most cynical approach is also the most realistic—viz., that the importance of the region is such that all sides will continue to vie for its favors and that the inflow of funds will not cease; but, given the present mood of the donors, it could slacken appreciably.

Income From Services

For thousands of years the Middle East has derived sizeable income from various "services" arising from its location, climate, culture, and religions. Transit trade between the Indian Ocean and Mediterranean has always been important, and has been channelled through the Suez Canal and airports. Pilgrims have flocked, and still flock, to the Christian, Muslim, and Jewish Holy Places—and before that to the shrines of Isis and Astarte. Tourists since the time of Herodotus have come to gape at the pyramids. Such long-established trades are not likely to be cut off by transient phenomena like the cold war!

Nevertheless two of these items, the canal and tourism, may be affected by mundane contingencies. It seems inconceivable that the canal should remain closed for very long. Equally, it has clearly lost not only its former monopoly but also its recent importance, based on oil. For the largest tankers that can at present pass through the canal fully laden are 80,000 tonners. And economies of scale are such that tankers sailing round the cape can deliver oil to Western Europe more cheaply than small ones using the canal. The shape of things to come is indicated by the fact that whereas on June 30, 1968, there were only 87 tankers of over 100,000 tons, aggregating 11 million tons, the number on order was 186, aggregating 37 million tons and including 26 monsters of over 250,000 tons.

Nevertheless oil will continue to flow in large quantities through the canal, because the volume of trade is bound to grow, because there is still a huge fleet of small and medium tankers, and because the canal route from the Persian Gulf to Southern and Eastern Europe is so much shorter than the cape route. As far as is known, the Soviet bloc does not own tankers of over 80,000 tons. Canal traffic will almost certainly not continue to increase at its recent rate of about 9.0 per cent per annum, but once restored it is likely to be maintained or even to rise slowly. And it is just worth mentioning one more possibility—the proposed Egyptian pipeline, estimated to cost $100 to $135 million. An Israel pipeline, estimated to cost $62 million in its first stage and another $61 million in its second stage, is also being built. So, short of an actual shooting war, Egypt is likely to derive substantial revenues from oil transit, probably exceeding the peak of $230 million collected in canal dues.

Tourism is more likely to wilt under the blast of the cold war since most tourists visit countries for fun—although many Middle East governments do not seem to have discovered this arcane truth. Except for a few countries—Israel, Lebanon, Morocco, and Tunisia—the region has not exploited its enormous potentialities, and its share of world tourism, about 3.0 or 4.0 per cent, is still very small. In recent years the rate of growth has accelerated, tourist receipts rising from about $300 million in 1963 to over $550 million in 1966. One can visualize tourism expanding very rapidly, or dwindling to a mere trickle.

In conclusion, the mainstays of the economy of the Middle East and North Africa in recent years have been oil and foreign aid, which have greatly helped to achieve a rapid growth in agricultural and industrial output. Barring a catastrophe, it is unlikely that either of these two stimulants will lose much of its force in the near future; for the world cannot do without Middle East oil and therefore its interest in the region is not likely to vanish, though it may be reduced, whatever the temperature of the cold war. From an economist's point of view, then, there would be good grounds for optimism provided internal stability and regional peace are maintained—an important proviso, and one not likely to be achieved.

This brings us to the heart of the problem. Tensions between the powers affect the Middle East not so much through the region's economic relations with the outside world as through their repercussions within the region itself. For they exacerbate the tensions between Middle East states, increase the threat of war, and, to take only one economic consequence, stimulate the arms races on which many countries are at present spending 10 per cent or more of their GNP. This is where the cold war hurts most, and this is perhaps where a détente would produce its most beneficial results.

Cultural Contest

The "Cultural Contest"

CHARLES FRANKEL

Although many approaches to the study and practice of foreign policy regularly ignore the point, foreign policy, of course, is not simply *foreign* policy. Neither in the United States nor anywhere else is it simply a program for securing the power and safety of a country in the light of the resources, the actions, and the intentions of other countries. Foreign policy reflects the domestic play of interests, and is influenced by myths about the world which have domestic sources and a domestic function. Indeed, even if the foreign policy of a country were constructed entirely on the basis of rational calculations about the intentions and capacities of foreign nations, it would still remain, in good part, a domestic concoction. Whatever a government may decide to adopt on paper as its policy, what it actually does is controlled and limited by the style and habits, the resources and the scale of values, of the society which it asks to support and implement that policy.

In no area is this more the case than in cultural diplomacy. In America, "culture"—the liberal arts, sciences and professions, education, literature, painting, the performing arts, architecture, and design—is the work of private citizens who are not employees of the government, and who produce what is not an official product. And this culture of the intellectuals, scientists and artists, furthermore, is distinguished by a distinctive political culture, a set of attitudes toward government, authority, and power. On the whole, intellectuals, scholars, and writers are suspicious of organization and tight centralized direction, and they are particularly jealous of their autonomy *vis-à-vis* government. Moreover, their culture is, in a broad sense, international in its perspective.

There is not, to be sure, any general consensus within the "cultural community" about the proper political solution of existing international problems. Nor do I mean to suggest that scientists, critics, and artists have little or no sense of themselves as Americans —as products, and perhaps as spokesmen, of American civilization. Many are willing and eager to be perceived as representatives of this civilization. Nevertheless, despite the fact that in many fields, such as poetry, sociology, philosophy, and political science, national cultural differences set up obstacles to communication across the borders, national frontiers, on the whole, have a more arbitrary, fictitious quality for members of the so-called "cultural community" than they do for members of, say, the foreign policy community or the professional politician's club. In comparison with other communities, the cultural community's audience, its standards of achievement, its professional associations, and sources of inspiration are all more independent of political boundaries and power rivalries.

A principle of fundamental importance emerges from this state of affairs. Cultural policy, and particularly the cultural policy of the United States, cannot be viewed as a technique of maneuver, or a tool that can be freely used as the government wishes to use it, for purposes defined within the traditional perspectives of diplomacy. Or perhaps it would be more accurate to say that cultural diplomacy *can* be viewed in this way, since, in fact, it often is. But the result of doing so is usually a cultural foreign policy at once clumsy and juvenile—an effort to win friends and influence people that is transparent to foreigners and irritating to most of the Americans who are asked to participate in it. To conceive cultural foreign policy in this manner is to weaken the capacity of the government to achieve the distinctive and highly important long-range purposes which cultural diplomacy alone can achieve.

It is for this reason that, in the title to this paper, I have put the words "cultural contest" in the topic that has been assigned to me between quotation marks. I do not doubt that there is a cultural contest in the Middle East; there are in fact several. Indeed, there is a cultural contest taking place in the United States, as there is one in the Soviet Union and Eastern Europe. And I believe it is highly probable that the cultural contest in the Middle East will continue for years and perhaps decades to come, no matter what happens to relations between the United States and the Soviet Union. Yet it is a fundamental error for American cultural policy in this area of the world, or anywhere else, to be guided by the slogans and spirit appropriate to a polemical contest.

To be sure, one cannot ignore the fact that the Soviet Union does not accept peaceful coexistence on the ideological plane; Americans must realize that their intellectual and cultural activities will be attacked, by the Soviets themselves, by their partisans, and by many other groups, not only on the left but on the right as well. Protective measures will be necessary. But the most effective of these, I am persuaded, is resolutely to refuse to take the bait. The proper approach is to display a culture which is not marked by aggressiveness or intolerance, which offers the advantages of diversity and flexibility, which is prepared for cooperative endeavors with others if they will be equally forthcoming, and which leaves people free to choose what they want from it without asking for any form of total allegiance from them. Over the long run, the central cultural contest on which the possibility of improvement in international relations in the Middle East depends—the central cultural contest on which the possibility of improvement in the United States or the Soviet Union, depends—is the contest between the dogmatists and the moderate men, between the ideologues and the skeptical reformers. To adopt a policy of contest and contention is to get into a fight we are not likely to win, and it is to sow the seeds of the whirlwind.

One can not, of course, predict that United States cultural policy will follow this course. National pride, America's itch to sell itself, America's dislike of losing any contest whether it belongs in that contest or not, may well push policy in the other direction. Moreover, the organization of international educational and cultural programs in the United States government reinforces these tendencies. Whatever the cultural policies may be that are established in Washington, operational control of cultural programs in the field is in the hands of the USIA, which has a built-in bias toward viewing cultural relations simply as one more public relations or propaganda weapon. Without the substantial modification of this system for administering cultural affairs, it will be difficult to prevent American cultural diplomacy in the Middle East from being carried on in the spirit of the cold war. There is likely to be bureaucratic momentum in this direction even if Soviet-American relations improve and American policy changes in other spheres.

Still, it is pragmatically desirable to project the possibilities for United States policy as though that policy were capable of being formulated in the light of objective needs and facts, and not simply in response to bureaucratic pressures. Taking this point of view, what are the possibilities for American educational and cultural policy in the next decade in the Middle East?

I

It is necessary first, in answering this question, to indicate what the general purposes and policies of cultural diplomacy can reasonably be said to be. Unless these are to be laid down in a wholly *a priori* fashion, it is wise to begin the effort to define the purposes by noting that there are certain general requirements, inherent in the nature of cultural diplomacy, which a well-designed policy must meet. For this discussion, it will be enough to mention three.

One imperative, which bears with particular force on a large power, is that cultural diplomacy must have a transnational flavor. In both the richer and the poorer parts of the world, it is a condition of successful cultural diplomacy that the culture presented not be merely a piece of exotica. It must have a quality of translatability, of applicability to conditions beyond the borders of its country of origin. It must have, in other words, an element of *universality*.

In the poorer countries particularly, people have little interest in American culture because it is American. They are interested in it for what it represents, for its significance as a product of a popular, democratic culture or a scientifically and technologically advanced society, for what it can do for them—what techniques it offers, what models it proposes, and what alternatives it offers to the existing dispensation. Where there is an interest in American culture for its specifically American quality, as in certain countries of North and West Africa, this is due to the fact that the leaders of these countries believe their societies to have been too much under the influence of one or another European country. They turn to American culture as a way of opening windows and letting new intellectual currents blow through. As a practical matter, therefore, cultural activities in the Middle East are likely to be successful the more they are focused on the needs of the local population. An excessive concern with spreading knowledge of American society or sympathy towards it can work against the success of the program, as, in fact, it often has. Conversely, in certain circumstances useful purposes can be achieved by working in cooperation with other countries in common educational or intellectual pursuits.

A second imperative that bears on American cultural policy everywhere is particularly important in the Middle East. It is the other side of translatability—receptivity. The United States is very powerful, and its technology has an immense thrust, as do its popular forms of mass entertainment like the movies and rock music. The United States, therefore, is always subject to the charge, justified or not, that it is "culturally imperialist." However unconcerned a nation might be about such charges in the nineteenth century, it cannot ignore them in the present century—particularly a country like the United States, which believes itself to be egalitarian and anticolonialist, and hopes to be perceived as such.

American cultural policy, therefore, has to be a *cultural exchange* policy. Not only must official policy and actions be such that smaller and weaker nations will not feel themselves imposed upon, but the framework for cultural policy should be binational or multinational, taking every opportunity to receive as well as to give. A certain hard-headed cultural self-interest, whether it is in possibilities for study or research by Americans or in receiving in our own country the representatives or the products of the other culture, is an excellent quality to display.

A third imperative is that cultural policy has to be cultural *policy*. It has to possess, that is to say, at least two characteristics—a set of consistent guidelines, not subject to drastic change without very strong reasons, and a set of identifiable goals. It is easy to assume that "culture" and "education" are such obviously good things that their deployment in the international arena cannot help but do good: everybody believes that literacy is desirable, that music is an international language, and that exchanges of students and scholars promote good will. Piety often has a tendency to substitute for policy in foreign affairs; educational and cultural affairs are no exception.

But beliefs such as those mentioned, though they may be more true than false, do not help policy makers to decide what their basic priorities are, to use their resources economically, or to measure their progress towards definite goals. On the contrary they have a tendency to encourage the irrational alteration of priorities from year to year, the scattering of efforts, and the choice of quick but evanescent benefits at the expense of slower programs that might leave a lasting deposit. Educational and cultural programs with other countries are best administered when they are consciously conceived as jointly devised plans for improving the educational and cultural enterprises of the United States and its partner. Within such a framework specific targets should be developed to give continuity and substance to the exchange program—e.g., improvement in the study of economic or comparative law, the mitigation of the brain drain, the revising of textbooks, or the development of teacher-training centers sufficient to give a nation the capacity for self-sustaining educational growth.

Given such requirements, a special group of purposes emerge for cultural diplomacy. The particular blend of these purposes will differ from region to region and country to country; but, overall, educational and cultural foreign policy, properly conceived, can be construed as an effort to achieve such goals as the following: (1) to build international contact, communication, and cooperation among educational systems; (2) to develop international communities of intellectual, professional, and artistic workers, actively cooperating in their common business; (3) to aid, by technical means, by government agreements, by international exchange programs and other means, the flow across borders of ideas and information; (4) to develop international arrangements designed to prevent the piling up of talent and knowledge in a few metropolitan centers of the world, and aimed at producing a distribution of educated leadership and specialized expertise adequate to assure the poorer countries that they can develop mainly through the exercise of their own capacities.

What are the reasons for regarding cultural diplomacy, so conceived, as a necessary branch of diplomacy? The rationale lies in the major changes in the nature of human societies that have taken place in the last fifty years. Science and technology have moved to the foreground as motors of historical evolution. The spread of literacy and leisure, the growth of urbanism and improvements in communication have meant that literature, the fine arts, the cinema and music have greatly increased in their power to affect the forms of human consciousness, and thus to influence the movement of opinion and the evolution of historical events. The school has emerged as a major instrument of national consolidation and social change, moving into areas of social power from which the home, the community, and religious authorities have gradually receded. Education has become an indispensable area of economic investment for good economic reasons. The intelligentsia has acquired critical forms of power and influence, not always inside governments, but over the larger societies within which governments function; and its power is not simply that of technical experts but of critics, moral commentators, and secular priests.

To try to arrange relations between nations without taking account of the perturbations created by such changes is to conduct diplomacy on premises about as useful to us as Lord Palmerston's. Indeed, the most decisive variable affecting American cultural policy in the Middle East over the next decade is probably not what happens in the Middle East but what happens in this country in our understanding of international cultural policy, and in the way in which the United States government organizes and administers this sector of foreign affairs.

II

Cultural policy in the Middle East, for at least the next decade, will have to function in a situation marked by two paradoxes. They will hold true no matter what happens to Soviet-American relations.

The first paradox is the perception of American culture by the Middle East intelligentsia as "reactionary-progressive." By and large, the intelligentsia and other groups will continue to identify themselves with causes like "socialism" and "anticolonialism." While the positive content of such words is vague, what they stand for negatively is not at all uncertain: suspicion of the rich and powerful states, particularly of those identified as "capitalist." There are, of course, differences from country to country with regard to the prevalence of such attitudes among intellectuals. The Turks are less suspicious of the United States than the Egyptians; the Tunisians are more friendly than the Algerians. There is little the United States can do to overcome this handicap, although extensive social reforms at home might have a minor effect. On the whole, any attempt to convince the intelligentsia in the Middle East that the United States has a social system they should copy will be a severe, uphill effort.

Yet, at the same time, American science, technology, and organizational capacities will continue to have an intrinsic attractiveness. Though we may be perceived as "reactionary" in one respect, we are also perceived as dynamic and modern in another. On the perhaps optimistic assumption that things will not get worse than they already are here at home, American technological culture and American know-how will probably continue to exercise appeal. Accordingly, the lure of American education and culture in the Middle East will probably be as great as the suspicions that exist toward them.

The second paradox can be caught in the phrase "alienation-attraction." In most underdeveloped countries, Marxism—or, at any rate, a way of looking at the world that is heavily Marxist in origin—now has special appeal. I see little reason to suppose that this will change. Marxism is at once a synthesis and a critique of Western thought and culture; it thus allows people to partake of Western culture while feeling that they have also liberated themselves from it.

However, in the Middle East, as elsewhere, this view will likely be more national or regional than international in its orientation. It will create barriers to the easy assimilation in the Middle East of American styles of empirical social thought, but it is not an insuperable barrier to communication provided that Americans become sensitive to the nuances of different varieties of Marxism. The possibility of communication is enhanced by the fact that American culture is not perceived, by most of the countries in the Middle East, simply as a storehouse of technical know-how. It is part of Western European culture, for which intellectual leaders continue to have immense respect and admiration, despite their efforts to de-colonialize themselves. Intellectuals in the Middle East do not want their countries to be second-rate. Western European and American culture, with its freedom and sophistication, therefore continues to attract them, and to make them uncomfortable with the doctrinaire aspects of Marxist ideology. In this context, Russian culture has shown little competitive power, and Chinese culture is not likely to do much better. Indeed, the very fact that the struggle in the Middle East is usually presented as a struggle against Western domination is the reflection of an underlying fact of equal importance: the Middle East states are culturally oriented toward the West, not Russia or East Asia.

III

Within these controlling imperatives, what are the specific problems and possibilities for American educational and cultural policy in the Middle East in the coming years? Let us assume, first, a condition of continuing dangerous rivalry between the United States and the Soviet Union in the area.

Under these circumstances, the major purposes of United States policy should be twofold: (1) to do what can be done to assure that alternative models for university organization, educational development, and intellectual activity are maintained, and (2) to be as useful as possible in helping to meet the educational needs of countries in the area. The openness and the utility of the American educational system and intellectual resources need not be preached, but they should be demonstrated in practice.

From this point of view, the American-sponsored private institutions in the area are important resources. They should be strengthened and encouraged to grow, provided that they are not built as enclaves but with genuine local support and the friendship of the host government. What is probably crucial in the strengthening of these institutions is that they be brought into active alliance with powerful colleges and universities in the United States, which would support them by sending faculty to teach at them, use them for important forms of research, and engage in regular programs of student exchange with them.

The resources of the Fulbright-Hays program should also be used in a planned fashion to keep the alternative of free educational development an open prospect. This means more than simply an increase of funds for these programs in the Middle East, although it certainly does mean that. It means the mounting of systematic exchange programs which can contribute to the filling, over the years, of definite educational needs, ordered on a conscious scale of priorities. Allowing for variations due to local conditions, I am inclined to think that the most long-range and far-reaching benefits will be obtained if emphasis is placed on the basic intellectual disciplines, rather than on their vocational or practical offshoots. If the Inter-

national Education Act passed in 1966 is ever funded, this would provide an additional framework for accomplishing these purposes.

AID programs, in contrast, can probably focus best on teacher
education. Indeed, if a reorganization of technical assistance programs takes place, as seems likely, attention should be given to the
creation of new administrative entities, more capable of giving the
requisite attention to long-range forms of educational cooperation
and assistance than those that have existed. The general impact of
better educated populations on the development process is so considerable as to justify investment in education as such.

The impact of a continuing cold war on such a nonpolitical cultural policy as that described here is difficult to estimate. The need
of countries in the Middle East for educational and cultural contact
with the West, simply in the interests of their own development, is
considerable. Moreover, linguistic, cultural, and political problems
make exclusive reliance on Soviet educational and cultural programs
unwise for most of them. Soviet influence over Middle East countries, even if it grows greatly, is unlikely to be sufficient in itself
to cause these countries to cut off contacts with the United States or
Western Europe. What is far more likely to cause such a breach in
relations is political pressures arising from local conditions, such as
the Arab-Israel conflict or factional disputes within or between individual states. To the extent that American cultural diplomacy can
succeed in establishing useful, domestically rooted programs of educational exchange and development in which the Middle East nations
develop their own vested interests, a measure of protection against
the breach of cultural relations is created.

For this reason, if for no other, concern about the impact of American cultural programs on the development of "socialism" in the area
is ill-placed. Perhaps Russian cultural programs in states friendly to
the Soviet Union will accelerate socialism, and American programs
in states friendly to the United States will retard its growth. Perhaps;
but perhaps not. The overweening cultural presence of the Russians
seems to have opposite effects, and so does the overweening presence
of the Americans. In any case, the central issue for educational and
cultural policy is not to stop "socialism" in the Middle East (whatever that term can mean in countries like Iraq, the UAR, or Algeria).
It is not capable of accomplishing such a task. What educational and
cultural diplomacy can more sensibly attempt is to build conditions

that will prevent the rigidification and polarization of disputes, and produce more moderate international policies on all sides.

IV

What would be the impact on cultural policy if there were a limited Soviet-American détente? On the whole, the ideological divisions among intellectuals might become somewhat less bitter, but they would persist, as would the political instability, economic turmoil, and nationalist hatreds that presently exist in the Middle East. Diminution of tensions between the two superpowers, however, may permit the increased adoption of two strategies: complementarity and multinationality.

The first of these consists in dividing responsibilities for educational assistance within individual countries between the United States and the Soviet Union, on the basis of either explicit or tacit understandings. The second consists in placing greater reliance in multinational agencies like UNESCO or FAO, which would become more easy to do if the major powers become less interested in using them as forums for polemic and contention. The easing of political tensions, in a word, will offer opportunities for a more affirmative policy of multilateralism and international educational effort. These opportunities should be sought and seized. Meanwhile, pending a relaxation of tensions, the offers to engage in such efforts should be on the table, and the seriousness of United States intentions should be shown in every practical way.

V

The negotiation of a general Soviet-American détente would not, to my mind, greatly alter the options available under a condition of limited détente. As already mentioned general political détente does not necessarily mean ideological détente. The present Soviet leaders, as their recent behavior toward Czechoslovakia once again reveals, still do not want to risk the effects in their own country of a more open-minded and uncontrolled intellectual and cultural dialogue.

On the whole, indeed, it seems more probable that gradual military disarmament, economic cooperation, and fundamental political agreements can be reached with the Soviet Union than that relaxed cultural arrangements can be reached with them. Pushed by internal necessities and also by overlapping interests on the international

scene, it is within the bounds of the possible that the United States
and its allies can, in concert with the USSR, liquidate large parts of
the cold war during the next decade. But in the area of cultural,
scientific, intellectual, and educational endeavor, they are dealing
with problems less susceptible to solution by formal international
agreement. For they are not the consequences, essentially, of conflicts
in policy, but of differences between two types of society. The
United States cannot negotiate away its own constitutional commitment to freedom of speech for its own citizens, nor can it abandon
its support for such international human rights as free movement
across borders and free access of all populations to ideas and information. The Soviets, on their side, are not likely to abandon the concept of a politically controlled culture. This does not require a cold
war, but cultural relations with Russia are not going to be like American relations with France, Japan, Mexico, or India.

In the long run, to be sure, new generations of intellectual and
political leaders in both the United States and Russia will gradually
succeed in reducing the anachronistic political fears and ideological
fantasies that affect relations between the two societies. It is, indeed,
one function of cultural diplomacy to produce precisely this effect. A
general détente may make the pace of progress toward such a goal
noticeably faster. However, United States policies in this period, if
they are realistic, should assume the possibility neither of a marriage
of love or even of reason so far as educational and cultural affairs are
concerned. They should seek business partnerships devoted to specific cooperative projects, such as population control or literacy. The
American view should be that ideological and cultural differences
are not insuperable barriers to intellectual or educational cooperation, if the projects are well chosen. The American view should not
be that these differences do not exist or are unimportant. This would
probably aggravate distrust and disbelief.

VI

But perhaps the greatest danger to educational and cultural policy
which is presented by the Soviet-American rivalry in the Middle
East is that it can lead to an obsession with cold war problems that
causes us to ignore other forms of "cultural contest" in the Middle
East. For these other contests may be more severe, and will almost
certainly be more significant in their effect on the general evolution

of events in that area. One is the contest between education and emigration. The Soviet-American "cultural contest" has a dimension that lies below its polemical surface. It is the race between the inflow of help to the Middle East and the outflow of people, the problem that has come to be known as "the brain drain."

Viewed in the context of East-West rivalries, the very lure of Western society is hurtful to it. People who are won over by the Russian model are not normally tempted to migrate to that part of the world, and usually encounter major obstacles if they wish to do so. On the other hand, people attracted by Western education, culture, or opportunity do often wish to migrate to the West.

The emigration of such people in large numbers impedes the development and liberalization of their countries, which is the most important consequence, and it also has the side effect of leaving the devotees of the cruder forms of nationalism and the more dogmatic forms of Marxism and socialism with fewer capable rivals. This tendency on the part of a certain proportion of the talented and sophisticated leaders of Middle East countries to leave their homes will probably persist in the next decade. Thus, a fundamental desideratum of American cultural policy, paradoxically enough, must be to create countervailing conditions which will reduce the bad side effects of American and Western culture's attractiveness.

From this point of view, certain general strategies are needed. Setting aside general political or economic pressures which push people into leaving their native countries, there appear to be four factors which, within an educational system itself, encourage emigration. These are (1) the small scale of a system, which makes it less interesting to people of superior talent; (2) its linguistic separateness, which deprives its members of the sense of membership in the larger intellectual communities where the main action is; (3) the rigidities in the system, which discourage the young, the innovators, and the reformers; (4) the physical isolation of the system, which prevents people from mixing as they believe they should with their professional peers. Educational assistance and organized exchange programs should be planned with these problems in mind.

In addition, attention has to be given to the balance between promoting educational development in the Middle East and bringing people abroad for their education. If a choice must be made between two abstract statements of policy, it is undoubtedly better for a nation that needs foreign educational assistance to bring foreign teachers and specialists to it than to send its students abroad. Unfortunately, however, such a statement greatly oversimplifies the issues. The costs of such a policy are often prohibitive. It is difficult to recruit the best people or to provide the supporting libraries and laboratories. Perhaps most important of all, such a policy ignores the invaluable function of study abroad. When a nation sends its best students abroad for study, it risks losing a proportion of them. When it fails to do so, it risks losing the worldliness, the drive and freshness of outlook, and the international associations that students trained abroad bring home with them. It is not just "skills" that students learn abroad. They develop attitudes of mind which are at least equally important to economic development.

Well-planned actions can reduce the effects that such study abroad can have in increasing the brain drain. For example, younger students are more likely to remain in the country where they receive their education than are older students. Those who stay abroad longer are more prone to wish to remain away from home. Grant programs should take these facts into account. The developing countries can do more to ensure that students who study abroad will have job opportunities commensurate with their training when they return home. The developed countries can be more careful to fit their scholarship and exchange programs to the needs of the developing countries, and can provide programs of instruction better fitted to motivate and prepare foreign students for work in their own countries. Through the creation of more adequate facilities for selecting and counselling students before they go abroad, both the sending countries and the receiving countries can also reduce the drain of talent.

Such measures, to be sure, are not likely to remove the problem entirely. The migration of skills to the richer countries is not, after all, a recent phenomenon; it is itself part of the price of development. But this price can probably be reduced with effective planning to the point that it is considerably outweighed by the flow of people and resources from the developed to the less developed world.

VII

Another "cultural contest" independent of Soviet-American rivalries which is nevertheless crucial for cultural policy is that between the values of mass popular education and those of higher education. It is now becoming plain that the tendency in most poor countries to emphasize primary education at one end and higher education at the other is a mistake. Primary education and the eradication of illiteracy are properly major goals of educational development. But the accomplishment of these goals, as experience in many countries has shown, requires more teachers, better conditions of communication, physical and psychological, between the cities and the countryside, and fundamental changes in family mores and in the mental horizons of the population at large. All this implies that, other things being equal, the advancement of primary education depends in part on the rapid development of education at higher levels. Particularly in the countries just starting out on the route to development, the greatest emphasis should be on secondary education.

It is of particular importance that expansion of higher education be accompanied by a considerably broader expansion of public secondary education, and an upgrading of its status. This ensures broader and more democratic access to university education. It can also provide employment for many university graduates who might otherwise be unemployed, and give them therewith an opportunity to bridge the gap between themselves and the rest of the population.

Closely connected to the need for expanded secondary education is the need to give special attention to the training of middle-level professional and technical people. It is a mistake to take over the model of advanced professional education in developed countries as the dominant pattern for professional education in the poorer countries. Even in the richer countries this model is no longer a sufficient guide to educational policy. In these countries, there is a need not only for doctors but for nurses, public health specialists, and hospital assistants, not only for research scientists but for laboratory assistants and skilled mechanics, not only for teachers but for teachers' aides and preschool supervisors. Manpower shortage in the richer countries is not likely to be eliminated unless better provision is made for attracting and training people at these subprofessional levels. All this applies even more strongly to the developing countries. And the training of such middle-level specialists also serves the additional purpose of producing people who can serve effectively as translators and communicators between the advanced intelligentsia and the population as a whole.

VIII

To discuss the relation between university development and the general course of social evolution is, however, to raise perhaps the knottiest problem of all. It is the emerging role of the university, in the Middle East, in Eastern Europe, in Western Europe, and the United States, as a center for political activism and for the articulation of radical forms of protest against major features of industrial society. Paradoxically, the universities, which in all societies are the indispensable agents of modernization, have also become the major centers for the revival of pre-industrial conceptions of politics and social organization.

It is possible that these tendencies, which have become so noticeable during the past year, will be with us for a long time. And if so, they may mean that both the Soviet Union and the United States will be bypassed as models for either political or cultural emulation. The issue for each of the superpowers will not be to push its own cultural cause and resist the advance of its rival's. The issue will be simply to stay in touch with emerging aspirations.

The consequences of this new cultural contest—a contest within the cultural establishment everywhere, a contest between that establishment and its environing society—are difficult to predict. It may lead in some countries in the Middle East to essentially conservative movements, sometimes led by students and intellectuals, sometimes against them. It may lead elsewhere to movements on the left. In either case, the impact on the development of the Middle East would be severe; tensions within countries would be increased, and, very probably, tensions between them.

Moreover, what the United States can do about such events will depend very largely on the course of a similar cultural contest in the United States itself. Disturbances in the universities may well lead people in the executive and legislative branches simply to the conclusion that American professors and students, artists and writers, are not to be trusted, and relations with their foreign counterparts not to be cultivated. Then educational and cultural policy will be more neglected than ever. The demonstration that it operates in an area of great historical importance will have produced the usual reaction; if a troublesome problem is ignored, it may go away.

However, a more affirmative response is at least theoretically possible. Such a response would have to begin not with foreign policy but with domestic policy, with educational reforms within American universities, and with efforts at larger political reforms, designed to bring the cultural and educational community closer to public policy. At this moment in the winter of 1968, the chances do not look good that such efforts will be made. If they are, it will be difficult for them to succeed. Even if they do succeed, a segment of the university community and the scientific and cultural estate may remain alienated.

Still, such a domestic policy would make possible a much larger degree of successful voluntary cooperation between government and the cultural community than is now imaginable, and this, in turn, would greatly promote the chances for sensitive and effective cultural diplomacy abroad. One of the prerequisites for such a turn of events, however, is the easing of the tensions that now divide the American cultural and educational community internally.

The prospects for educational and cultural diplomacy are not good when choice is polarized, thanks to both governmental and academic attitudes, between intellectual alienation and intellectual helotry, between governmental suspicion of intellectuals and government efforts to tame them to the needs of bureaucracies and the irritabilities of conservative Congressmen. The great problem is whether the educational and cultural community will know how to retain its independence and its critical stance while recognizing, at the same time, that its opportunities to use its powers to the advantage of the national and international scene are greatly augmented by the resources that government can put at its disposal. The great problem is whether the government can come gradually to the view that there are cultural relationships between the United States and other societies on which their mutual destinies depend, and which cannot be properly cultivated if they are bureaucratized or politicalized. An American cultural policy organized on the basis of such understandings would have considerable magnetism, here and abroad. It would be a policy that could contribute significantly to the progress and peace of the Middle East, and to the establishment of less precarious relations with that part of the world.

Soviet Cultural Effort

FREDERICK C. BARGHOORN

The dearth of detailed, factual information available to students of Soviet-Middle East relations, particularly the social and cultural aspects, makes this analysis somewhat impressionistic. Nevertheless, material in Soviet publications on cultural policy toward the Middle East, though fragmentary and limited, provides a general picture of some aspects of Soviet intentions, strategy, and organization.

Like the overall Soviet policy to which it is subordinated, the Soviet cultural effort in the Middle East has been only partly successful. However, the effort has been vigorous, persistent, and broad in scope. To the outsider, at least, it appears to have been well coordinated. Thus, such varied activities as exchanges of artists, athletes, students, and assistance in the development of medical services, and impressive technical and economic aid projects, such as the Aswan High Dam, project a positive image of "Soviet culture." All seem to serve major, long-term ideological and political goals. But what are these goals?

I

In broadest terms, all Soviet Middle East policy since the closing stages of World War II seems to have been subordinated to the primarily negative objective of weakening the influence of Western powers in the area. Stalin pursued this objective mainly by conspiracy and threats. Khrushchev, operating under conditions more favorable to the Soviet cause than those that confronted Stalin, but also displaying much greater flexibility and resourcefulness than he had, resorted to a mixture of force and persuasion, with the emphasis on persuasion. However, despite the conspicuousness in Khrushchevian policy of evangelism and blandishments, one must not forget that Khrushchev laid the foundation for substantial Soviet influence in the Middle East largely by the export of arms to Egypt and Syria. Somewhat ironically, the Soviet Union had earlier, in the Stalin era, made Israel the beneficiary of its use of the instrument of arms supply. In both cases, the objective was reduction of Western influence, and in both cases, as John A. Armstrong notes, "The direct supplier at first was Czechoslovakia, a circumstance which appeared to dilute the USSR's formal commitment."[1]

If one were to attempt to compare post-Khrushchev with Khrushchevian policy in the Middle East, one would probably conclude that the continuity has been considerable, but that the Brezhnev-Kosygin-Podgorny team has partly reverted to the Stalin pattern of primary reliance on the military as opposed to the propaganda or other instruments of foreign policy. Particularly since the Arab-Israel war of 1967, Soviet policy in the Middle East and in the Mediterranean also seems more concerned with projecting an image of power than with demonstrating the applicability of the Soviet model of modernization to the countries of the area.

However, this generalization must be qualified. During the last two or three years and perhaps especially in 1968, Soviet policy has been concerned, among other things, with the assiduous cultivation of friendly relations with the governments of Turkey and Iran. The contrast between Soviet efforts to use military advisers and naval visits to impress the Egyptians, Syrians, Algerians, and other peoples with the pursuit of quiet and tactful diplomacy *vis-à-vis* the countries of the "northern tier" illustrates, perhaps, both the complexity of conditions in the area and the increasing sophistication of Soviet policy. It also illustrates an abiding characteristic of Soviet policy in the Middle East, and indeed throughout the world, since the consolidation of Stalin's empire in Eastern Europe following World War II, namely, the subordination of the interests of non-Soviet Communist parties to those of the USSR as a world power. Generally in the

[1] John A. Armstrong, "Soviet Relations with the Middle East," in Kurt L. London (ed.), *The Soviet Union* (Baltimore, 1968), 423-456.

underdeveloped world, Moscow has placed its bets mainly upon "bourgeois nationalist" leaders, such as Gamal 'Abd al-Nasir and since 1965 Moscow has hailed the efforts of the 'Abd al-Nasir government and that of Algeria, to achieve "the socialist development" of their countries. Also, as Armstrong has pointed out, since 1966 Soviet theory has placed the United Arab Republic and other Middle East states in the category of "developing countries." Armstrong interprets the use of this "definitely non-Leninist category" as part of a "reconsideration of the desirability of encouraging regimes that did not follow the complete Leninist revolutionary model but that had taken the non-capitalist path."

Both the trend of Soviet theory regarding underdeveloped countries and much in Soviet practice seemed to indicate the willingness of Moscow to accept, at least for some time, the continued dominance of "national bourgeois" leaders and parties in the political life of those countries. It would appear that the Soviet leadership, while by no means rejecting the concept of the inevitable triumph of world Communism at some future point in time has come to realize that the interests of the Soviet Union, in its global rivalry both with Communist China and with the United States and other Western powers, can be served best by peaceful coexistence with the established regimes in such countries as Iran, Turkey, Pakistan, and the United Arab Republic.

Although by its very nature the policy of coexistence and cooperation—subject, of course, to ideological reservations—probably cannot, in the foreseeable future, lead to the expansion of the sphere directly controlled by Soviet Communists, it has substantial achievements to its credit, from the Soviet point of view. It has already gained for Moscow considerable influence over the internal and foreign affairs of the UAR, Syria, and Algeria. It has led to greatly improved relations with Turkey and Pakistan. In Iran, a favorable target for Soviet penetration during the Musaddiq regime, which later cooled toward Moscow, the new emphasis in Soviet policy has paid off handsomely, although one should bear in mind the wariness and sophistication of the shah's government.

The Soviet Union will probably continue to pursue a reasonably successful policy, even if it has not produced brilliant results and involves many difficulties and frustrations. However, the continuance of such a policy line appears to be contingent upon several factors.

One is the ability of the established regimes in the UAR, Iran, and Algeria to contain and guide their own internal political and social development. Another is the potential attractiveness to the most radical and discontented elements of Chinese Communist militancy. Also, the ability of the United States and the USSR to move toward a greater degree of cooperation than hitherto will largely determine the possibilities for stable development in the Middle East and other areas. That there are elements in the intellectual and political elites of both the United States and the USSR who desire a kind of relationship that would permit cooperation—not unmixed with rivalry—in helping the Middle East to achieve its legitimate aspirations, there can be no doubt. Moreover, even among those in both countries not much inclined toward policies of détente, there is a sober realization that tensions must not be allowed anywhere to reach a breaking point.

II

Before analyzing the strategy of Soviet cultural diplomacy in the Middle East, it might be useful to briefly consider the advantages and disadvantages to the Soviet Union in applying to the Middle East methods tested earlier elsewhere. Although there is considerable difference in Soviet methods and techniques as between "imperial dependencies" and "developing" countries and although Soviet planners take careful account of national traditions and local circumstances, Soviet strategy in any area or state develops within the unified framework imposed by a centralized political system and an official ideology. At any given time, there is a high degree of consistency and apparent coordination among Soviet propaganda policies throughout the world. Usually, there is one major antagonist, and since 1945 it has been the United States. It may be true, as many political analysts point out, that the Soviet Union should fear Communist China more than the United States, but the principal target of Soviet propaganda has remained "imperialist reaction," which is accused of pursuing, in international cultural relations, policies analogous to those attributed to it in military-political relations.

The imperatives which appear to follow from concern with "imperialist reaction" include vigilance and sensitivity toward the vulnerabilities of the "imperialist" antagonist. It is known that the Soviet Ministry of Foreign Affairs, the Soviet Intelligence Services generally, and Soviet research agencies keep well-informed on political trends everywhere. They are thus in a position to quickly pour cultural resources into areas and situations which offer a potential for political exploitation. They did this in Egypt and Syria in 1955-1956, for example. In this sense, Marxist-Leninist ideology, which, despite many defects, furnishes a general framework for analysis, may represent an advantage to Soviet cultural warriors.

Specific features of Marxism-Leninism may also confer advantages on Soviet propagandists and practitioners of cultural diplomacy. Since Marxism-Leninism is nominally a revolutionary doctrine, despite the rigidity and conservatism increasingly characteristic of Soviet society and cultural life, it has appeal to the many groups adversely affected by the poverty in most of the world and by the stresses and strains in societies bent on development. However, the Soviet Union confronts the mounting danger of being "outflanked on the left," particularly by the Chinese Communists and their supporters.

A less obvious advantage which Soviet propagandists and cultural diplomats perhaps enjoyed in the Middle East consists in the fact that the Soviet Union itself, despite its enormous progress, is still to some degree underdeveloped. Moreover, only twenty or thirty years ago the Soviet Union was a very poor country. It may well be that the relevant Soviet personnel have a somewhat surer "feel" for the psychology of the intelligentsia, in particular, in such countries as Egypt, than their American competitors. However, if the Russians possess such an advantage, its significance should not be exaggerated. There seems little doubt that Soviet and American personnel engaged in international informational and cultural activity have often behaved ethnocentrically.

It may also be argued that because the Soviet Union is a multinational society, its representatives have a somewhat better comprehension of the implications of the extreme cultural and national diversity of the Middle East. There are in the Soviet Union many Middle East peoples—Armenians, Arabs, Kurds, Iranians, and Turks. One of the traditions of Soviet foreign policy in the Middle East has been sensitivity to nationality problems and assiduity in exploiting them.

Finally, it must be pointed out that the greatest advantages of the Soviet Union over the United States and other Western powers in the struggle for influence in the Middle East have derived from the difficulties inherent in the situation of the Western powers in a revolutionary age, and from the defects and shortcomings of Western policy. Although these shortcomings were in part unavoidable, it is hard to escape the conclusion that Soviet successes have been gained largely by default. One thinks of the Anglo-French attack on Egypt in 1956 or of American indifference to the opportunity seized by the Russians when they agreed to construct the Aswan High Dam. To mention another, less significant example, can the failure of any major Western power, except West Germany, to exhibit at international fairs in Egypt and Syria, at which, of course, the Soviet Union and other Communist countries were represented, be regarded as anything but self-defeating?

In the cultural contest in the Middle East, Moscow also suffers important disadvantages. While Marxism-Leninism supplies a clarity of view, however specious, it also fosters rigidity and standoffishness toward "bourgeois" culture and its exponents. In attempting to account for the habitual aloof behavior of Soviet cultural emissaries living abroad one cannot know how much weight to give to the vigilance against "imperialist" machinations, and how much to traditional Russian suspicion of foreigners. The Soviet practice of sticking strictly to business and avoiding local involvements may reduce friction, but it must also inhibit the cultivation of fruitful relations. According to the New York Times of May 13, 1966, the Russian policy of isolation in Egypt was working well and the Soviet experts had "Egyptian respect for sticking to business and steering clear of politics." Apparently, the Soviets follow a similar policy even in Communist Cuba.

The most serious handicap to the Soviet Union's cultural efforts in the Middle East is the fear of the vast majority of the elites of the countries concerned, whether they are "socialists" or not, regarding ultimate Soviet intentions. It is presumably with this in mind that Moscow in recent years has increasingly played down the theme of world revolution. However, Moscow is ambivalent over the proper attitude to take toward this and other fundamental elements of official doctrine.

Many basic differences between the culture patterns in the Middle East states and the somewhat synthetic pattern of "Soviet culture" clearly present obstacles to Soviet success. The continued vitality of the Muslim religious tradition is obviously one such element. The generally Western orientation of the middle classes and intellectuals in most of the countries of the area, and the close ties of kinship between such peoples as the Lebanese with the United States, are other aspects of local cultural patterns which militate against Soviet influence. Also, it is probably true that to most of the politically relevant elements in the Middle East states Soviet culture appears rather unsophisticated. However, one may also guess that there is considerable disdain and suspicion among many upper- and middle-class elements toward the culture, way of life, and intentions of all outside powers. Within this framework, Soviet policy appears to take advantage of all opportunities to blacken the image of the West, especially of the United States, and to reinforce pro-Soviet predispositions.

The cultural exploitation of political opportunities is pursued in various ways. Some, such as educational and medical assistance, are, in principle, highly commendable. Others, such as the fulsome and obvious flattery of rulers and politicians or the frequent attempts to exacerbate anti-Western sentiments, are much less attractive. Heavy stress is placed, in Soviet sources, on the benefits derived by underdeveloped countries from Soviet medical assistance. The attempt is made to create the impression that this assistance, which is described as having begun very early in the history of the Soviet Union, has always been unselfish. For example, it is asserted that even in the most difficult early years, Soviet Russia sent medical workers, laboratories, vaccines, medicines, and the like to Iran to help combat the plague and that this aid was given "without any economic advantage." Reportedly, the USSR has assisted the UAR and Iraq in building plants for the manufacture of drugs and surgical instruments. In Iran the USSR built and helped operate a hospital. More than three hundred Soviet "medical workers" were in Algeria "together with their Algerian colleagues" in 1966. Soviet sources devote considerable attention to aid given by the Union of Societies of the Red Cross and Red Crescent of the Soviet Union to countries that have suffered from earthquakes and other natural calamities. This society exchanges delegations with appropriate medical and other personnel of various Middle East states.

The Soviet Union has long conducted a wide range of indoctrinational and educational programs with foreigners, and some Middle East students have been enrolled in such programs. As of 1966, more than 24,000 foreign students, from almost 130 countries, were reportedly enrolled in more than 300 Soviet higher and secondary educational institutions. Also, it was asserted that about 5,000 undergraduate and graduate students were enrolling annually in Soviet higher educational and technical institutions and that 25,000 foreign students had been graduated from such institutions in the decade ending in 1966. Moreover, it was asserted that "many foreign citizens, primarily from the developing countries, are also studying in lower technical schools and schools of professional technical education, acquiring necessary specialties." Since most foreign students in the Soviet Union come from Communist countries and many of the rest come from such areas as sub-Saharan Africa, it would not appear that the Middle Easterners are very numerous.

Occasional bits of data, however, indicate that there have been many students from the Middle East in Soviet Russia. For example, the Iraqi press reported in October 1961 that there were 1,500 Iraqi students in Communist countries. Apparently, these included many in technical training, for fewer than 1,000 Iraqis were believed enrolled in the universities of Communist countries. The source reporting this information noted that "Iraqis shared with other Arab students in Bloc countries the problems of language, poor living conditions, indoctrination, and isolation." In December 1960, the UAR and the Soviet Union signed a two-year agreement providing, among other things, for sending to UAR specialists, including thirty-eight scientists and university professors, as well as specialists in music and dance, Russian language instructors, and others, including "three circus specialists." Also, the Soviet Union agreed to accept 240 UAR graduates to work toward higher scientific degrees, although, according to the same source, there was no indication that this quota was filled. In addition, other Egyptians, including four university presidents, visited Soviet universities.

One indication of the establishment of close and enduring relations between Soviet citizens and citizens of Africa and Asian countries, presumably including Middle Easterners, was the report in 1965 that up to 1963, 250 African and Asian students had married Russians. The government of Jordan in the same period sent ten students to study in the Soviet Union on Soviet government scholarships. Soviet experts in geology, physics, and technical studies taught in Algerian universities at the request of the Algerian government, and Soviet experts helped build a school, opened in 1964, to train Algerian industrial and agricultural personnel.

Romanovski asserted, "In a number of Afro-Asian countries, in special faculties of the Russian language, dozens of Soviet teachers are at work," and he also stated that in the UAR, in the Institute of Foreign Languages, a faculty of the Russian language had been established, and it was offering courses in Russian.[2] The USSR seeks to popularize the study of the Russian language in nonindustrial states, and in Soviet higher institutions, where large numbers of foreign students are studying, there are "preparatory faculties," such as the Preparatory Faculty for Foreign Students, which began teaching at Moscow State University in September 1959. Later, similar faculties were established at Kiev State University, at Leningrad State University, at Tashkent University and elsewhere. In these faculties students spend a year studying Russian and basic courses before continuing their regular higher education.

With the movement toward "socialism" in the UAR and Syria beginning in the early 1960s, educational exchanges between the Soviet Union and these states expanded visibly. Apparently, Moscow felt that educational and other types of contacts with these states and with most others in the Middle East, were becoming safer and more profitable. In 1965, the Communist party in the UAR voluntarily dissolved, and Communists since then have tried to function within the dominant Arab Socialist Union. It was not until that year that a USSR-UAR Friendship Society was established. It was also around this time that Moscow began to propound the doctrine of "revolutionary democracy" and to preach the gospel of cooperation among a wide range of "revolutionary" and "socialist" elements. However, Moscow from time to time indicated that it had reservations about the degree to which Egyptian and other forms of "Arab socialism" corresponded to the Soviet model of socialism, which, though cautiously and tactfully, continued to be officially viewed as the only correct form. For example, in 1965 and again in 1967 authoritative Soviet publications, while expressing appreciation of the "progressive" tendencies of Nasirist policies and doctrines, also criticized the survival of "illusions," particularly those related to the role of private property in the national economy.

By 1965, it was estimated that between sixty and eighty Soviet professors and instructors were teaching at UAR universities, and at the same time at least twenty-four vocational centers, largely financed

[2] S. K. Romanovski, *Mezhdunarodnye kulturnye i nauchnye svyazi sssr* (Moscow, 1966), Tom I, 67.

with Soviet funds and employing large numbers of Soviet instructors, were operating in that country. Reportedly, more than 7,400 Egyptian students were being trained in these vocational centers. In Syria also, the early and mid-1960s saw a large expansion in cultural and educational contacts with the USSR, and also with Peiping. For example, in 1965 the Syrian Minister for Foreign Affairs and Culture made a lengthy tour of China after the signing of a cultural agreement in March. In numbers of academic exchanges with Communist countries, however, as of December 1965, Iraq led all the Middle East states. Thus, 1,205 Iraqis were studying in Communist countries, while the figures were as follows for other Middle East countries: Syria, 405; Lebanon, 360; the UAR, 280; Turkey, 40. Startling were the figures for Yemen, 550, and for Cyprus, 170. It should be noted that many students from Lebanon were apparently Armenians. Of the total number of academic students from the Middle East as of December 1965, 2,125 were said to be enrolled in the USSR and 955 in Eastern Europe. Of "technical trainees" from the Middle East, 510 were reported in Soviet institutions and 105 in Eastern Europe. In both cases, the overall figures for 1965 were somewhat smaller than those for 1964.

Despite the highly unsatisfactory data on the scope and character of Soviet cultural relations with the Middle East states, the evidence brought together here is sufficient to convince one that a substantial and well-organized Soviet program—part of a worldwide effort—to establish links that will prove useful to the Soviet Union in the future is well underway. However, on the basis of the available information, it is most difficult to evaluate the results. It would certainly appear that the maximum objective of the program, especially in the educational field, is the building of a Communist elite, or at least of an elite predisposed to pursue domestic and foreign policies satisfactory to the Kremlin. Moreover, as a student of Soviet policy in Africa points out, "It is clear that the Soviet Union cannot profess to encourage industrialization without assisting in the training of the personnel necessary to develop modern industrial-based economies."[3] Hence, the Soviet effort to assist youths from underdeveloped countries to acquire technical education.

Harry Ellis quotes a Western official to the effect that "the com-

[3] Roger E. Kanet, "African Youth: The Target of Soviet African Policy," *The Russian Review*, XXVII (April 1966), 167.

munists are satisfied if two out of one hundred students become convinced communists, who can be sent home to work for the cause. If the rest are not against communism, that is enough. This is cadre building, from the communist point of view."[4] According to Ellis, "The bulk of the students from underdeveloped countries simply absorb their academic training and go home, neither for communism nor against it, but neutral. A very few become reliable communists, a very few others turn passionately anti-Marxist." Ellis also expressed the view that while African students were very likely to become discontented in the Soviet Union or other Communist countries, this was not so often the case with Arab students. Ellis also pointed out that the Soviets had become increasingly sophisticated in their dealings with students from the Middle East and other underdeveloped areas. He saw this change as having taken place around 1960. It is perhaps indicative of increasing Soviet sophistication and tact in the handling of foreign students that Premier Kosygin, in his address to the first graduating class of the Patrice Lumumba Friendship University in 1965, emphasized that it was not Moscow's intention to impose its ideology on foreign students. Kosygin said, *inter alia,*

> We are confident that the University graduates as well as the two thousand foreign specialists graduating this year from other Soviet educational establishments will show themselves and their countries to be not only excellent engineers, doctors, teachers, economists, but also frontrankers in the struggle for the national revival of their countries, for the social progress of their peoples. . . . We would like the University graduates forever to remain our friends, to become the bearers of an inviolable friendship between their peoples and the peoples of the first country of socialism.[5]

On balance it would appear that the Soviet educational-exchange program in the Middle East, as elsewhere in the developing world, pays dividends to Moscow. It would also appear that of all facets in the Soviet cultural program, the Kremlin regards education the most significant.

III

The process of policy making that underlies the cultural exchange program, like Soviet policy formation, is most difficult to assess.

[4] Harry B. Ellis, "African Students Vault Iron Curtain," *The Christian Science Monitor*, February 25, 1967.

[5] U.S. Department of State, *Research Memorandum, RSB-10* (Washington, D.C., 1967), 34-35.

There are probably scores of Soviet agencies and organizations that have some role in cultural exchange policy. All are subordinated to the leadership of the Communist party. Under the monolithic surface, dissension and squabbling undoubtedly take place. According to American graduate students and scholars who have participated in exchanges in the USSR, the secret police, the conservative apparatchiki and specialists on propaganda in the party organization generally take a dim view of cultural exchanges. On the other hand, Soviet intellectuals, especially natural scientists and liberal writers, favor the exchanges. Presumably, this general balance of forces operates with respect to the Middle East as it apparently does with respect to the non-Soviet world in general. Unfortunately, it is as difficult to document the degree of differentiation by region and country, which undoubtedly plays an important role in Soviet policy, as it is to demonstrate, on the basis of Soviet-published sources, the differences of emphasis which undoubtedly exist in exchanges generally, between the more rational, cosmopolitan, and sophisticated elements of the Soviet elite and the more traditional, orthodox, and parochial elements.

However, one can perceive in Soviet exchange policy in recent years a tendency toward "normalization." This is, perhaps, not as apparent in dealings with the United States, where relations are complicated by the war in Vietnam, as it is in relations with most other countries of the world, and perhaps in particular in relations with the developing nations. Perhaps, too, somewhat complementary trends might be identified. On the one hand, the role of organizations designed primarily to exploit revolutionary movements and militant and radical sentiments appears to have diminished. Thus, for example, the significance of the Soviet Committee of Solidarity of the Countries of Asia and Africa, founded in 1956, appears to have diminished steadily. The waning influence of this organization seems to be, in large part, the result of Chinese Communist opposition. It has also run afoul of the revolutionary pretensions of Fidel Castro, who in 1966 staged his own flamboyant Tri-Continental Conference in Havana and subsequently launched a Cuban-dominated Latin-American Solidarity Organization. However, it seems that the Soviet Solidarity Committee would have been doomed in any case, in view of improving relations between the "establishments" of the Middle East states and the nominally "revolutionary" but in fact increasingly conservative regime in Moscow.

The establishment, in 1960, of Lumumba University might appear to contradict this line of interpretation. Indeed, in some ways the strategy represented by Lumumba University did contradict the generally conservative evolution of Soviet policy. However, Lumumba University serves a useful purpose, which illustrates the complexity, many-sidedness, and adaptiveness, of Soviet foreign cultural policy. It enables those in charge of Soviet cultural exchange policy to separate from the more or less conventional body of students admitted to Soviet higher educational institutions those of inferior academic background but with superior "revolutionary" qualifications. Some of these, of course, may well have been persons of superior native intelligence, despite their lack of conventional academic background. Thus, Moscow was able, at the same time, to meet the needs of the more or less "proletarian" types accepted by Lumumba, while at the same time it could continue to offer conventional higher education to students of middle-class background from developing as well as from more advanced countries.

From 1957 to 1967 the most powerful agency in the administration of Soviet cultural-exchange policy appears to have been the State Committee for Cultural Relations with Foreign Countries, established in 1957, apparently for the purpose of facilitating cultural relations with the United States and the United Kingdom. Although the "unofficial" VOKS organization expanded rapidly, particularly after its transformation, in 1958, into the SOD (Union of Soviet Societies of Friendship and Cultural Relations with Foreign Countries), it was clearly outranked by the State Committee. In the fall of 1967, the functions of the State Committee were taken over by a section of the Ministry of Foreign Affairs, headed by G. A. Lunkov, a former Soviet Ambassador to Norway. In the post-Stalin years, it has become standard Soviet practice to regularize cultural relations, both with "bourgeois" and "socialist" states by means of formal treaties and agreements.

IV

The prediction of any aspect of Soviet policy, whether domestic or foreign, has been rendered even more difficult than it already was by the Soviet invasion of Czechoslovakia. Coming a little more than a year after the Arab-Israel war of June 1967, it underscored the Kremlin's anxiety over the dangers of close or intimate contact between Soviet citizens and "bourgeois" foreigners. It highlighted the dilemma of a leadership which professes to be the "vanguard" of "progressive mankind" but which continues to fear free and intimate contacts between its citizens and citizens of other countries.

Nevertheless, it would still seem reasonable to forecast a continuation of a large Soviet investment of human and material resources in cultural relations with the Middle East and other developing areas. Like tsarist Russia, Soviet Russia feels more at home in dealing with the nonindustrial world than it does in its contacts with the more industrial nations. It may even be possible that under favorable conditions a useful division of labor might develop between the United States and other Western industrial countries on the one hand and the USSR and other "socialist" countries on the other hand in assisting the nations of the third world to achieve their legitimate aspirations. The development of such a division of labor, which could have salutary consequences for world tranquility and welfare, depends upon the improvement of relations between the superpowers and the achievement of a reasonable level of stability in the nonindustrial countries.

Internal Contest in the Middle East

JOHN S. BADEAU

Since World War II, American-Soviet rivalry in the Middle East has been a recurrent force affecting most of the area's major developments. This is so obviously true in foreign policy, international relations, and political and economic development as to require neither argument nor illustration. But is it also true in the field of culture? That rapid and extensive cultural change has taken place during the postwar decades is obvious, but how much of this has been a product of the cold war competition, and to what extent does it display the marks of Soviet or American cultural competition?

The question arises partly because of the value set by the cold war competitors on their own cultural activities. All embassies now have informational services; the Soviet and American missions, together with some of the other major countries, also conduct elaborate and expensive programs of cultural activity. The chief Cultural Affairs Officer holds a diplomatic rank akin to his colleagues in the political and economic sections. In American embassies he is usually one of the Embassy Counsellors and thus of the Ambassador's inner circle. Obviously those who conduct foreign policy in Washington and Moscow believe that cultural activities and influences are valuable adjuncts to traditional diplomacy. Libraries and reading rooms, publications, educational exchange, film showings, performing arts troupes, art and scientific exhibitions, and language classes, have thus taken their place by the side of economic assistance and political persuasion as activities "in the national interest" of the supplying country.

What has this done to the Middle East? The annual report of any cultural officer, American or Soviet, would answer chiefly in quantitative terms, the variety of cultural operations and the measurable response to them. Comparisons would be made between what "we" and "they" have accomplished as regards the numbers of readers using the library, the number of books sold, the circulation of informational material, the number of students studying in the home country, the size of audiences at performances and film showings.

This, of course, is a legitimate and necessary exercise, but it does little to illumine the question as to how far foreign cultural programs have affected local cultural development. "Learning," contends one educational philosopher, "is any change in behavior *which persists.*" On this definition, has the cultural competition of the cold war taught the Middle East anything? It may be possible to point to some immediate changes in local cultural activities resulting from Soviet or American programs, but have these persisted and do they represent integral elements of continuing cultural development?

The answer to both questions is a qualified no. To be sure, frequently there has been a ready response to cultural programs conducted by embassies. Students do go abroad to study, libraries are used, books are sold, dramatic troupes draw interested audiences, yet there is little to show that these responses lead to permanent alterations in the national pattern of cultural development.

I

Consider the impact of Soviet programs. Their most obvious success thus far seems to be in the field in which Russia was already unique before it became a Communist country—the ballet. Not only do Russian ballet performances receive a warm welcome wherever they appear, but a number of Middle East countries have been stimulated by them to develop ballet troupes of their own, turning to the Soviet Union for help and support. There can be little doubt that in sophisticated centers such as Cairo, Istanbul, and Tehran, local development in the dance will continue to show the impact of Soviet culture.

Other aspects of the Soviet program have been less effective in lasting influence. After the first surge of students going to study in Soviet universities, educational missions to the Communist world dwindled. They are now supported chiefly by the need for training technicians to operate Soviet equipment, or to work with Soviet advisers in administering national programs. There has been no continuing stream of students seeking to study medicine, law, engineering, science, history, business, or general culture in Soviet universities. As things now stand, when the Soviet machines wear out or are no longer used, and Soviet cooperative programs cease, there is little reason to believe that any significant number of students will still go to the Soviet Union for their higher training.

In national school systems, there are few Soviet advisers or teachers. Only occasionally are Soviet educational materials used by local authors of textbooks and manuals. The Russian language is not generally taught, even in universities. Soviet educational principles, systems and institutions, although studied by some of the area educators, have not been copied by Ministries of Education. In some countries, Soviet scientific books are bought by university students, but this is usually due to the fact that they are cheap in contrast to the expensive books from the West, especially from the United States. It is difficult to tell what priority the Soviets have given to penetrating national systems of education, but it does not appear to be high.

Soviet films are rarely seen on local television programs or in commercial cinemas. They serve chiefly as program material for embassy showings to invited audiences. A study of the techniques and themes of Middle East film production does not reveal elements which can be traced to Russian film makers, despite the excellence of some of their work. Soviet book shops and publications may reach urban middle-class and student groups, but there is little popular interest in Soviet literature. There is no evidence that Soviet literary patterns are being widely copied or are furnishing models for the new national writers—except possibly in political pamphlets. The classical Russian authors (in common with those of Western Europe) have contributed some themes and literary forms to modern literary developments in the area, but this was not due to any special interest in Soviet culture.

In contrast to this paucity of permanent cultural influence emanating from Soviet programs, it would appear that Western programs in general, and those of the United States in particular, have had a lasting impact on cultural developments. Students and exchange professors stream to Western universities whenever the way is open to them. The expanding systems of national education continue to draw forms of organization, institutional concepts, and materials from the French, British, and, more selectively, American systems. When

Asyut University was opened in Egypt early in the 1960s it sought to introduce the American system of engineering education, to be launched by an educational mission of fifteen American professors. New technical universities in Turkey and Iran have copied elements of the American university pattern. The English language, followed by French, continues to hold its place as the second language of culture, being taught in secondary schools and universities. English and French literature have long been studied in Middle East universities, and several institutions are now offering courses in American literature. American films and television programs are widely popular and are copied by local producers.

This is true not only in countries which are considered politically pro-Western, or at least neutral; it is almost equally true in those with close Soviet connections. It is significant that when American-Syrian diplomatic relations were near the breaking point a few years ago, the American cultural program in Aleppo flourished and was eagerly sought out, especially by the university community. Although the UAR broke its relations with the United States during the Six Day War in 1967, it has continued to send students to America to study, allowed the American University at Cairo to continue, and has been eager to have the Fulbright exchange program revived.

Impressive as this record is, it does not prove that the Western direction of Middle East cultural development is derived from the cultural competition of the cold war. Western government funds for educational exchanges, libraries, book translation programs, and other cultural activities have in some cases expanded the scope and increased the availability of Western cultural resources used by the Middle East. But they cannot claim to be the reason why such resources are accepted in the area and utilized so steadily in its cultural development. What underlies the continuing Western direction of Middle East cultural development is not the cultural propaganda engendered by the cold war, but the character of the modernizing process the Middle East has chosen to follow. This modernization antedated the cold war and has continued through it with remarkably little change of direction. Soviet cultural offerings are seen not so much as alternatives to traditional ways, as departures from a modernizing (Western) pattern already well established in the Middle East.

In many cases Soviet cultural activities were not accepted by local governments because of an innate desire to profit from them, but for political reasons. Accepting the Soviet diplomatic presence and seeking Soviet political and economic assistance carry as a corollary the acceptance of Soviet cultural programs. Moreover, to welcome and give public display to cultural activities sometimes has been a useful way of keeping political fences mended. More than once it appeared in Cairo that the government attitude toward foreign cultural programs and the press reports concerning them were really designed to give the ambassadors something to write home about as indicating Egyptian good will or displeasure. In other words, the response to cultural programs born of the cold war, both Soviet and American, has frequently been more tactical than strategic, not so much concerned with long-range cultural goals as with sustaining political relationships. Consequently local response to cultural programs can oscillate from appreciative warmth to studied frigidity without affecting the general continued direction of cultural development.

II

Estimates of how a prolongation of the cold war into the 1970s may affect Middle East cultural activities must be based on factors other than the continued competition of the American and Soviet embassies and their programs. The questions to be asked are: Why has the Middle East chosen a Western pattern of cultural development? Why have the Soviets been unable to challenge this pattern thus far? What future developments may alter the present situation?

The basis for the pro-Western preference of the Middle East in cultural development has been ascribed in part to the fact that Islam and European culture are historically related. Islam, within whose religious framework Middle East culture arose, is sister to Judaism and Christianity and many of its fundamental concepts are rooted in the same Semitic source. Medieval European and Middle East scholars drew much of their intellectual materials from the same corpus of classical, Greco-Roman learning. When the desert Arabs overran the Mediterranean basin they found advanced civilizations from which they adopted social and cultural practices to weave into the fabric of their own civilization. Consequently, European culture never seemed strange and foreign in the Middle East as it did in India, China, and Japan.

Yet this historic fact must not be overestimated. For all their common heritage, Europe and the Muslim Middle East were never two parts of a single cultural unit. Islamic civilization had a character and existence of its own. It selected what it considered useful from the common stock of ideas and fitted this to its own needs and outlook. The result was not a repetition of European culture. It would be a mistake to think that modernization in the Western pattern was chosen by and sustained in the Middle East basically because of the medieval connection. A more immediate and influential factor was the political relationship of Europe to the Middle East throughout the modern period. Beginning with the decay of the Ottoman Empire, Middle East societies increasingly fell under the control of Western powers. Military occupation, colonial status, spheres of influence, privileged economic position, placed the destiny of much of the Middle East in Western hands. This was naturally accompanied by a continued and increasing penetration of Eastern life by Western ways.

Under this impact in the nineteenth century, the Islamic world awakened to the weakness and degradation of its position, intensified by memories of a proud and powerful past. The response of Muslim leaders was to turn toward the technology and culture of the dominant European as containing the secret of his success. The West had once quailed before the Turkish sultan and his armies; now it turned the tables. Obviously something had happened to push Europe ahead of the Middle East. An Arabic book published in the nineteenth century under the title *A Guide to the Good Qualities of Europeans* asked, Why have the Europeans been able to dominate us? and answered that the strength and success of the West were due to its political institutions, parliament, prime minister, cabinet, and party organization. If the Middle East wanted to regain control of its destiny, it would need itself to adopt such institutions.

Modernization in the Western mold was thus partly a defensive reaction against the West by which the Middle East hoped to throw off the Western yoke. But beyond this pragmatic objective, there was the psychological need to demonstrate that "we too can be modern." Islamic culture, highly regarded in medieval Europe, had sunk in the nineteenth century to the image of the Terrible Turk and his harim. Many Muslim intellectuals felt deeply what Taha Husayn wrote: "We must rid our minds of the evil suggestion that there are two mentalities—eastern and western." Mastery of Western ways, adoption of Western modes of dress and headgear, ability to speak Western languages, and operating a great canal which the French said was too complicated for any Egyptian to run, were necessary elements for the restoration of dignity. It was here that the memory of the historic relation between European and Middle East culture played a role. Eastern intellectuals, Christian as well as Muslim, knew that during the Middle Ages their culture had been the equal, at times the superior, of European culture; indeed, had made significant contributions to Western development. What it had been once, it could be again, indeed must be, or admit cultural bankruptcy.

But what started as a reaction against and competition with the West became an indigenous force in many aspects of Middle East cultural development. Where the occupying Western power was in a position to do so, as the French in Syria and Lebanon, it tended to reproduce its own systems of education and cultural institutions. Large numbers of Europeans in business, government and military service lived amidst and mingled with the upper classes of the Middle East for extended periods. The British occupation of Egypt, for example, lasted from 1882 to 1956. Government civil service on a Western pattern and Western business enterprises demanded personnel with Western training. As a result, many of the upper class, and later of the emerging middle class, became bicultural to a degree, speaking a Western language, educated in Western institutions, practicing Western social customs, enjoying Western literature and music.

Thus over the decades, aspects of Western culture became indigenous to Eastern life. They were practiced without any feeling of strangeness and were accepted not so much as European imports as marks of a progressive Islamic or Middle East culture. When European political control ebbed and Middle East states became fully independent and in a position to direct their own development, the Western path to modernization had become so established that it was followed with little attempt to return to earlier and more "native" patterns, despite the rise of nationalism.

This mood of accommodation and acceptance was reinforced by the fact that what was regarded as "Western" culture in the eighteenth and early nineteenth centuries, gradually was transformed into a world culture. The scientific method developed in Europe has universal validity and any modern man can claim it for his own. Indians, Japanese, and Africans have won Nobel prizes, written modern novels, debated in the United Nations on a par with any other modern man. What would be unpalatable as "Western" or "European" became acceptable as "modern" since the latter carried no geographical tie or political implication.

In summary, modernization in the Western pattern was a response to an urgently felt challenge—political, intellectual, economic, psychological—to pass from the traditional past to the modern future, casting off aspersions of backwardness or underdevelopment. In this endeavor, only one pattern of modernization was available—that of the dominant and successful West. Through its controlling political position in the Middle East, the West was able to introduce, stimulate, and support cultural developments in Western patterns and institutions. Prolonged and intimate contact between the two cultures took place over more than a century, with colonies of Europeans mingling with the Middle East elite. European languages, chiefly English and French, became the second tongue of the new, modernizing group. These languages were taught in the schools and became the vehicles for introducing Western literature, both classical and modern, to the upper classes. In consequence, the groups in the Middle East involved in the process of change felt at home in many aspects of Western culture, even while they resented and opposed Western political control. By the time the cold war was instituted, a current of modernization built on Western patterns had been set in motion which was too strong and deep easily to deflect.

III

In their cultural endeavors, the Soviets have faced a very different situation. The modernizing process they brought did not appear chiefly as an alternative to a traditional and backward system; it was mainly seen as a rival to the already existing pattern of Western modernization. The Soviets themselves recognized this. During his visit to the UAR in 1964 for the opening of the High Dam, Khrushchev repeated the theme in public speeches that the Soviet program of modernization was more effective than that of the West because the Russians had proved its power in modernizing their own backward society—hence they could help developing countries in their problems. This appeal to Soviet accomplishments raises the question as to whether these are so preeminent, in fact, that they strongly attract the Middle East.

Here many in the Middle East have had serious doubts. That Russia under the Soviet regime has made enormous progress is beyond argument, but not because its methods and their results are innately superior to those of the West. Soviet space exploration has been a dramatic witness to the strength of Soviet science and has impressed the scientific community in the Middle East, but Soviet heavy machinery, for instance, is a different matter. In the final drive to finish the first stages of the High Dam on schedule, the UAR finally used some of its scarce hard currency to purchase Western rock-drilling equipment because Soviet drills proved too slow and inefficient. Given a preference, and uninhibited by political and fiscal considerations, most Middle East countries and leaders still opt for Western methods, equipment, and technology.

Moreover, the Soviet Union has had neither the extended period nor the depth of penetration of political control in the Middle East that the Western powers have had. Significant Soviet political presence in the area is only two decades old and is still confined to a limited number of countries, important as some of these are. Even in those states where the Soviet Union appears firmly established, it has as yet nothing comparable to the position of Great Britain and France when they controlled the area through their colonies, protectorates, and mandates. Thus far Soviet advisers have been limited to the military establishment and technical aspects of Soviet economic programs. They have not appeared in Ministries of Education, Culture, Guidance, and other parts of the government dealing with cultural affairs. Since the Soviet Union does not occupy a position with colonial or mandatory controls, it has not been able forcibly to introduce its own institutions into the process of national development.

To the brevity and paucity of political control must be added the limited number of Russians living in the Middle East. Before the June 1967 war, there does not appear to have been more than two or three thousand Soviet nationals in the UAR, all of whom were connected with official Soviet programs. They were military trainers, technicians working on the High Dam, and technical advisers of other aspects of Soviet aid. As a matter of policy, their government did not allow them to live at random throughout the country but insisted that they reside in compounds and organize their education and recreation on a tight, inward-looking community basis. There has been little opportunity for personal, friendly, daily, unofficial contact between individual Russians and Egyptians. Thus the major contacts between the Soviet community and the Middle East community have been controlled and have not had that natural, sustained relation which did so much to insinuate European culture into the Middle East.

This situation is reflected in the small number of Middle Easterners who have been trained in Soviet institutions, either at home or in Russia. Unlike the European powers during the nineteenth century, the Russians have not established a series of schools in the Middle East in which the local populace could be trained in a Soviet-tinged education. Were they to attempt to found such institutions now, they would have to compete with the national systems of education which have developed rapidly during the past decades and which increasingly are jealous of sharing the process of national education with foreign institutions. Very few of the leadership class, or any other class, have had university education in the Soviet Union. Most important, the Russian language has not become popular except for those who need it to deal with Soviet technicians. Russian is not taught in secondary schools; it is not a language of scientific instruction in the universities like French and English; its literature is still a closed book to intellectuals. A striking example of how the English language continues to hold its preeminence was seen at the American University in Cairo in the fall of 1968, when Soviet influence in the UAR was reputedly at its height. The university had over 4,500 applications for the 2,500 places in its advanced course in English for graduate students, professional and business men.

In view of such conditions, it is not surprising that the program of the Soviet Union has thus far failed to make significant inroads into the continuing Western direction of Middle East cultural development. The fact is that in most parts of the Middle East, including the Soviet client countries, a serious conversation with the social, technical, and cultural elite will usually reveal that what they envision as most desirable for their societies is something akin to what the West now has. Politically they may resist and resent the West and be highly critical of its claims as against its realities. But when all is said and done, they still want to live in a society which can generally be considered "Western" even when they adopt the vocabulary of socialism and nationalism. There is little evidence that, aside from Communist party members and supporters, anyone in the Middle East yearns for the pattern of the Soviet Union as the final goal of national development.

IV

Will this situation continue? If the cold war abates or remains so balanced that those caught in its tensions retain a reasonable freedom of action, it is unlikely to change. Yet it would be a mistake to envision future development as an uncritical adoption of Western patterns—which it too often has been in the past. What began as a slavish copying of Western ways has become increasingly a selective program of modernization, based on indigenous needs. Eager to discover and assert their own identity in the modern world as well as to achieve national progress, Middle East societies are seeking patterns of development which they can consider truly theirs—indigenous, native to their own past, focused on their own needs as they see them.

This process tends to move in two different directions. One is a salute to the past, embodied in attempts to revive and utilize elements of traditional Middle East culture. Thus a recent conference of Arab university leaders, after reviewing curricula and discussing the responsibility of the universities for serving national progress, called for the development of a unique Arab element in higher education. The increasing use of Middle East languages for advanced teaching purposes, especially in the sciences, the expanded production by Middle East authors of scientific textbooks, the accelerating revival of literature in the Middle East languages with experimentation in new literary form, the sharp curtailment of foreign educational institutions, are evidences of an uneasy feeling that in adopting Western forms the Middle East may be losing its cultural birthright.

The difference between the current adaptions and those of the past is that most Middle East states are now free to make their own choices in the light of their own needs and to weave the foreign elements they select into their own pattern. It is in this sense only that Arab socialism is "Arab." There are, in fact, no elements of the system which can be derived specifically from the Arab past. The principal features were drawn from the experience of a variety of European states, including Scandinavia, Yugoslavia, and Italian Fascism. Arab Socialism is not a slavish copy of any one of these. "It is not," said an Egyptian leader, "Karl Marx, Leon Blum, the English Fabians or Norman Thomas." It is "Arab" in the sense that it is put together by Arabs from elements which Arabs selected for the particular needs of an Arab society. It seems inevitable that this process of adaption and absorption will take on a stronger nationalist and local character in the future, while still using Western technology and culture as its basic source of supply.

Given the drive for modernization, the freedom to choose, and the urge to produce indigenous patterns of development, under what conditions of the cold war would Soviet culture be likely to play a more significant role? Basically this would depend upon the creation of a situation in which the Soviet Union could have a more extended, penetrating, and exclusive contact with Middle East states than it has had in the past.

The contact needs to be *extended* because Soviet culture, where it differs from general Western culture, must displace the current Western-oriented forms of development which have become accepted in most of the Middle East. This cannot be done in a few years of relationship—as the past two decades make apparent. But if to these two decades another twenty years are added, the sustained intermingling of Soviet and Middle East technicians, officials, programs, educational exchanges, and publications might well place marks of Soviet culture in areas where they do not now exist. An illustration of this process can be found at the present time in the UAR. The Soviets have had significant relations with Egypt since 1955, but only within the last year have merchants in Cairo (especially in Zamalik where the Russian colony is) begun to use the Russian language. Language lessons have been available for a long time but there was no profit in taking them. Now there are enough Soviet citizens buying in shops and bazaars to make a command of Russian useful for the shopowner. This, in miniature, is the process through which a long sustained foreign presence enables cultural transmissions to take place.

The contact must also be *penetrating*, that is, reaching deeper into the cultural structure of the country. The virtual exclusion of the Russian language and Soviet methods, advisers, and teachers from systems of national education in Middle East countries has been a major handicap to Soviet cultural impact. Were the Soviet Union to have a position of political influence similar to that the British once held in Egypt, it could foster its own institutions and introduce its own methods into the domestic programs of its client states. Under these conditions local authorities and the national leadership class would find it to their advantage to Sovietize aspects of their culture as they earlier Anglicized and Gallicized them.

Both sustained and penetrating contacts imply a more *exclusive position* for the Soviet Union in any Middle East country than it has had in the past. Where the Soviet presence is counterbalanced by a Western presence, as it was in Egypt between 1960 and 1966, the local government can play off one side against the other with freedom to choose from both. But if the West abandons the field to the Soviet Union (as the United States did in the UAR after the 1967 war), and thus precludes any significant cultural assistance except that furnished by the Communist world, the Russians would have a corner on foreign cultural influence. Under these circumstances it is probable that a Soviet client state would gradually adopt many aspects of Soviet culture which it thus far has eschewed.

If the cold war continues into another decade, it could create a situation in which the Soviet Union would develop the closer and more exclusive relations just discussed. To interpolate from present and past trends (but not to prophesy) this situation principally would arise out of the continuance and development of Soviet-Western polarity in the region. Polarization has been a Soviet objective (at least tactically) in the past, with the United States identified as the guardian of fading traditionalism and conservatism and the Soviet Union as the apostle and supporter of radical change. During the past two years, the American position has weakened, especially in the Arab world, while the Russians have an enlarged influence in the UAR, Algeria, and, to a lesser extent, Syria, thanks to the Six Day War. Current American policy does not seem concerned to challenge the new Russian position by restoring relations with and assistance to Soviet client states in the Middle East. By default, the United States may find that when it is ready to move, the time will have passed when the counterbalances of the cold war can be restored.

This would leave the Soviet Union in a position to influence more deeply the internal affairs of their host countries. Such influence would probably not be directly political, built upon control of the country's administration in the way Britain and France exercised power through their colonies, mandates, and occupations. Current regimes in the Arab world are too nationalistic readily to surrender to the

Russians what remains of their freedom of action, and none is so ideologically Communist as to collaborate in a Moscow-controlled take-over. Whatever position of influence the Soviet Union might attain in fields directly related to major national interests where Russian help is indispensable (the military, foreign policy, and economic development), it is improbable that this would give it leverage to insist on the adoption of Soviet-oriented cultural and educational institutions.

In fact, cultural penetration is more likely to emerge as a by-product of the Soviet presence than as a direct and planned policy, based on Russian control of local governments. Here the economic and technical monopoly of the Soviet Union in some of its client states, like the UAR, furnishes an opportunity which cannot help but engender some absorption of Soviet culture. It is not that Russian technicians are used directly as political and cultural missionaries. In fact, on many occasions in the past they have carefully and deliberately eschewed this role. What does happen is that increasingly the technical and economic processes of development take on Soviet patterns, especially under long continued and relatively exclusive Russian assistance. Soviet engineers naturally approach problems of construction and planning in terms of their own technology, and local engineers and administrators who work with them must do likewise. This places a premium on the use of the Russian language and a knowledge of Soviet methods and developmental theory which makes it difficult for technicians of the country to maintain the Western-oriented professional connections of the past. Western-trained engineers who have worked with Soviet technicians on the High Dam have noted this with concern, saying that after a decade of close co-operation with Soviet colleagues, they have lost contact with Western science and engineering which cannot now be revived.

A similar process would go on in the field of economic organization and those involved in it. For example, the Russians will not approach the economic, technical, administrative, and labor problems of the Cairo Steel Mill in the way that Kopper's Koke, an American firm, did. If the Russians run the steel mill long enough, the nationals in the organization must run it the Soviet way, and the economic principles they learn and use will be considered for other projects in the country. While the economic structure of the host country may not become Communist in theoretical form (the Arab Socialism of the UAR is not Communism), it will bear the imprint of the principles, values, and institutions by which the Russians approach the problems of development. Those who are caught up in this process over extended periods of time cannot help but feel the impact and adopt some of the contents of Soviet culture.

This is particularly true because in the more radical countries like Algeria and the United Arab Republic where the Soviet Union is ensconced, the traditional order has broken down under the onslaught of revolutionary development. The new regimes are faced with a double task. They must create institutions to fill the void of those discredited and supply instruments to serve new ends, and also to mold the populace into a revolutionary pattern, accepting and assisting the new order. In other words, the challenge is to bring into being a new structure of society and a new individual to work within it. This means that governments like the UAR are in search of new programs and institutions in a way that the more traditional states are not. There is apt to be a premium on newness and a pragmatic willingness to accept whatever is deemed useful, regardless of its source. In this situation, the Soviet Union often has the advantage. It maintains a revolutionary stance in contrast to the capitalist establishment of the West; it has worked out devices for the centralized, mass control of society, and it is *there*, closely related to the radical regimes of the Middle East, from which the United States is too often absent.

Under these circumstances it would not be surprising if a number of Soviet-inspired institutions may be adopted, or utilized, by client states. This can be seen in the development of the Arab Socialist Union as the projected political base of the UAR radical regime. The Union is not a Communist institution, yet some of its organizational features reflect Soviet practice and its relation to cabinet government has been envisioned as similar to that of the Communist party to the Soviet government in Russia. At various times the UAR has followed the Soviet lead in calling for "solidarity conferences" of writers and intellectuals, especially from Africa and neighboring Arab states, in which the political responsibility of literature was stressed. Given the need to control public opinion and develop a mass revolutionary character, it will not be surprising if Soviet practices in mass media and popular cultural institutions inspire their counterparts in some Middle East countries.

Such developments may seem remote from a carefully calculated program of cultural penetration. Yet it is precisely in consciously noncultural situations that the deepest and most lasting impact may be made. It is here that foreign language is accepted because it is needed, that education in foreign patterns becomes desirable, and that foreign institutions and programs are absorbed into local life. Cultural transmission takes place as it did during the last century, when the winds of trade and political contacts from Europe broadcast the seeds of Western ways throughout the Middle East. Given the closer, more sustained, and more polarized Soviet position the cold war of the future can create, it is to be expected that Soviet culture can penetrate the area more deeply than it has done in the past.

This possibility concerns more than the obvious and visible forms of cultural activity. The questions at stake are not so much what foreign language shall the Middle East learn, what foreign literature shall influence its cultural development, what kind of cinema and television programs it shall watch, and what form of cultural institution it shall adopt. Involved in these, and underlying them, is the truly critical factor of mind and outlook, of intellectual concepts and final values. Insofar as the present leadership of the Middle East has been modernized, it has accepted many aspects of the Western value-structure, both personal and social. Twenty years hence the young university students and technicians of today will be the leaders and key men in their societies. Will they also act within the general framework of Western thought and values—or will the authoritarian, state-centered, mass-controlling concepts so interwoven into the Soviet system produce the framework of their response? The matter is of great moment both to the Middle East and to the West. For them, it will determine whether the momentum of the past century is to be maintained through future rapid change, shaping national development by those concepts of freedom, responsibility, and creativeness which have thus far been the goal of their most far-sighted leaders. It will decide whether America can maintain understanding through communication with Middle Easterners, even across the barriers of political differences.

The heart of the matter lies in the extent to which the West allows the Soviet Union to preempt relations with the Middle East, especially with some of the more radical countries. If the American course in the future is to accept the polarization of the Soviet-American and Western positions, allowing the Russians to bear the burdens and accept the opportunities of countries like the UAR, Americans will have no one to thank but themselves if the Sovietization of culture, together with politics and economics, proceeds apace. But if the Americans are willing to bypass or overleap political difficulties, maintaining cultural relations in spite of them, the Western-flowing current of national development will continue, taking on a more national character than in the past, but moving onward into a world in which both parties can be at home, if not in perpetual harmony.

Quest for Stability

Britain, France, and the Last Phase of the Eastern Question

ELIE KEDOURIE

When, in 1915, the British Government had to consider its policy regarding the future of Ottoman territories in Asia, Lord Kitchener, then Secretary of State for War, suggested that Mosul should be given to France. His reason was that this territory under French control would act as a useful buffer between Britain and Russia in an area which, as past experience indicated, was likely to occasion friction between the two empires. In making this suggestion Kitchener was, in fact, following the logic of the classical Eastern Question.

For a century or so the Eastern Question was in the forefront of European diplomacy, because the Middle East was vital or important to a number of European great powers, and because the Ottoman Empire, which controlled the area, was too weak to defend it against foreign ambitions and encroachments. In spite of the fact that it involved the vital interests of two great powers, namely Britain and Russia, it was only during the Crimean War in the 1850s that the Eastern Question resulted in armed conflict between the European great powers. The reason for this comparative stability, we may suspect, lay in the fact that more than two great powers were involved in the Eastern Question. For besides Britain and Russia, France, Austria-Hungary, and Germany also had substantial interests in the area and were able to bring their influence and might to bear in such a way that if any power were tempted to expand at the expense of the Ottoman Empire, it would find ranged against itself a combination of two or more powers ready to oppose and checkmate its expansion. It was perhaps the beneficent operation of this balancing mechanism which led Kitchener to propose the award of Mosul to France.

But World War I was in some respects to transform fundamentally the Eastern Question. Because Britain still ruled India, the Middle East remained of prime importance to her. And at the end of the war, it seemed as though her interests were infinitely more secure than they had been before 1914. This was because Russia, which had been Britain's main rival, was now *hors de combat*, and unlikely for many decades perhaps to intervene in the area.

In 1918, then, only two remained of the four or five great powers whose rivalries, quarrels, and combinations constituted the classical Eastern Question. These two powers were Britain and France, and the first seemed much more powerful in the area than the second. This made balancing mechanisms such as the one mooted by Kitchener in 1915 now seem less attractive, seem indeed superfluous if not downright harmful to British interests. Britain, therefore, did not resist the temptation to whittle down and, if possible, to do away with such French interests as had been traditionally recognized and secured by the Sykes-Picot Agreement of 1916.

To do this, Britain adopted a highly adventurous policy, the consequences of which on British imperial interests were not perhaps then properly appreciated. This policy consisted of using Arab nationalism and Zionism as weapons with which to combat French demands and undo the French position in the Middle East. It is true that at the beginning of the war, Britain had encouraged the Sharif Husayn of Mecca to act as the standard-bearer of Arabism, but their purpose in this policy had been to foment internal disorders for their Ottoman enemy. At the end of the war, British encouragement of Arab nationalism had an entirely different purpose. Britain allowed Faysal's so-called Northern Arab Army to claim the capture of Damascus and to occupy and control the city. It allowed Faysal himself to set up a more-or-less independent regime in Syria which it then financed and armed. In pursuing these policies in Syria the British were clearly seeking to discomfit the French and to discourage them from pursuing their claims in the Levant. As for Zionism, it is safe to say that if the Sykes-Picot Agreement had not ensured for France a voice in the disposal and administration of

Palestine, Britain would have been much less tempted to issue the Balfour Declaration. In any event, this British policy, did not prove entirely successful. France, while giving up its rights in Palestine, tenaciously asserted and finally made good its claim to Syria. But for this partial victory, the British were to pay a heavy price. In encouraging Faysal and the Zionists they were encouraging an ideological style of politics quite at variance with the interests of an imperial power. And in simultaneously sponsoring both Zionism and Arab nationalism, they were committing themselves to the support of large and incompatible claims, the clash between which proved very damaging to British interests.

By the late 1930s, with the increasing belligerency of Italy in the Mediterranean, and of Germany in Europe, the incompatible claims of the Zionists and the original inhabitants of Palestine began to seem to the British government increasingly inconvenient and embarrassing. The government abandoned the partition plan which the Peel Commission had proposed in 1937, and which it had begun by favouring. Since the Palestinians and their fellow Arabs outside Palestine were the majority, and were intransigeant in their opposition to Zionism it was easier and safer to disregard the Zionists and to coerce them if necessary.

This policy, which became clear in the Round-Table Conference and the White Paper of 1939, sought to deal with the difficulties which Britain had created for itself by the ideological adventure of the latter half of World War I. But this new policy, in its turn, encouraged just as dangerously doctrinaire a view of Middle East politics. The policy proceeded on the assumption that the dispute in Palestine was the central issue in Middle East politics. This was an erroneous assumption since British relations with Egypt, Iraq, and Saudi Arabia, for instance, were bedevilled by difficulties which had little to do with Palestine; and to insist on making Palestine the central issue in the Middle East could alleviate none of these difficulties. Another erroneous assumption which underlay this policy was that the so-called Arab states were in earnest, and of one mind, concerning Arab unity—in other words, that a coherent pro-Arab policy was possible and profitable for Britain. Again, as events were to show, the call for Arab unity was a weapon which various states employed in prosecuting their local rivalries, and a pro-Arab policy *tout court* was, for Britain, literally nonsensical.

But once this policy was adopted certain consequences followed which could not easily be undone, and which did great harm to Palestine and to the Middle East, as well as to British interests. The Palestine Round Table Conference of 1939 was the first fruit of this policy. By inviting Palestine's neighbors to this Conference Britain acknowledged—what it had so far strenuously resisted—that these neighbors had some kind of right to intervene in the affairs of a British-mandated territory. This set a precedent for further intervention in Palestine and elsewhere, whether Britain liked it or not. Also by greatly increasing the number of parties in the Palestine dispute, this policy fearfully complicated the problem which finally became well-nigh intractable. It ended by making the Palestinians the dupes and victims of their neighbors' interested solicitude.

One thing may be said in justification of this policy as it operated from 1938 when the international situation became very critical to 1942 when the Axis threat to the Middle East finally receded. During this period, erroneous and unrealistic as were its assumptions, the motive at least of this policy was prudential and defensive. The Axis Powers in their public statements and propaganda, if not in their actual commitments, which were cautious and restricted, were setting the pace in the Middle East, and this policy was designed to lessen the attraction which the Axis had for many governments in the area. After 1942, Britain did not abandon this so-called pro-Arab policy. On the contrary, the policy became more ambitious and adventurous. Here is an interesting parallel with World War I. On that occasion, the encouragement of Husayn had initially for its purpose the disruption of the Ottoman Empire, while the subsequent encouragement of his son Faysal was essentially aimed at the French. In World War II, too, pro-Arab policy was initially designed to checkmate the Axis, while in the latter part of the war it was meant to eliminate the French from the center of the Middle East—and it succeeded; and to ensure the sole dominance of Britain in the area—and it was speedily seen to have failed.

The period between Rommel's defeat at 'Alamayn and the end of the war saw the apogee of British power and influence in the Middle East. In the autumn of 1943 the Lebanese government adopted a provocative policy toward the Free French who reacted forcefully. But Britain intervened on the Lebanese side, thereby irremediably damaging the French position in that country. A similar episode in

Syria in the spring of 1945 completed French humiliation in the Levant. It left Britain seemingly the only great power in the Middle East and the sole patron of the Arab states now organized in an Arab League, the formation of which Britain had itself suggested and encouraged.

This dominance soon proved deceptive. Britain emerged from the war victorious but enfeebled, and with a government wedded to welfarism at home and retrenchment abroad. With the giving up of India, there simultaneously disappeared the main *raison d'être* of British interest in the Middle East, and the British ability ultimately to bring superior force to bear on the affairs of the region. But there were local reasons for the British decline. These had to do with the pro-Arab policy which had been adopted in 1938, and to which the war had given a prodigious extension. When, soon after the end of the war, the Palestine problem once more became acute, Britain found that support for the Arabs in Palestine ensured no advantage in relations with Egypt or Iraq—witness the Egyptian complaint to the United Nations in 1947 and the fate of the Portsmouth Treaty with Iraq in 1948. Again, it proved very difficult to give content and substance to a pro-Arab policy, so far as Palestine itself was concerned. When the United Nations decided to partition Palestine, the British government announced that it would not help to enforce a scheme unacceptable to the Arabs, that it was giving up its mandatory responsibilities and withdrawing from the territory by a fixed and stated date. This decision made of Palestine a battlefield not only between the Zionists and the native Palestinians, but also between the rival and irreconcilable ambitions of King 'Abdallah and King Faruq. These ambitions led to the intervention of Arab regular armies in Palestine and clearly showed up the hollowness of a pro-Arab policy on Britain's part. For it became apparent that the issue was not whether the Arabs as a whole should be supported, but rather which particular faction among them.

The injury done to British interests in the Middle East by the Palestine war of 1948 was thus in large measure a self-inflicted injury. It resulted from a misunderstanding of the Middle East situation, from a deliberate encouragement—in the sponsoring of the Arab League—of an ideological, hence extremist, style of politics, and from a faulty estimate of the power and capacities of the various contending parties. But even so, the British position in the Middle

East in 1950 was by no means negligible. Cyprus and Aden were British possessions, Britain was supreme in the Persian Gulf and had bases in Libya, Egypt, and Iraq. But in the last two countries in particular there was great pressure for the revision of the treaties which sanctioned these bases. In seeking this revision, the British negotiated if not from strength, certainly not from weakness. They agreed to evacuate the Suez base against a promise to allow it to be reactivated in an emergency, and, with the intermittent and qualified support of the United States, took the lead in setting up the Baghdad Pact.

This treaty had in fact originated in American preoccupation with the Soviet threat to the Middle East. The best way to cope with this threat, United States officials held, was to organize what was then called the Northern Tier of Middle Eastern States into a Middle East Defence Organization complementary to NATO and to SEATO. The scheme was clearly not well thought out. The countries concerned were absorbed in their own local rivalries, and had their own divergent preoccupations. This made their cooperation in countering a Soviet threat, which some of them regarded as remote and none of their concern, somewhat problematic. The consequence of these Western attempts to organize Middle Eastern defense was precisely to provide an opening for the Soviet Union successfully to intervene in the area.

The Baghdad Pact represented an end and a beginning. It was an adaptation of the Northern Tier scheme in which Britain was glad to take the lead. But by choosing to support Iraq—and thus to affront Egypt—the British government tacitly admitted that a pro-Arab policy was, as such, meaningless. It is ironical that as Foreign Secretary, Eden, who encouraged and promoted the Arab League in which Egypt obtained the primacy, should have, some ten years afterwards, presided over a government which abandoned the earlier policy and the assumptions on which it was based, and that he should have taken the lead in prosecuting a violent quarrel with Egypt which wrecked his political career.

Egypt having been affronted retorted by seeking arms from the Soviet camp. The Baghdad Pact thus ended the long Russian absence from the Middle East, and, in the vastly changed conditions since 1917, bade fair to involve the other superpower more deeply in Middle East affairs.

The year 1955, therefore, marked the end of the classical Eastern Question. The Middle East is no longer important because it is the road to India, and because a weak Ottoman Empire gives scope to three or four European great powers to jockey for position. It becomes one more area, no doubt with its own peculiarities, where the two superpowers confront each other more or less suspiciously, more or less belligerently. Before the Suez War of 1956, Britain still had respectable assets in the Middle East to put at the disposal of her American ally. So much was this the case that, when Bulganin and Khrushchev visited London in the spring of 1956, Eden felt able to utter a warning to the Soviet visitors that Britain had important interests in the area which it would not tolerate being tampered with. The challenge to Eden's assertion came sooner than anybody expected. But it did not come from the Soviet Union. It came from Egypt. The nationalization of the Suez Canal, which the British government considered an intolerable affront, was the consequence, however, not of an Anglo-Egyptian but of an American-Egyptian quarrel. But in the war which followed, the United States took the lead in denouncing the British and French aggression, and in demanding the immediate evacuation of their troops from Egypt. This policy, which dealt a mortal blow to the British position in the Middle East, remains still quite obscure in its aims and motives. For if Britain had remained relatively powerful and respected in the Middle East she would, at best, have proved a precious auxiliary to the United States, or at worst, have acted as an intermediary or a buffer between the superpowers, in the manner which Kitchener envisaged when he suggested in 1915 the award of Mosul to France. As it was, in consequence of American policy, after Suez the superpowers confronted one another, each with its own local and troublesome clients, without intermediary or buffer. This bipolar situation is inherently more unstable—and therefore, in modern conditions, potentially more catastrophic—than what used to obtain in the classical Eastern Question when three or four powers combined with one another to checkmate or contain an aggressive or ambitious rival. And what adds further to this bipolarity is that France, evicted by Britain from the Levant, decided between 1955 and 1962 to give up the two protectorates of Tunisia and Morocco, and to abandon Algeria to the FLN.

Whether this bipolarity will in fact lead to disaster remains, of course, to be seen. The record since 1956 is obscure and inconclusive. In July 1958, following the Iraqi *coup d'état*, which was an indirect consequence of the Suez fiasco, the United States was compelled to intervene in Lebanon to arrest Egyptian expansion. At that time there was no Soviet fleet in the Mediterranean, and the Soviet Union was either not inclined or not ready, to pursue a forward and active policy in the Middle East. By 1967, this seems to have changed. The Russians were now much more intimately involved with the United Arab Republic and Syria, and it is generally agreed that they had some part to play in precipitating the Six Day War. The war has shown that in groping for a policy in the Middle East, the Soviet Union can miscalculate just as badly as its Western rivals. Indeed the parallel to the Soviet miscalculation in 1967 is the British miscalculation over Palestine in 1948. The war has also clearly shown that the Suez fiasco has meant that the two superpowers now starkly confront each other in the Middle East, and in the Mediterranean as a whole. In 1967 they were wise enough or lucky enough to avoid an armed clash. But, as has been said, the situation is inherently unstable and the risk of conflict is not negligible.

The risk may perhaps arise not so much out of the Israel-Arab dispute (in which Soviet support for the Arabs has been unequivocal, at least publicly, but American support for Israel ambiguous), as from two other situations. Both situations have been created by a British government which, like its predecessor of 1947, is bent on welfarism at home and retrenchment abroad, and again like its predecessor, is given to public advance notification of its intention to withdraw from overseas commitments, according to a rigidly fixed schedule. The consequences of such a proceeding became evident in Aden. That the situation in South Yemen has not yet given rise to international tension may perhaps be due to the closure of the Suez Canal which has, so to speak, sealed off this highly volatile area for the time being from international rivalries. Similar instability may be apprehended in the Persian Gulf from which the British government has announced its withdrawal in 1971. Such instability may tempt the Soviets to pursue an adventurous and ambitious policy, and may thus heighten tensions and make for a confrontation between the two superpowers.

It may be asked whether the risk of such a confrontation may not be diminished by the presence and policies of other outside powers; whether, in other words, a state of affairs similar to what obtained before 1914 would not be conducive to greater stability in the area. The answer is that what obtained before 1914 is dead and gone, and cannot be artificially revived. In the Middle East now, only the superpowers can intervene decisively. It is true, to be sure, that other outside powers (such as Britain, France, Germany, or Italy) can, especially if tension is relaxed, pursue their own local interests and cultivate friendships with this or that Middle East state. It is also true that these outsiders (who, with the negligible exception of Britain, have no physical foothold in the area itself) can through arms supply and diplomatic support, affect the local balance of power. French policy toward Israel before and after 1967 is a case in point. But as the French record itself shows, such intervention does not seem decisive either in local matters, or *a fortiori*, in changing or deflecting the aims and policies of the two superpowers.

American Search for Partners

JOHN C. CAMPBELL

        In the two decades from the Truman Doctrine to the Six
Day War, the United States set as its major task in the Middle East
the blocking of the expansion of Soviet power into the area and the
prevention of Soviet dominance or control over one or more Middle
East states. In view of the fact that no Middle East state was reduced
to the status of a Soviet republic or of the European satellite states during the later Stalin years, this policy may be judged successful. On
the other hand, considering what was the American grand design,
the combining of its own growing power in the area, certain remaining positions of its Western allies, and the assertive forces of local
nationalism in a comprehensive collective security system directed
against the Soviet Union, the conclusion cannot be avoided that the
design failed. The Soviet Union in this period broke into a region
which was previously a Western preserve, improved its military position, increased its political influence, and became the principal outside power playing a role in the affairs of a number of Arab states.
A rough political map of the region drawn in 1947 would show
American influence moving in to replace that of Britain in Greece
and Turkey, which would soon become members of NATO; Britain
and the United States both present in Iran, from which the Soviet
Union was excluded after its withdrawal from Azarbayjan and its
failure to get an oil concession in northern Iran; Cyprus still a British
crown colony; Britain the leading power in the Arab East, with
American influence growing especially in Saudi Arabia; France out

of Syria and Lebanon, but the successor regimes generally cooperating with the West; Britain ready to give up the Palestine mandate, but with the Soviet Union playing no role there, other than its support of an independent Jewish state; France still in full control of the Maghrib; and no Soviet military presence anywhere in the Middle East.

A comparable map drawn in the spring of 1967 would show Turkey still loyal to NATO and to its American connection but increasingly restive, seeking a more independent policy, and establishing a new relationship with the Soviet Union marked by high-level visits, Soviet economic aid to Turkey, and a favorable Soviet attitude toward Turkey's line on Cyprus; Iran looking to the United States as its major foreign ally but also "normalizing" its relations with the Soviet Union to the point of making important economic deals and buying some arms; Cyprus a bone of contention between two NATO members and providing a possible additional point of entry for Soviet influence in the Eastern Mediterranean; the Soviet Union very strong in the UAR, Syria, Iraq, and Algeria, owing to its political support and its position as major or exclusive supplier of arms to all of them; Jordan still holding to its Western ties but under increasing pressure to repudiate them because of its inability to defend itself against Israel; Yemen in its fifth year of civil war which could provide openings for anti-Western forces; the British in trouble in Aden and about to withdraw; Western influence relatively strong in the major oil-producing Arab countries (Saudi Arabia, Kuwayt, Libya) and in Tunisia and Morocco, but adversely affected by the Palestine issue which no Arab government could ignore; and a growing Soviet naval force in the Mediterranean.

This stark contrast suggests a succession of Soviet advances and Western retreats equivalent to a decisive change in the balance of military and political power in the region. Such was not the case. What happened was that the Soviet Union had become a Middle East power whereas before it had been virtually excluded. As in other parts of the third world, the Soviet Union from 1955 onward was no longer just a military threat from outside or a manipulator of subversive Communist organizations within. It was actively engaged in competition with the West, seeking friends and partners and using all the methods of its rivals: governmental relations, military and economic aid, trade and cultural ties.

It was inevitable that the Soviet Union, as one of the superpowers, should have asserted itself in a strategically important area bordering on its own frontiers. It was also highly unlikely that the United States could have succeeded in its design of organizing the Middle East in an alliance comparable to NATO. Turkey, a member both of NATO and of the Baghdad Pact, was to be the iron link between them, but the demise of the latter and the weakness of its successor, CENTO, proved that the political foundations for a security system did not extend beyond Turkey and Iran. The resistance of local nationalism to Western imperialism and even to its ghost, the attractions of neutralism, the conflicts among local states, and the general instability of governments provided openings for the Russians which they did not fail to exploit. The hostility of Arab nationalist leaders toward the West and toward Israel made it natural for them to turn to Moscow as a counterweight and a provider of help, and for Moscow to assume that role. The Soviet policy of "peaceful coexistence," moreover, inclined Middle East governments, even the allies of the United States, to discount the possibilities of Soviet aggression and to seek more room for maneuvering in the changed climate. This transformation of the area into one of active competition did not spell Soviet domination, but it proved that the old system of Western domination was ended and would not be replaced by an American substitute, even in the guise of alliances and economic cooperation.

It was all too apparent that the great-power balance in the Middle East was not the making of the great powers alone but was dependent in large measure on the attitudes and decisions of local governments and political forces. The disposition of outside military forces and the possession of bases continued to have some significance, but the crucial aspects in what was primarily a political competition lay in the standing of each of the competitors on the local scene. The interlocking of global and local cold wars, moreover, was not without risks for the great powers, for they could become the captives of the policies of their smaller partners. The historical parallel with the Balkans before 1914 is suggestive.

The Six Day War and Its Aftermath

The Arab-Israel war of June 1967 illustrated several points: (1) that local states can push a crisis over the brink into war despite the urgings and efforts of outside powers to prevent it; (2) that such a local war may bring the United States and the Soviet Union, because of the depth of their involvement with respective parties to the conflict, to a point of grave danger of conflict with each other; (3) that a shift in the local balance of power need not result in a comparable shift in the great-power balance in the area; that the Soviet Union, indeed, could take advantage of the defeat of its clients to establish an even stronger position.

Thus, the United States tried to restrain Israel from going to war but was unsuccessful. The Soviets tried, at a very late stage in the game, to restrain the UAR and Syria from provocative acts but failed to do so. Both great powers then made sure, by direct communication, that neither wished nor intended to become militarily involved. The speed of Israel's victory fortunately removed the question from further testing.

The Six Day War was disastrous for Moscow's clients but not for Moscow. Israel decisively defeated three Arab states, two of which were closely associated with and supplied by the Soviet Union. Humiliated by defeat and loss of territory, the UAR and Syria broke relations with the United States and drew even closer to the Soviet Union, which rapidly replenished their supplies of arms. The regime in Jordan was so shaken by defeat that it was unable to act independently of the UAR or to keep order in its remaining territory; it maintained its ties with the United States but was pressured at home to turn instead to Russia. Thus in all three Arab states the United States was relatively worse off than before the war. The other radical nationalist states of the Arab world (Iraq, Yemen, and Algeria) also broke relations with the United States, as did Sudan, which then for the first time sought arms from Russia. The moderate Arab states were less sympathetic than before because of what they regarded as open American support of Israel against Arab rights and interests. Meanwhile, the United States position toward Israel was no stronger; if anything it was weaker because Israel had shown it could disregard American advice and successfully defend its vital interests, establishing its own position of strength as against its Arab neighbors.

On the conclusion of the war, the United States took the position that an attempt should be made to reach a durable peace settlement instead of merely restoring the armistice arrangements, which had proved inadequate to keep the peace. The desired settlement was to include, in addition to withdrawal of forces, all the major issues which were at the heart of the Arab-Israel conflict: frontiers, refugees, freedom of navigation, renunciation of belligerency, recognition of the right of all states to exist, and limitations on arms shipments. The United States has pursued this end largely through the United Nations, supporting the Security Council Resolution of November 22, 1967, and the efforts of Dr. Gunnar V. Jarring to promote an agreement between the parties.

There were sound reasons for making that effort. An agreed settlement would reduce the danger to peace and limit the advantages the Russians could gain from exploiting the Arab-Israel conflict. It would basically satisfy Israel while opening the way for the restoration of more normal and fruitful relations between the United States and the Arab world. By the same token, the inability of Dr. Jarring or of the United States to bring the parties to a settlement would leave Israel dissatisfied with the results of American diplomacy as it had long been dissatisfied with the United Nations, and would leave the Arab states still resentful of America's failure to press Israel to withdraw from their occupied territories. That is where the situation stands at the time of writing. The United States still seeks a position between the extreme claims of Israel and of the Arab states and a means of preventing the erosion of its influence among the Arabs. It does not wish to be totally identified with Israel's cause but its apparent acceptance of the Israel view that no Arab territory need be given up except as part of a comprehensive settlement is to the Arabs convincing evidence of total partiality.

For these reasons the period since the Six Day War has seen a strengthening of Soviet influence in the UAR and Syria through the provision of arms, military advisers, economic aid, and political support. In return the Soviet Union has been able to use certain naval and air facilities in Arab states which give added flexibility to its military position in the area. These developments, by giving encouragement to Arab militants and involving the Soviet Union more deeply on behalf of their cause, increase the danger that a new round between Israel and the Arab states may break out and the greater danger that it may draw in the great powers.

It is apparent also that since the crisis of 1967 the Soviet role in other parts of the Middle East has not diminished. The British have left Aden and have declared their intention of withdrawing from their positions and commitments in the Persian Gulf by 1971. Soviet influence in the Yemen Republic and in South Yemen is already evident. Soviet interest in the Gulf has been publicly declared and made manifest by visits of Soviet naval vessels. The policy of peaceful coexistence with Turkey, Iran, Pakistan, and Afghanistan continues, untroubled by Soviet conduct in Czechoslovakia.

Appraisal and Reappraisal

Any appraisal of the future problems and policies for the United States in the Middle East in the context of rivalry with the Soviet Union requires some estimate of Soviet aims and strategy. It is of no help to speak broadly of the aim of spreading Communism. It is too confining, however, to tie one's consideration of American choices to any fixed and necessarily arbitrary description of the Soviet "threat." Let us be content with some broad assumptions about Soviet policy over the coming decade. We may reasonably expect that (1) the Kremlin will continue to have the general aim of increasing Soviet influence in the area and diminishing that of the United States; (2) it will, however, set no master plan or schedule for reaching the point where it exercises exclusive influence or dominance, and may come to regard it as no more than a nominal aim; (3) it will not launch direct military aggression against Middle East states but may engage in limited military intervention in cases where the political gains to be made or losses to be avoided are considerable and the risks of international conflict are low; (4) it will regard Soviet military forces in the area primarily as a useful tool to influence the attitudes and decisions of local governments and movements, to counterbalance United States forces, and to discourage any local interventions by the latter; (5) it will continue to avoid situations which carry a substantial risk of armed conflict with the United States; and (6) it will not exclude the possibility of common or parallel action with the United States in the Middle East, if it sees that its own interests will be advanced thereby.

How those aims and policies are pursued over the years, and with what success, will depend in large degree on the obstacles which they encounter on the part of Middle East states themselves or of other outside powers. Thus we do not need to picture American policy simply as a response to Soviet attacks, military buildup, or gains in this or that country, but rather in the context of a developing situation in which outside powers and local states will all be engaged in an interplay of initiatives and responses. The United States has to define the nature of its interests in that situation, then consider more specifically how its policies can be related to their protection or advancement. Do America's interests require a more determined cold-war policy of strengthening its military forces in the region, tightening up alliances with Greece, Turkey, and Iran, and making stronger efforts to gain the cooperation of Arab states (or, alternatively, strengthening support of Israel as a dependable partner), or are they better served by a diminution of commitment and involvement? Are current policies adequate, or are quite new approaches called for?

Major United States interests in the Middle East may be stated broadly in three propositions: (1) that there be no nuclear war in the Middle East or growing out of conflicts in that area, (2) that there be no major shift in the world balance against us through Soviet advances in the area, and (3) that the independence of certain nations to which the United States is committed be maintained, within the terms of those obligations.

The first proposition needs little explanation or comment. It is directed at the conduct of both the Soviet Union and the United States. It postulates that both powers share the interest but that the avoidance of war is not automatically assured; thus, the United States must always be alert to the need for persuasion and deterrence in order to minimize the risks.

The second proposition is less definite. It does not refer only to the possible military effects of the loss of valuable resources and strategic positions. It stresses rather the disastrous political and psychological effects on American power, influence, and interests all over the world of a shift of the entire region or a large part of it into a dependent or exclusive relationship with a great power hostile to us. Such a result could come from an American withdrawal from the region in a general reappraisal of commitments, responsibilities, and resources, or from the rapid spread of radical movements growing out of political breakdown, economic stagnation, and the momentum of Soviet successes.

The third proposition refers to Turkey under the terms of the North Atlantic Treaty; to Iran, although the treaty commitment in its case is less precise; and to Israel, with which no written security treaty exists but rather a general conviction on the part of successive United States administrations that this country will not permit Israel's independence as a nation to be destroyed. If outside powers, including the United States, were to guarantee any part of an Arab-Israel settlement, living up to that guarantee should also be considered a major American interest.

The United States has other important interests in the Middle East: containment and control of local disputes which carry the threat of wider conflict; independence, development, and social progress for the peoples of the region; access to the territory of allies and continued availability of certain military bases and installations; maintenance of access to Middle East oil for its major consumers (Western Europe and Japan) on reasonable terms; protection of the United States investment in Middle East oil and its contribution to the United States balance of payments; freedom of movement and transit for ships and aircraft, both military and commercial; preservation and expansion of cultural ties with Middle East peoples; furtherance of United States trade with the region; protection of American citizens, and so on. Some of these interests are related to the two major interests mentioned above. None of them, however, should be regarded in absolute terms, and none is of such a nature as to require the use of military force as a suitable means of safeguarding it. Together they form a pattern which reflects the totality of the American position in the Middle East. The pattern will shift from time to time, and as it does the various interests should be attuned to the shape of developments in the region itself and to the ways in which its governments and peoples see their own interests. We cannot protect our interests effectively if they are conceived of as static positions—bases, oil concessions, or ties with particular regimes or factions—to be rigidly held against all comers. Much will depend, of course, on whether the future brings cold war or détente.

Assumption 1: Continuing Cold War

The very fact of continuing cold war as a worldwide phenomenon will require the maintenance of the United States global deterrent, a part of which will include the strategic striking power of the Sixth Fleet and of Polaris missiles in the waters of the general Middle East area. Technological or other developments may in time change this requirement, but for the near future it remains. Thus there is a need for powerful military units in or near the area wholly unrelated to the Middle East situation itself.

Additionally, decisions will have to be made on what United

States military posture is suited to the continuing cold war in the Middle East. The presence of American and of Soviet forces there provides a backdrop to what is likely to be primarily a political competition. The main purpose of the Soviet buildup is to provide a counterweight to American forces, to remove any impression that the Mediterranean is an American lake and that the United States possesses ultimate power over the Middle East because of its military superiority. It may be inferred that the Soviet military presence is intended to deter military moves by rival powers comparable to the United States landings in Lebanon and British move into Jordan in 1958. Possibly the Soviet forces would themselves intervene in local situations, particularly if they could act first and place on the United States the onus and the risk of counterintervention which could bring on a direct clash of United States and Soviet forces. Possibly Soviet forces would be drawn into a local war involving a client state in whose fate Soviet prestige was deeply engaged.

What conclusions may be drawn concerning American military posture and dispositions? The guiding aims should be (1) to maintain military forces adequate to reassure allied and other governments that the United States will continue to be present in the area, and to prevent their acting in fear of Soviet military pressure, and (2) to deter the Russians from adventurous moves such as those mentioned above. Such requirements cannot be precisely calculated in military terms, but maintenance of a clear naval and air superiority in the Mediterranean and in the Arabian Sea-Persian Gulf-Indian Ocean area seems essential to these aims. The idea of superiority conjures up thoughts of an unending and futile arms race. That need not be the result. The United States has had superiority in the past, has it now, and should be able to maintain it without great difficulty.

Particularly in the Mediterranean area NATO members other than the United States are wary of the possible adverse effects of growing Soviet military strength there on their own security and interests. Great Britain, France, Italy, Greece, and Turkey are the states most concerned. Any decisions on their part, within or outside the NATO structure, to strengthen their own forces would be helpful, especially from the political standpoint since it is important to show that there is a recognized Western solidarity on the question of security in the Mediterranean. Militarily, steps taken (e.g., the joint reconnaissance plan recently adopted in NATO) or to be taken are not likely to be a major factor in the balance of power. The main counterweight to Soviet power will remain the United States Sixth Fleet in the Mediterranean, and it should stay there.

So much for the military component of an American policy. A related question is whether the United States should attempt to revitalize its military alliances and seek to play a more dynamic role of leadership to prevent further Soviet gains and erosion of Western influence. Let us concede at the start that we cannot turn back the clock to the 1950s or to the goals which we set and did not reach even at that time. We cannot reverse what has happened in Turkey's and Iran's relations with the Soviet Union over the past few years. Even if the American Congress and public could be persuaded to support a vast arms program to strengthen those countries against the Soviet Union, they themselves would not choose to break off their present normal and cooperative relations with Moscow in order to follow our leadership (although they would be happy to accept more arms) unless the Russians themselves revert to a policy of hostility and threats of force.

More promising opportunities for a revitalized American leadership lie in building political relationships with Turkey and Iran which have the best chance of thriving over the years and surviving changes on the domestic or the international scene. Such relationships must rest on a foundation of common interest in the security and independence of those nations and require a studied effort by the United States to see their interests as they themselves see them. In the case of Turkey, such matters as military planning and the strength and the role of various armed forces in case of war should be less important than the nature of relations between the two governments, their respective diplomatic and military representatives, and their citizens. It may be more useful to reduce the size and visibility of the United States military presence than to insist on "logical" military arrangements likely to prove politically abrasive. Military and economic aid should not be rigidly set at what we feel they need (or that the United States can afford), but should be responsive to their local concerns, to their sense of values, and to relations of confidence and good faith. Obviously, the United States cannot give full backing to all the interests of Turkey or Iran as each sees them, especially when these interests are in conflict with those of neighboring states as in the disputes over Cyprus or Bahrayn. But here again there are ways of dealing with such problems that break down confidence and other ways which maintain and strengthen it.

With the Arab world the task of restoring confidence and building constructive relations is infinitely more difficult because of the record of the past, the burden of the Palestine question, and the interlocking of the United States-Soviet cold war with the Arab-Israel conflict and the cold war among the Arab states themselves. Those who say that it is hopeless, that no ground can be gained with the Arabs so long as American policy is tied to Zionism, can make a strong case. But it would be sheer defeatism to write off the entire Arab world on this hypothesis. Even if the assumption be made that an independent Israel will continue to exist and that the United States will defend its right to existence, there remain possibilities of change in Israel policy, in American policy, in Soviet policy, and in Arab affairs which make it anything but a fixed conclusion that the United States is doomed to "lose" the entire Arab world and that the Soviet Union will inevitably inherit it. American prestige is at a low point, but the United States is by no means excluded from the Arab world.

The first task is to keep the situation from growing worse in those states where mutual interests remain strong. These are Saudi Arabia, Kuwayt, Libya, Lebanon, Tunisia, and Morocco. The means will vary according to differing conditions. Where American initiatives and action can reinforce those mutual interests (e.g., in arrangements concerning oil production in the first three countries, tourism and financial stability in Lebanon, and aid for national development in Tunisia and Morocco), the effort should be made. Because these states are somewhat removed from the center of the Arab-Israel conflict, such cooperation should be possible. On the other hand, they are very sensitive on that issue and their relations with the United States, continually sapped by it, are always at the mercy of a flare-up caused by events on the front line of the struggle. Here, of course, the main road to improvement can only be in progress toward settlement of the Arab-Israel conflict, including concessions that give some satisfaction to the Palestine Arabs, or in an American policy which takes greater account of Arab views. The secondary road, that of explaining again and again to the Arab governments that we understand their concern and are hoping for a settlement, has not led anywhere in particular and has taken its toll mainly in the credibility of American diplomats.

Current reasonably good relations with the conservative or moderate Arab states should not induce the United States to become their partisans and backers in their cold war with the radical states. If Soviet military intervention in support of the latter takes place, that is another matter, but the continuing contests between the UAR and Saudi Arabia or between Algeria and Morocco, and civil struggles in such places as Yemen or South Yemen or the Persian Gulf shaykh-doms, should be left to work themselves out without being drawn into the center of world politics. The lineup in the inter-Arab cold war is not set in concrete; hence the danger of assuming long-term friendship or enmity with one state or another. This lesson should have been learned through experience.

One reason for a policy of aloofness from inter-Arab strife is that it would be a mistake for the United States to deepen the gulf that already divides it from the radical Arab states. Those states, now considered in the pro-Soviet camp, carry the main weight in the Arab world. They occupy the central areas: the Nile Valley and most of the Fertile Crescent. In population, education, social development, and influence, they tend to overshadow their moderate rivals in everything but oil wealth. In spite of all the difficulties of today and of the hostility shown by the governments of those states, it is not in America's interest to ignore them or to be cut off from them. It would be a mistake to consign them automatically to the Soviet camp. At a minimum, the United States should be in communication with them and should be prepared to listen to their point of view.

As things stand now, the close ties between the radical Arab states and the Soviet Union constitute a formidable handicap for the United States in a period of continuing cold war. As long as the Arab-Israel conflict is in an explosive state, that situation is not likely to change, certainly not by any initiative from the United States unless it decides on a shift in its policy toward Israel. The passing of time, however, may have its effect on Soviet-Arab relations. There is nothing unbreakably permanent in what has been a marriage of convenience. Soviet help and advice and the massive Soviet presence, in the absence of a Western counterweight, may be increasingly resented and opposed. Arab nationalism, even with a socialist label, does not accept Soviet any more than Western domination. 'Abd al-Nasir or his successors and other radical leaders may discover that the Soviet Union is not able either to bring about the restoration of their lost territories or the fulfillment of promises they have made to their own peoples. Amid economic troubles at home they may be more inclined to look to the international financial institutions, to the world market, to compromises with the moderate Arab states, and to improved relations with Western nations. The United States cannot predict such developments but it should not foreclose them.

In attempting to narrow the gap with the Arab world and to check the advance of Soviet influence, the United States should encourage the interest of other Western states in a more active role in the Middle East. This does not mean a concerted Western effort to carry out a cold war strategy. The Middle East nations would resist such an effort even if the Western states were prepared to make it, and they are not. What is more practical and useful is that individual Western states should establish stronger ties with individual local states. France is trying to re-establish ties with the Arab world broken for two decades. French and Italian oil enterprises are in the field. West Germany is increasing its economic connections. All this creates a certain amount of competition among Western firms, and new ventures on the part of General de Gaulle have not always been welcomed by the United States. Nevertheless, Western influence may profit by its variety. Arab states may make arrangements with Europeans which they would not make with the United States. Turkey and Iran may prefer to diversify their Western connections more than they have in the past. The result should be a basically stronger American position over the long run. The reduction of the Soviet cold war challenge depends ultimately on the strength and resiliency of the web of relationships between the Middle East and the West.

Assumption 2: Limited Détente

The two powers might be said already to have an agreed area of common interest in the Middle East, as in other parts of the world. Both wish to prevent developments in the region from growing into a nuclear conflict. Perhaps that area of common interest is wide enough to include avoidance of any direct military conflict between themselves even if limited to the region and below the nuclear threshold. The conduct of both powers in the crisis of June 1967 indicated a strong determination not to be drawn in.

One can hardly justify, however, calling that common determination to avoid mutual annihilation a limited détente. It is rather an accepted limitation on the conduct of the cold war. More convincing tests of the willingness of the Soviet Union and the United States to move toward limited détente may be found in the field of arms control and in the handling of the Arab-Israel conflict.

Control of the local arms races in the Middle East, which is discussed elsewhere in this volume, need be mentioned here only to stress its relationship to the overall Soviet-American military balance and to the status of any negotiations for limitation of strategic weapons or for arms control in certain regions of the world. It seems more likely that agreements reached in other areas might spread possibilities of détente to the Middle East than vice versa. In Europe, for example, the trend toward détente has had a basis in a territorial status quo which from the standpoint of security has de facto acceptance on both sides. Even so violent and shocking an act as the Soviet invasion of Czechoslovakia may not destroy the desire on both sides for a détente which will provide greater stability despite the absence of a durable political settlement. Regional arms control could contribute to that stability. In the Middle East, by contrast, there is no equilibrium between recognized alliance systems or tacitly accepted division of spheres of interest. There are conflicts in progress, wide areas of contention, neutralist states leaning in one direction or another, and an intensity of struggle within the region that would make it extraordinarily difficult for the two superpowers, if they could agree on a common approach, to get the cooperation of the local states.

Washington is well aware that its policy of arms deliveries in the Middle East has elements of inconsistency. It provides no guarantees of stability, no resolution of conflicts. Each part of it—arms to Turkey and Iran to strengthen the frontier zone, arms to Israel to offset massive Soviet deliveries to Arab states, and arms to Jordan to stabilize the regime and keep it looking westward—has a different justification, and they cannot be easily changed unless the circumstances that brought them into being change first. Here there is little the United States can do unless the Arab-Israel dispute moves toward settlement or the Soviet Union modifies its use of arms deliveries as a main weapon of political competition.

The Soviet government has indicated its interest in arms control in the Arab-Israel area but only after Israel has withdrawn from the occupied territories. Thus the main test of limited détente is the Arab-

Israel conflict itself: first, the current effort at settlement following the war of 1967; later, the development of longer-term policies toward the conflict, which is bound to continue in one form or another whether or not there is some kind of settlement in the near future.

For the United States the present problem is how to move from the United Nations Resolution of November 22, 1967, and the painfully slow efforts of the Jarring mission to a political settlement. That will require a basis of agreement between the two sides somewhere in the middle ground between their present extreme positions. It is at least possible, judging from what is publicly known of Soviet and American views, that a compromise satisfactory to both powers could be found. But would it satisfy the parties to the dispute, even if it included a Soviet-American (or possibly a four-power) guarantee of the settlement? The big powers could not impose a compromise if it were strongly resisted, but they might persuade the disputants that they had more to gain by acceptance than by refusal. If so, the consequent defusing of the more explosive aspects of the Arab-Israel dispute and the common obligations undertaken by the two big powers to preserve the settlement could usher in what we may call here a limited détente. Whether the acccent would remain on the adjective or the noun would depend on how the two powers chose to pursue their interests under the new conditions.

The fact of an Arab-Israel settlement would not wipe the slate clean of their conflict. It can be assumed that significant political forces on both sides would be dissatisfied with the settlement and would seek to undermine it; that Arab nationalists would continue to regard Israel as a group of intruders in the Arab East; that the Arab boycott would be continued; that heavy propaganda and violent incidents would not cease, especially if the Palestine Arab community and its leaders remained unreconciled to the settlement; and that both Israel and the Arab states would attempt to go on with their arms race. Soviet-American rivalry would probably persist throughout the Middle East, but we cannot be sure what forms it would take.

From the Soviet side might come a major "peace offensive" designed to take advantage of the new atmosphere and to strengthen the Soviet political and economic positions in states previously associated largely with the West. More intensive Soviet efforts might be expected to woo Turkey and Iran away from their military ties with the United States and the West, and to make new arrangements with the oil-producing Arab states. At the same time, the Soviet Union probably would be offering arms to many countries and building up rather than reducing its military strength in the Mediterranean and in the waters east of Suez.

The United States would not find it easy to cope with that kind of dynamic Soviet policy. It might be difficult to hold the old alliance system together after a demonstration of the fact that the two big powers could agree to reduce the dangers of war and to cooperate in keeping the peace between Israel and its Arab neighbors. A military buildup alone would be no adequate response. Perhaps the best strategy would be a general economic offensive, combining the resources of international institutions with the efforts of individual countries (including the Soviet Union if it were willing) to support a comprehensive development program in the Middle East. This is no new proposal. Many in the past, including Dag Hammarskjold, have seen it as the only way to solve the refugee problem. Timing has been the critical factor. With an Arab-Israel settlement, many of the obstacles to tackling the problems involving Israel and its Arab neighbors (expansion of water resources and agreement on their use, settlement of refugees, Israel-Jordan trade, reopening of the Suez Canel and so on) might disappear. Egypt's economic problems could be made more tolerable by effective outside aid. Regional projects could encourage the better use of the area's own resources, in particular its oil revenues. No miracles should be anticipated. We know from experience that economic and technical aid and even marked economic progress will not solve tough political problems. But a partial Arab-Israel settlement and a limited degree of Soviet-American cooperation would at least open up long dormant possibilities.

The United States should have two principal purposes. The first, as suggested above, is to appear in the Middle East with a broad appeal to all its peoples, not just as the backer of a few allies and friends such as Israel or Saudi Arabia or Iran. The second is to consolidate and expand whatever common interests it can establish with the Soviet Union: in keeping the peace, in arms control, or in cooperation for the economic development of the area. Progress in those directions could conceivably lead to a situation approaching general détente.

Assumption 3: General Détente

There are two ways in which a general détente might come about in the Middle East. The superpowers might decide that the region was no longer crucial to their security; having introduced bipolarity with all its consequences, presumably they could reduce it by a gradual process of relaxation. Or they might undertake the more difficult and constructive task of building a new international order in the Middle East.

In the first case they might simply reduce their commitments and their concern with local affairs, allowing local problems to be dealt with by the states of the area, and local disputes to flicker or to flame, without feeling the need for competitive action or for intervention except in situations where their joint guarantees were involved. One difficulty is that each would tend to wait for the other to demonstrate its noninterest first, and much would depend on what happens elsewhere than in the Middle East. If a greater stability could be achieved in their own bilateral strategic relationship and in Europe and other areas, the leadership in both countries might be less concerned with the threat posed by the other to its security in the Middle East. A contributing factor would be the tendency of Middle East states themselves to loosen or reduce their military ties with the two powers. If Turkey and Iran moved gradually toward a more neutral, buffer-state position and the radical Arab states restored a balance in their relations with the Soviet Union and the West, a certain decoupling of the large and small cold wars could take place.

In the second case, that of joint efforts to build a stable international order, the two powers would have to develop the means and the will to act in concert to control threats to the peace and to attack the causes of insecurity and war. It is hard to imagine the United States and the Soviet Union having sufficiently close cooperation to take up this approach as a joint policy, no matter how much the spirit of détente may soften past attitudes. If settlements between Israel and its Arab neighbors or among other states of the region were backed by four-power guarantees, then something like the old "Concert of Europe" might come into being, but one may doubt the Soviet government's willingness to function as one among four. If the United States and the USSR choose to work together, they would more likely do so in the United Nations, thus giving the world organization an authority to act in the Middle East more effectively than it has been able to in the past. In this way certain Western European, Asian, and other nations would be in a position to take part and to share some of the responsibilities. Over time, the United States might hope that most Middle East states would find it less promising to play off the outside powers against one another than to look for security and economic cooperation to a group of such powers acting together through the United Nations.

Two major questions would remain, even under the dream-like picture of collaboration just conjured up. One is the predictable unwillingness of certain Middle East states to accept a new order in the region which seemed to stack the cards against them. For example, Israel would have doubts about a system in which it would be dependent on a world concert for its continuing security against growing Arab strength, especially since both the Soviet Union and the United States might favor the Arabs. Israel might insist on keeping the guarantees of its security in its own hands and thus try to force the United States into a continuing pro-Israel and anti-Arab policy. Another possible example is Iran, which might be determined to pursue a policy of hegemony in the Persian Gulf region; to that end it might strive to get support from one or another great power, or simply ignore them all.

A second question concerns the amount of change that may be expected in Soviet leadership and policy over the next decade. The kind of general détente postulated here would signify a major change, not only an erosion of doctrine on national liberation movements, the struggle against imperialism and all that, but a real shift in thinking about the Middle East and its strategic, geopolitical significance to the role of Russia as a great power. Such a change could possibly take place in the context of an overall détente with the United States affecting all parts of the world, and of a Soviet acceptance of the idea that the real problems of the future could be met only through cooperation of the advanced industrial states to cope with strife, poverty, and chaos in the rest of the world. Some individuals in the Soviet Union are thinking in those terms, but their reflection in attitudes of governmental and party authorities is not discernible.

Soviet Search for Security

PHILIP E. MOSELY

One way to organize an attempted projection of the Soviet search for security and influence in the Middle East over any arbitrarily selected period, say, the next ten years, is to visualize two extreme possibilities. One extreme may be called the cataclysmic, the other the utopian. Although both projections represent overstatements, each of these possibilities may be projected by a close but selective scrutiny of Soviet ways of thinking about Moscow's role in world politics. Indeed, at each shift in the political environment Lenin systematically resorted to the device of defining a maximum program and a minimum program, and Soviet thinking about policy is deeply marked by Lenin's political genius.

Obviously, for a convinced Soviet Communist the maximum program in the Middle East of the next decade is a drastic one. It would end the risky and costly cold war of the past two decades by inflicting decisive political defeats on the United States, thereby expelling American influence from one area after another. In the Middle East, the ultimate goal would presumably be a Communist-led federation or confederation of the entire region, or perhaps a subconfederation or a sub-federation of the Arab countries. Each country would in turn be governed by a Communist party, and all the parties would be generally obedient to Soviet influence and to applying the Soviet pattern, with some adjustments, to the reconstruction of their societies. Western influence and power would, of course, be extruded from the area. The oil of the area would be organized under a regional monopoly in order to exact favorable terms of trade from Britain and Western Europe, which might still need it, and to exert political pressure upon West European policy.

In this "maximum" situation, Israel might conceivably be preserved but it would be confined within narrow and indefensible boundaries, without defenses or power of its own. It would probably come under some form of Soviet protection, and under Soviet-style planning it might serve as a highly skilled sweatshop to help pay the costs of industrializing the Arab countries. Since the Soviet leadership attaches great importance to the Brezhnev doctrine enunciated in September 1968, and by it reserves to itself (or "the international Communist movement") the ultimate right to determine which Communist parties or regimes are pursuing truly "internationalist" policies, the Kremlin would be able to make its political interests and its political strategy the dominant factor throughout the Middle East. Soviet exponents of doctrine would determine whether a given Communist regime within the region was or was not in good odor with Moscow. A united and Communist Middle East would also, of course, open broad highways for extending Soviet influence westward into North Africa, eastward into South Asia, and southward into Central Africa.

This, one should hasten to point out, is not an operational Soviet program of today. But behind and beyond each minimum program there must be some grander vision, and the day-to-day actions must not be inconsistent with the larger goals. Within Communism the leading elite is trained to believe in the sole right of Communists to rule, and their claim to a monopoly of power rests on the insistence of Marxist-Leninist doctrine that its loyal and correct adherents possess and act upon a uniquely correct interpretation of the course of history. In an ideocracy such as Communism, it is the possession of the correct ideology, plus the will to act on it, that justifies the use of vast amounts of force against one's own and other peoples. A Communist leader who says that there is some truth in other, non-Communist, ideas would forfeit the right to rule.

While Communist leaders must believe in the desirability and the inevitability of the doctrinally maximal program, they operate at any given time within an extremely complex setting and in both cooperation and conflict with many forces that are beyond their own control. Yet, even when Communist leaders dream of achieving the maximum goals they may suffer from certain doubts and qualms. They may wonder at times whether it would, in fact, be advantageous to the power of the Soviet state, and to their own leadership, to extend Communism throughout the Middle East. For one thing, the Soviet state would thereby take upon itself a moral obligation to modernize the economies and raise greatly the standard of living of very large populations. Any prolonged delay in achieving these benefits might be politically dangerous, and to achieve fairly rapid and striking results would exact great sacrifices from the Soviet economy and the Soviet people. It is doubtful that the Soviet Union can afford to undertake the industrialization of a large number of underdeveloped areas of the world.

If the Soviet Union were to succeed in enrolling a large number of poorly endowed countries, with their vast needs, ambitions, and frustrations, under the banner of Communism, this would certainly impose tremendous burdens on the economic and organizational resources of the Soviet Union and would tend to slow down its own development and the achievement of a more satisfactory standard of living for its own people. This dilemma has already caused grave political embarrassments and severe political losses to the Soviet leadership. When Mao Tse-tung insisted that the Soviet Union should slow down its own rate of economic growth in order to provide vast assistance to the "fraternal" Chinese people and thus enable China to enter the idyllic stage of "full Communism" arm-in-arm with Russia, the Soviet leaders pointed out with some bitterness that this was not a reasonable claim. The charges of "bourgeois degeneration," levied by Communist China against the Soviet Union, are only one reflection of this bitter argument over the nature and extent of the "proletarian internationalist duty" of the Soviet Union toward the Chinese People's Republic.

There will be other risks and dangers to the power and prestige of the Soviet Union if its maximum program in the Middle East is achieved. Once a generation or two come to maturity under a Communist system, the new generation may no longer give automatic obedience to Soviet dictates or Soviet whims. Indeed, the Soviet leadership might be reluctant to promote the development of a Middle East or an Arab federation or confederation. A consolidated region-wide leadership, created in place of numerous small rival states, might assert its independence of Soviet power that much more effectively. A precedent can be found in the history of Southeast Europe since World War II. After having advocated the creation of a Balkan Communist Federation as a major goal over more than two decades, the Soviet leadership since 1947 has been deeply suspicious of any attempts to form any groupings that might escape in some degree from its close supervision.

The emergence of Soviet-certified Communist regimes in a number of historic nations of Muslim culture might even have some repercussions—undesirable from the standpoint of Soviet power—within the Soviet Union. A large confederation of basically Muslim tradition might come to exert a considerable influence among the nearly thirty million people of Muslim background within the Soviet Republics of Azarbayjan, Uzbekistan, Turkmenistan, and Tajikistan. The emergence of a large new center of attraction to the south of Soviet Central Asia could conceivably upset the balance of social and political forces there, with potentially serious disadvantages to the Soviet state and its prestige.

Finally, any systematic and deliberate Soviet effort to achieve the maximum program might prove cataclysmic in another and undesirable sense. It might well lead to a nuclear war with the United States, and, of course, in that case, all reliable predictions about the future location and structure of world power are simply impossible. So it may safely be assumed that the maximum program is not a Soviet goal at present, but is rather a picture of what the Kremlin leaders dream of as an ultimate but remote achievement of complete and lasting security. Anything short of that may be regarded by them as an unstable or incomplete fulfillment of an ideal system, but they have constantly tempered their utopian dreams to take account of hard facts.

The opposite extreme is the hope for a détente which would lead out of the present situation of turbulence, uncertainties, and perils into a period of genuine peace. In a Western definition of détente, this would mean, basically, consolidating and improving the status quo, lessening and removing the present dangers to peace, and finding cooperative solutions to the national and social strains of the area. Basically, détente would require acceptance of the status quo by the Soviet Union and putting a halt to the recent expansion of its influence. This program might be initiated through an agreed limitation of the arms race within the Middle East, a step that the United

States has urged directly and indirectly for many years, so far to no avail. Another cornerstone of détente would be to bring about a negotiated settlement of the Arab-Israel conflict, with or without a great-power guarantee. Under any such settlement Israel would be assured of its right to exist within agreed boundaries and with an accepted international status. For the Arab countries this would mean accepting a settlement which would give them far less than they now claim, for they have been adamant in rejecting Israel's existence or its right to exist. Acceptance of a settlement would at least give the Arab nations a long period of relative stability, perhaps under some type of international guarantee, and this might set free human and economic resources to promote and sustain a more rapid process of development.

The major factor in a stable, long-term and agreed policy of détente would be a large-scale cooperative program of assistance to the Middle East, to help its peoples achieve their full human and material potential. Obviously, the cost of such a program of cooperative assistance would be much less than the waste and risks of continuing great-power rivalries and local conflicts; its cost would be immeasurably less than that of a single hour of nuclear warfare. An effective and consistent policy of détente would constitute a beneficent and reliable program of cooperation between the United States and the Soviet Union, with assistance from other advanced countries and from international organizations. A policy of full and lasting détente might, however, appear to people in the Middle East as an unwelcome political consortium or condominium of the two strongest powers, for even its beneficent purposes would limit severely their freedom of maneuver and action.

The dream of a complete détente is one that the Soviet Union does not share, but perhaps it could see in a partial détente some advantages for itself. There are a few hopeful precedents. At Tashkent Premier Alexei Kosygin did succeed in persuading India and Pakistan to put an end to their direct military conflict. All the world, except Communist China and Albania, applauded this statesmanlike initiative, which also served Soviet interests, logically enough. Yet even when Soviet and United States policies have run along parallel lines, as in the Tashkent settlement, the Soviet leadership has taken great pains to differentiate its policy from that of the United States. It remains sensitive to any accusation that it may be diluting its ideological purity or relaxing its insistence on the uniquely righteous or self-righteous quality of its own goals.

Furthermore, the Kremlin is clearly nervous about consorting openly with a status quo power such as the United States. In its simultaneous efforts both to deal with the United States as one great power with another and to mobilize on its side the discontented and disinherited of the world, it must constantly keep one eye cocked to the Chinese Communists, waiting impatiently on the sidelines to recruit potentially revolutionary forces for which the Soviet Union is becoming a satisfied and middle-aged regime. Just because United States and Soviet policies today run along parallel lines in a few areas, the Soviet Union is especially sensitive to Peking's raucous accusations of having entered into an agreement either for joint rule or condominium in world politics or for a division of spheres in complicity with "American imperialism." Thus, there are grave disadvantages and future risks, in the eyes of the Kremlin, in seeking or accepting a genuine détente in the Middle East. Détente would mean adoption by the Soviet leadership of a self-denying ordinance and Soviet support for the status quo at a time when the balance of influence in the Middle East is changing in favor of Soviet prestige and goals. It would imply the denial by the Soviet leaders of the validity of their doctrine, just at a time when Soviet policy can hope to make significant new gains, in addition to those it has chalked up since 1955. Détente may be a Western pipe dream; it is a Soviet nightmare.

Since neither the cataclysmic nor the utopian extreme can have much current attraction for the Kremlin, the most likely prospect is for the continuation of the present in-between situation, neither peace and stability nor all-out war. The in-between status has certain limiting if not stabilizing factors built into it. One is the Soviet and American desire to avoid being trapped into a nuclear war. Both the Russians and the Americans miscalculate frequently, and perhaps Soviet miscalculations have occurred more often. On the other hand, Soviet policy has recovered more quickly from its miscalculations, as witnessed by its quick footwork in the months since the June 1967 war.

Soviet commitments in the Middle East, though growing, have remained limited. The Kremlin has so far not committed itself to achieve goals for any client state that it could not achieve for itself with limited amounts of Soviet aid—political, military, and economic. There has been no direct military participation by Soviet forces in struggles within the area. Even the few exceptions to this rule have tended to confirm it. After the withdrawal of Egyptian forces from Yemen, Soviet pilots were reported to have taken a brief part in combat and then to have been recalled. It is possible, however, that Yemeni pilots were talking Russian to each other, because they had been trained in Russia, just as in the Korean War there were Korean pilots who communicated with ground stations in Russian. Whatever minor exceptions have been detected, the Russians have so far been careful to avoid any military participation in Middle East conflicts. The Soviet Union recognizes, as it did in June 1967, the importance of maintaining a firebreak between local conflicts and a potentially global conflict, and it has so far avoided taking the first steps in the path that could lead to a United States-Soviet confrontation in or over the Middle East.

There is one other factor of the recent past that may provide some grounds for optimism. While the Soviet Union has had a relatively short period of experience in the Middle East, its leaders seem to have been learning new lessons fairly rapidly in the years since 1955. Issues that they pressed hard have been relegated to obscurity when they proved unproductive of advantage to Soviet policy. For a number of years Soviet propaganda gave all-out support to the Afghan claims to a large part of West Pakistan, to the Pushtunistan concept. In recent years nothing more has been heard in the Soviet press or radio about these claims, and the Soviet government is now courting Pakistan with great ardor, much to the disappointment of many Indians. In a similar instance, for many years the Soviet government gave full support to the Indian view in the dispute over Kashmir. Later, as it reexamined its own interests, the Kremlin withdrew to a position of evenhanded finger-shaking, parallel to the British and American positions. The Soviet Union gave vigorous backing to Greek claims against Turkey over the Cyprus problem; more recently it has adopted a position which is sufficiently uncommitted to satisfy both or neither side.

In the light of these precedents, it is possible that some day the Soviet Union may decide to adopt a more evenhanded stance in the Arab-Israel conflict and may attach serious significance to the cooperative search for an agreed or even a guaranteed solution. In the later months of 1968 the Soviet press has, on occasions, issued critical warnings to its Arab allies. It has attacked the frequent Arab appeals to destroy Israel and has maintained that Israel exists and will continue to exist. It has criticized Arab appeals for an early war of revenge, pointing out that such threats make it less likely that Israel would agree to withdraw to its prewar boundaries. In late 1968 the Soviet press expressed clear disapproval of the Arab commando movements; such attacks, if persisted in, could bring new defeats on several Arab states. Incidentally, the Soviet process of self-education is sometimes reflected in changes of political personnel. After the Arab miscalculations and defeats of mid-1967, several Soviet subleaders who had previously been identified with Moscow's policy toward the UAR were suddenly demoted or transferred to functions remote from the problems of Soviet policy in the Arab world.

Soviet policy in the Middle East is heavily concentrated today on the Arab-Israel conflict, with its great stakes and its unpredictable range of future perils. But Soviet policy is broader and more diverse in its concepts and methods. Ever since the reign of Peter the Great, Russian, and now Soviet, policy has given great attention to its three immediate neighbors in Western Asia. In recent years the Soviet Union has continued to be the most important outside factor in Afghanistan's strenuous program of development. It has more recently adopted a policy of reconciliation and cooperation with both Turkey and Iran. Having recognized and reversed the mistakes of Stalin's time, the Soviet Union has been striving actively to demonstrate a friendly attitude toward Turkey and Iran and thus to encourage them to adopt a less committed position, which in turn makes them less dependent on American support and therefore on American policy.

The new Soviet policy is making some valuable contributions to the economic and social development of all three of its southern neighbors. By removing the Soviet bogey, the Kremlin can overcome their yearning, so strong since 1945, for a firm United States guarantee. Domestic issues and social demands, muted perforce in a period of national danger, have reemerged within Turkey and Iran. This in turn encourages a turning-inward, a primary concern with domestic issues, and, with that, a process of decommitment or depolarization in world politics. It is not clear that the sudden Soviet invasion of Czechoslovakia, in August 1968, has checked, within Turkey or Iran, the turning toward a psychological though not diplomatic detachment from the great-power conflict. In any case, in a period of grave conflicts, both recent and potential, in the Arab-Israel zone, it is clearly to Soviet advantage to reassure its direct southern neighbors that these clashes and alarums have no direct significance for their relations with the Soviet Union by turning to them an untroubled and benevolent visage.

In the Arab-Israel zone, the prospect is for "no war, no peace," but perhaps for greater Soviet caution. After the drastic failure of Soviet political estimates in 1967, Moscow has been reviewing its past policies, as well as canvassing the use of new methods. The Western press has written a good deal about the large number of Soviet advisers that are now in the UAR, estimated to be between 3,000 and 5,000. This innovation is clearly designed to assure more efficient use by the UAR of the very large Soviet supply of military and economic aid; it may increase both Soviet influence over Egyptian policies and Soviet commitment to Egyptian goals. Soviet advisers are reported to be solidly ensconced in their positions. Soviet management experts are said to be actively engaged in efforts to improve the operations of Soviet-supplied and state-owned enterprises in order to make them into a source of strength, rather than serving as a drain on the economy as a whole. After the June 1967 war the Soviet press attacked the Egyptian upper-class bureaucrats and called for a "truly revolutionary deepening" of the UAR regime. It also drew attention to the "merits" of the Egyptian Communists and criticized the continuing policy of repressing Communists and excluding them from positions of influence.

Moscow's reliance on large numbers of its own bureaucrats to strengthen the UAR may or may not turn out to be effective. It seems doubtful that Moscow would go so far as to organize a political-military cabal or coup within the UAR power structure. Yet continuous interference within 'Abd al-Nasir's military and economic apparatus is likely to irritate and anger potential Egyptian leaders, rather than persuading them to place their political future in Moscow's hands. In addition, Soviet bureaucrats are often heavy-handed, stubborn in insisting that Moscow's way of doing things is the only correct way, and insensitive to local customs and national pride. Having gotten rid only recently of the British advisers and officers, who were by comparison gentlemanly, worldly, and often pro-Arab in outlook, the cultivated and sophisticated educated class in the UAR will not find it easy to accept the airs of self-righteous and provincial superiority typically displayed by Soviet bureaucrats.

Another factor that may make a policy of caution more attractive in the Kremlin is its growing concern over the high cost of a number of its foreign policies. The annual cost of its support for Castro, in uncompensated deliveries, is estimated to be running at about $350 million a year, and yet Castro's aims and methods in Latin America, and even in some African countries, run directly counter to the Soviet line within the Communist movement. Large Soviet investments in support of its policies in Indonesia and Ghana have gone down the drain. In its advice to radical African regimes, as in Guinea, Soviet commentators have even issued strong warnings against the hasty confiscation of "imperialist" enterprises. They have even urged some developing countries to seek Western support for their development and for strengthening their ability to export and to earn foreign exchange. Soviet spokesmen have said rather bluntly that simply confiscating Western enterprises is not in itself a progressive step; it may lead to a decline in production and to higher costs, thereby undermining the prestige of the "socialist path."

The Soviet leaders today show a visible sensitivity about explaining to their own people that, when they provide large credits to a developing country, they are also laying the basis for a future increase of exports to the Soviet Union, as a means of eventually compensating the Soviet economy and the Soviet consumer for their current sacrifices. Visitors to the Soviet Union report a rather widespread resentment against foreign aid, against the diversion of resources to other countries, at a time when the Soviet Union itself is in many ways still a relatively underdeveloped country.

Finally, there is the question of the relative power-vacuum that has been emerging in the Middle East, and the related question whether the vacuum will necessarily be filled by the injection of Soviet strategic and political power. At present the overall strategic balance in world politics is not favorable to a direct insertion of Soviet military power or direct Soviet control into the Arab-Israel zone. The relative strategic weight of the Soviet Union has been growing, but it is not clear that it will ever achieve a clearcut preponderance. The indirect growth of Soviet influence has been marked and is continuing, but one cannot predict at this time that any Arab country, even Syria or Yemen, will surrender to Soviet influence its own power of decision. So far the radical Arab states have exploited Soviet influence and Soviet resources for their own purposes. The main advantage derived by Soviet policy has been the knowledge that Western influences have been retreating and that its own influence—along with responsibilities—has been growing. Yet, we must not forget that Western influences had declined markedly even before the Soviet government embarked on its activist course in 1955.

The basic problem in the Middle East is whether the relative power-vacuum of the present will be filled by forces injected from outside the area or by the growth of indigenous forces working to develop their own strengths. Basically, power means the ability to provide security for one's own people and to satisfy its expectations. In these respects both Turkey and Iran have demonstrated their ability to grow from within and thus to avoid being engulfed in a power-vacuum. The countries of the Arab-Israel zone are not in this relatively happy situation. Since they are involved in a presently unresolvable escalation of claims and hatreds, they invite, even demand, the injection of outside support and resources. If conflicts in the Arab-Israel zone can be kept or brought within the realm of peaceful means of resolution, then there will be no power-vacuum, and there will be no inrush of strategic power from outside the region. The United States has generally sought to promote peace and stability in the Middle East both because the preservation of the status quo has been more favorable to its interests and sentiments than any conceivable alternative and because it has seen that an intensified conflict within the Arab-Israel zone only serves to exasperate or multiply the intraregional demand for intervention by outside powers, in particular by the Soviet Union.

In any fair and peaceful competition the West, and in particular the United States, would not need to fear the growing Soviet presence in the Middle East. The West provides, potentially, the biggest and most profitable markets for the exports of the region, the best sources of technology and management skills, and the main opportunity for the Middle East to benefit from international economic specialization. Indeed, the Soviet Union recognizes its own need to benefit from Western technology and management science. The cultural and educational facilities and traditions offered by the West are more attractive than Soviet models to people in the Middle East. After all, these are people with centuries of cultural and historical achievement behind them, and they have their own ideas about how best to overcome the temporary lag in their ability to assert their role in the world.

The West has another important advantage. It accepts the idea and the goal of full national self-determination in the Middle East, as elsewhere. The last doubt on that score was dissipated by the clear United States stand in the Suez crisis of 1956. The Soviet Union accepts the same stated goal of national self-fulfillment, but it does so within the confines of Communist dogma, to which it now attaches the ominous Brezhnev corollary of September 1968. According to this recent restatement of Soviet doctrine, national self-determination is vouchsafed to a Communist regime or party within limits set for it by Soviet interests and by Soviet interpretations of what is permitted or not permitted to non-Soviet Communists.

The one thing the Soviet Union offers, and the West does not, is a simple or simplistic recipe for rapid social evolution, or revolution, under total political control. The Soviet example, and Soviet doctrine, may persuade some people in the Middle East that, under the Communist recipe, they can achieve a military power disproportionate to their population and their economic resources, and that they can thereby achieve a political role greater than their natural strength would otherwise support. This promise of power may prove to be attractive to some key groups in the Middle East. The Soviet Union can add to that revolutionary recipe the backing of its military power, its naval presence, its economic strength, and its political support. Basically, aside from this one major and not-to-be-underestimated attraction offered by Soviet policy, the vacuum of power in the Middle East can and should be filled by the peoples of the region. One of the main tasks of United States policy thinking must be to examine each of its own policies to be sure it is helping the peoples of the Middle East to move, however uncertainly and erratically, toward achieving their goal of national self-fulfillment through peaceful and constructive methods.

Persistence of Regional Quarrels

MALCOLM H. KERR

The Middle East is an area fraught with its own internal deep-seated problems and conflicts which are not more than marginally susceptible to management from the outside. It is an unstable area par excellence. This instability has naturally attracted the intervention of both cold war superpowers, but in different ways, on different premises, and with different results for each. The United States has largely—if not altogether consciously—sought to inherit the British role, with modifications of style rather than substance. It has imagined that it was moving into something called a "power vacuum," only to find that politically if not militarily speaking, much of the region, somewhat like a boiling pot, offered the very opposite of a vacuum: everything in flux, at a high temperature. Hence the United States burned its fingers. The Soviet Union, by contrast, has sought not so much to intervene in the cooking process within the pot as to warm its hands above the fire.

What this rough analogy is intended to suggest is that the political processes of the region are not subject to very much manipulation. It is not within the power of outsiders to adjust the flame under the pot to their liking, let alone turn it off, nor to determine the contents. Some fuel can be added or withheld from time to time, and some seasoning; but the basic processes and components of Middle East politics are there as given. One can only try to examine the limited possible effects of competitive versus coordinated efforts by the superpowers to interfere.

I

Little need be said about the affairs of Turkey, Iran, Pakistan, and Afghanistan before moving on to areas of more critical contemporary concern. The author sees no chance that the relatively tranquil international position of the border states (except Pakistan) can provide any clues regarding the future of the Arabs and the Israelis, or guidelines for great power policies toward them.

Each of the border states except Pakistan, unlike most of the Arab countries, is a reasonably self-contained and coherent national society. While three of them have formal treaty ties with the United States and are at least nominally its military allies, all four have also evolved fairly stable relations with the Soviet Union. Admittedly, in each case there are certain potential dangers which could upset the stability of its external relations (Pakistan's quarrel with India, Turkey's quarrel over Cyprus, internal opposition to the shah's regime in Iran, Afghanistan's ethnic divisions), there is no particular reason to believe that any existing or likely future regime would seriously try to attract the involvement of either superpower in its problems more than is already the case, or that either superpower would welcome an opportunity to force its own way in.

One exception might seem to be Pakistan, but here the deterrent lies in the efforts of both Moscow and Washington to cultivate good relations with India. Another more serious exception might be Iran. Should the shah's regime collapse (although there is no sign at this moment that it is in danger of doing so), and particularly should a successor regime be confronted with serious internal divisions, as well it might, one faction or another might feel strongly tempted to appeal for Soviet assistance. The Soviet Union might find the temptation to intervene overwhelming. American intervention, on the other hand, seems a ludicrously implausible eventuality, especially in the aftermath of Vietnam; and it is not at all clear what the Soviet Union would really hope to accomplish, other than a renewal of unwanted previous tensions with Turkey.

The loosening of the cold war alliances of Turkey, Iran, and Pakistan with the United States and their building of better relations with the Soviet Union has not, after all, reflected the instability or vulnerability of their international postures, so much as gradual drift toward normalization. The alliances are gradually becoming obsolete, and no one mourns the fact. The most likely prospect, therefore, appears to be that Turkey, Iran, and (with luck) Pakistan will increasingly become what Afghanistan has been all along: stable buffer zones, making visible and reasonably harmonious progress, which neither Moscow nor Washington wishes to see disturbed.

II

Just as there are multiple arms races in the Middle East, so also are there multiple political divisions among the Arab states. The most spectacular and familiar is of course that which separates the revolutionary from the more conservative regimes: the UAR, Syria, Algeria, Iraq, the Yemen Republic, and South Yemen on one side, and Saudi Arabia, Jordan, Kuwayt, Lebanon, Libya, Tunisia, and Morocco on the other. The two groups are far from monolithic, and the solidarity of the members of each group ebbs and flows according to circumstance. Lebanon, for instance, has tried traditionally to avoid being identified with any faction, despite the undeniable conservatism of her own internal political and socioeconomic structure and of her international relationships. At the present moment, furthermore, the UAR and Jordan are closely aligned in their common adversity at the hands of Israel, while the relations of the UAR with the militant Syrian and Algerian regimes are rather distant.

Still, it seems sensible to assume that the radical-conservative division is a long-term, deeply rooted reality that will persist, in varying degrees of intensity, well into the future. The division arises, after all, not simply out of tactical diplomatic jockeying but out of an internal social, cultural, economic, psychological, and moral crisis within Arab society as a whole, a crisis that expresses itself most dramatically in political terms. It is a crisis of legitimacy and authority, of participation and representation, of collective self-identification and self-assertion, of social equality and economic welfare, and many other things. Mixed into this, of course, is a large component of ambition, opportunism, self-delusion, and vested interest on the part of old and new leadership groups. But one should not allow his recognition of these things to blind him to the historic reality of the revolutionary movement and the issues of principle, outlook, and program which it raises. One must assume that regardless of the comings and goings of individual leaders and regardless of the policies of outside powers, these issues will continue to undermine the tranquillity of individual Arab states and of their relations with one another and with the great powers. No relationship of the radical military dictatorships with either the neighboring monarchies or with the United States has much prospect of being close for long. Still, neither must these relations always be hostile. Whether they are depends on the shifts in other conflicts and alignments in the area, as well as in the international cold war itself.

Another inter-Arab conflict has been evident in the long series of quarrels within the Arab left over the years: among Communists, Nasirists, Ba'thists of various stripes, and nonparty groupings such as the regime of 'Abd al-Karim Qasim. During most of President 'Abd al-Nasir's period of rule in the UAR, for instance, he has been in conflict with one or another enemy on the left, and often with several at once. These conflicts have frequently been explained by their participants in ideological terms, with one's rival being castigated as insufficiently revolutionary, antinationalist, atheistic, undemocratic, and the like. But it is probably more to the point simply to characterize them as rivalries for leadership, within a pattern of conflicting ambition and mutual mistrust of which Arab society has long had more than its share, for historical and cultural reasons that one need not try to explore here. It goes without saying that conflicts of this kind have not been confined to the left, but over the past decade it has been among the radicals, rather than among conservatives, that feuds have been most in evidence. There is good reason for this, reason which has every prospect of asserting itself in the future as it did in the past. The conservatives operate within a more or less clearly settled pattern of authority, values, and constraints. Their ambitions are limited by definition: to preserve and consolidate what they can of the existing social, political, and territorial order. Their aims are easily compatible with one another. The old days when the Sa'udis quarrelled with the Hashimis and the Hamid al-Dins over legitimacy and territory are surely gone.

The radicals, by contrast, are an array of individualists whose ambitions seem to be commensurate with the obscurity of their backgrounds and the uncertainty of the foundations of their political support. "Today, Hamah; tomorrow, the world" hardly seems a plausible proposition, yet the man from Hamah who seizes power in Damascus—and immediately must worry about some rival from Latakiyah—is unlikely to be content to sit quietly and resist the impulse to deliver an ecumenical message. Indeed, so great is the impatience with mundane local problems, and the preoccupation with transcendent causes, that the more appropriate slogan might be "to-day, the world; tomorrow, Hamah." Ambitious men from the Hamahs, Latakiyahs, Kirkuks and other obscure corners of Arab society have come and gone with great rapidity, and have shown a considerable tendency to get in one another's way as they vie for leadership, prestige, and political support. It is hardly to be expected that they should close ranks according to some yet undiscovered orderly pattern merely because workers, peasants, intellectuals, or Soviet diplomats wish they would do so.

Parties to these rivalries have often sought tactical support from within the conservative Arab camp. As long as 'Abd al-Nasir was quarrelling with Qasim and the Syrian Ba'thists; he tried to mend his fences with Husayn and Sa'ud; he sent Egyptian troops to protect the Shaykh of Kuwayt; he maintained an alignment with Imam of Yemen. These liaisons quickly vanished after the 1961 Syrian secession, but some of them were revived in the "Arab summit" period of 1964-1965 after 'Abd al-Nasir's fight with the Ba'thists had broken out again, under different circumstances, in 1963. Again the ties to the monarchies were broken in 1966 under the pressure of the continuing Yemen war and the rise of Faysal's "Islamic Pact," until the war with Israel in 1967 introduced drastic changes in the scenario.

It seems clear, then, that in the years prior to the June war, while the radicals and the monarchs were incapable of building sustained cooperation, so were the radicals among themselves. The solidarity of the left against the right showed itself only in the period of opposition to the Baghdad Pact and the Eisenhower Doctrine in the years 1955-1958, and again in 1966 and early 1967, after the erosion of Egyptian-American relations culminating in the termination of American surplus food sales. Correspondingly, it was primarily in these two periods of radical-conservative polarization among the Arab states, that the two superpowers were most closely drawn in.

There appears to be a mutually reinforcing relationship of cause and effect here, with both local and outside powers looking for partners to assist them in securing their own objectives. This is not the place to assess the wisdom of American involvement in local Middle East alignments, but it is relevant to draw attention to the considerable sensitivity of both conservative and radical Arab regimes to what they perceive about American intentions. The conservatives, who feel threatened by the Red Tide of radicalism and feel impelled to lay a claim on American protection, have an "orphan complex," while the radicals, who imagine that the CIA is about to engineer their encirclement or overthrow, and who then rush to Moscow for countervailing support, have a conspiracy complex. This process of escalating bipolarity that was evident in the 1955-1958 and 1966-1967 periods was stimulated in both instances by local ideologically defined divisions ('Abd al-Nasir vs. Nuri, and 'Abd al-Nasir vs. Faysal) into which the British and American governments were dismayingly ready to jump, thereby increasing the attraction for Soviet involvement on the other side.

Admittedly, given the chronic problems of the region, and with the great powers at any given time inheriting commitments from previous years, it may be too much to expect them to take positive steps to avoid getting dragged in on opposite sides of radical-conservative quarrels even if they should prefer not to. A mere lack of will by the great powers to make matters worse cannot suffice to make them better, for the dynamics of local instability not being of their making, neither can they be of their unmaking. The radical-conservative split, however, is one which generally has provided much better opportunities and fewer risks to the Soviet Union than to the United States. It is therefore hypothetical at best to refer to a common desire among the powers to minimize this sort of conflict and to abstain from involvement in it. One can only say that even if Russia lost some of its interest or its tactical opportunities in the radical Arab movement, this would only reduce the prospect of the superpowers' being drawn in against their better judgment.

In the absence of a substantial détente with the USSR, the United States has attempted periodically to head off confrontations of Arab radicals and conservatives by cultivating its relationships on the radical side—primarily with the UAR, and most notably during periods when 'Abd al-Nasir, for reasons of his own, was already at odds with other Arab leftists and too embroiled in other difficulties to follow as activist a foreign policy as his inclinations might otherwise have dictated. It will be no surprise should some such liaison reemerge in the future under certain circumstances; but it should be even less of a surprise if subsequently it again collapses. For as the United States has learned by past experience, there are few stable bargains to be had with the Arab radicals, whose political bases and policy aims are unstable and whose constituencies respond most readily to a defiant posture toward the Western powers. Those who clung to the hope that 'Abd al-Nasir and other revolutionary leaders would see their interest in concentrating, with American help, on poverty, ignorance, and disease, to the exclusion of disruptive political adventures, simply failed to perceive the restlessness, frustration, and insecurity that have contributed so vitally to the dynamics of left-wing Arab politics.

However, the inability of the United States to do much to restrain conflict between the Arab left and right, together with the lack of interest of the Soviet Union in doing so, need not mean that the conflict will proceed unabated, for there are other likely restraints. One is the jealousy and mistrust which the radicals feel toward one another. A second is the problem of Israel, whose impact upon the Arab states tends on the whole to blur rather than sharpen the ideological differences among them.

One could therefore draw an ambiguous conclusion. The continuation of general tension between the superpowers, or even the absence of more than a de facto détente, undoubtedly leaves us with some dangerous prospects of reescalation arising out of inter-Arab conflicts. But these prospects are not inevitable. They are likely to come and go in accordance with unpredictable tactical shifts in the regional alignments of Arab regimes largely unrelated to Soviet and American policies; and whether they escalate beyond the local stage may depend heavily on the extent of American willingness to run the risks of inaction and to avoid the temptation to counter every Soviet effort to capitalize on inter-Arab conflicts. In any case, one's ability to forecast the strategic environment is beclouded by the completely open question of who will be ruling in any Arab capital at any given time in the future.

What of a significant détente between the superpowers, in which positive and coordinated efforts were made in Washington and Moscow to damp down inter-Arab tensions? In the first place it strikes this writer as most implausible that such an agreement should be reached, since it would seem to amount to a renunciation by the Soviet Union of its historic opportunity for influence in the Middle East, with nothing in return. More to the point is the question of what kind of meaningful agreement could be made. No one can guarantee the internal stability nor the external good-neighborliness, nor certainly the underlying freedom from anxiety, that would be required of Arab regimes. Nor, if the Arabs are going to continue to contend among themselves and appeal for outside assistance, can great powers really promise in advance that they will not respond to such appeals in as yet undefined situations. It would perhaps be easier for both superpowers to pledge not to become involved in Arab affairs, were they not both so deeply involved already.

A Soviet-American agreement to impose a particular solution to a particular territorial, economic, or legal quarrel might be expected to carry considerable weight—in persuading Syria to drop its claims to Alexandretta, for example, or in adjudicating individual aspects of the Arab-Israel problem. In the quarrels between Arab factions, however, there is little to adjudicate: the quarrels are over rival claims to legitimacy and fitness for leadership, and they rage within as well as between national societies. The power of outsiders to grant or withhold advanced weapons is a clumsy lever of control. Armaments have been used by contending Arab regimes mainly for purposes of prestige; indeed, in some Arab capitals the chief function of the tank has seemingly been to provide basic transportation, from the nearest army base to the presidential palace. Were the great powers miraculously to withdraw all the hardware they have supplied, Arab leaders would still be able to throw one another out of office and insult one another over the radio. This is perhaps the simplest reason why a détente has limited potential for stabilizing the inter-Arab scene.

Nonetheless, it seems undeniable that a general and overt Soviet-American rapprochement, even if not specifically applied to Middle East problems, would have some considerable psychological impact on contending Arab radical and conservative factions. For one thing, it would be likely to arouse suspicions in every faction's mind that the superpowers were plotting deals together at its expense. In this respect much would depend on the tenor of the détente elsewhere in the world. Presumably, however, a détente would have to carry some implication of the great powers' underwriting of the status quo, and thus of a Soviet abandonment of third-world revolutionaries. In the short run, this might be expected to take some of the steam out of the Arab left's efforts to undermine conservative regimes. Conversely, it might destroy the confidence of the conservatives who have felt dependent upon American sympathy. Or it might provide the Chinese with opportunities for involvement. A more likely prospect is that whatever understanding the superpowers thought they had developed in the Arab world would simply break down.

III

Unlike the Arab factions that contend for dominance, in the Arab-Israel confrontation both sides are vitally dependent upon outside support. The armaments they buy are actually used on occasion in full-scale warfare; the Israeli, Egyptian, and Jordanian economies are not viable without large-scale assistance; and the threat of Soviet or American military intervention is weighed in the balance in times of crisis.

These considerations create a prima facie argument that the great powers acting in concert could impose a settlement of some substantial kind on the Arab-Israel problem. One would have to assume, of course, that not only the two superpowers, but also lesser states like France, Britain, China, and others cooperated or at least effectively prevented disruption. To simplify the argument only the superpowers will be discussed here.

Disregarding for the moment the unlikelihood of a Soviet-American agreement to impose a solution, it does indeed appear that acting together the two powers could accomplish a great deal. They could force a measure of demilitarization on Israel and her neighbors; they could adjudicate questions of frontiers, navigation, and the settlement of refugees; they could extract pledges of nonaggression from both sides, and some form of at least de facto recognition of Israel from Egypt and Jordan. It is very doubtful that they could accomplish much more than this, such as the establishment of full diplomatic and commercial relations. Syria, Iraq, and other Arab states might remain as hostile as before; and in the end, Arab "acceptance" of Israel, and Israel's "de-Zionization," come down to nonnegotiable questions of moral attitude.

Still, to defuse the crisis would be a major feat. The difficulty might lie in some of the longer-term indirect effects of stuffing solutions down Middle East throats. It would mean a kind of return to the colonial era, with a great deal of policing to be done. The Russians and the Americans would collectively be assuming a role parallel in some ways to that of the British between the wars—a role that had its constructive aspects but was not altogether tranquil and certainly not widely appreciated in the Middle East. One could anticipate any number of unsettled problems raising their heads—disputes over the rights of Israeli Arabs, or over continued Jewish immigration, for example, similiar to those of the 1930s, but which this time would have to be dealt with on a continuing basis not by just one imperial power but two mutually suspicious powers together. Dissatisfied local parties would always seek opportunities to play the superpowers off against each other and to appeal beyond both of them to potential allies further afield. Such alignments, once established, would certainly bring in their wake a renewed division among the Arab states, with outside powers drawn in, and with no assurance that Moscow and Washington would be able to coordinate their response. The global structure of the détente could break down.

This speculation suggests that forced and unwanted solutions, even if America and Russia could ever agree on them, would run the risk of becoming unstuck in unforeseeable and explosive ways. It would make a difference on whom a solution was really being forced, and one can imagine a range of formulae relatively favorable to the Arabs or to Israel. It might be said that since it is the Arabs who are much the more numerous and widely distributed, their resentments against an imposed solution would be the most dangerous. It would be much easier to sit on dissatisfied Israelis than on dissatisfied Arabs, and therefore the solution should be a substantially pro-Arab one. But this was the position of the 1939 White Paper, issued on the basis of rather similar considerations, which did not survive the end of World War II. It serves to suggest that Russians and Americans together, like Britain alone during the mandate, might find Jews no easier to dictate to than Arabs. Again like the British, Americans—if not Russians—would surely lose the stomach for trying. Thus even an imposed pro-Arab settlement might not last.

In any case, this discussion is beside the point, for no Soviet-American agreement to liquidate the Palestine problem is remotely in prospect. Rather than asking what kind of solution might be imposed, it is more significant to ask what lesser steps (if any) are likely toward limiting the Arab-Israel conflict, under conditions of a partial or general Soviet-American détente.

Here the answer seems to be that there is not a great deal to hope for, because of the very considerable pressures that would have to come from both Moscow and Washington to accomplish much more than what little has been accomplished to date, i.e., the passage of the November 1967 Security Council resolution, with its ambiguous formula, and the not very hopeful mission of Ambassador Jarring. This mission, or a subsequent one, may yet succeed in liquidating the 1967 crisis, but the larger one would remain. However relaxed their relationship may become elsewhere in the world, and however unwelcome a new Middle East war might be to both of them, Russia and America are unlikely to accomplish more than to keep the pot somewhere below the boiling point.

Even with a détente the Arab animosity toward Israel and her supporters abroad provides too great an opportunity for the Soviet Union to ignore. Should the Soviets ignore it, Arab militants will certainly look elsewhere for support. But more than being an opportunity, association with the Arabs against Israel has been built up since 1955 as an ongoing Soviet investment, and therefore an obligation, which cannot lightly be discarded. Furthermore, this Soviet investment is closely tied to Moscow's deep interest in the future of the radical Arab regimes. To reformulate the point in its local context, one might say that whatever regime may rule five or ten years from now in Cairo or Damascus, the ongoing Arab radical political movement and the Arab Palestine cause are likely to continue to provide each other with special momentum. In so doing, they will continue to present difficulties for the United States, and commitments and opportunities for the Soviet Union. Meanwhile the United States carries a parallel historically based commitment to Israel. Neither of the local contenders will make it easy for its outside protector to disengage itself, even if the latter wishes to do so. May and June 1967 were excellent examples of the ability of client states in the Middle East to take their own initiatives, either against the advice of their patrons or without consulting them, and then to engage the full diplomatic support of their patrons in the aftermath of the crisis they had created.

Thus even under conditions of some degree of détente, the Arab-Israel problem must pose a continuing danger of open conflict in the Middle East to which the superpowers cannot agree in advance how they will react. Arabs and Israelis will threaten to engage Soviet and American interests and commitments whether the superpowers welcome it or not. The cold war has intruded into the Arab-Israel conflict, as it has into other conflicts in the region, because these conflicts defy solution or even stabilization; and as long as they continue to be unstable, it will be exceedingly difficult for Moscow and Washington to legislate their own extrication.

The converse of this argument is that if one assumes a continuing cold war in the world at large, it is doubtful that this would add much to the dangers that the Arab-Israel problem would already pose. The great powers and the local contenders have learned how to live with one another's conflicts—not happily, but tolerably—and one need not assume that they will not continue to do so.

There is, however, an imbalance of relationships, inasmuch as the Israelis have come to expect very little of anything from the Soviet Union, while both Jordan and the UAR have in the past expected a great deal from the United States, and may well develop further hopes in the future. The case of Jordan is rather obvious: she depended on American financial aid until the June war, and still depends on American arms supply. Besides, she is a monarchy. Of course the replacement of King Husayn by more radical elements could end the pattern, but this would be likely to leave Jordan in a relationship to the United States more similar to that of the UAR than that of Syria.

Syria has never needed or wanted anything from the United States: she is essentially immune to Israeli attack, apart from the Golan Heights which are of little consequence to her. Egypt and Jordan, by contrast, have both always been keenly aware that only the United States possesses a strong restraining influence over Israel —not strong enough, or without enough will to use it, they would say after 1967. Still, this restraining influence is of major policy importance to them, something they cannot afford not to cultivate to the best of their ability. Hence, despite the break in diplomatic relations in June 1967, Cairo left a few doors open to Washington. The realization remains, and will probably continue to remain, that if American military power neutralizes that of the Soviet Union in the Mediterranean, the Arabs are left at Israel's mercy—subject only to what Washington is willing to do to help.

Thus unless the Egyptian and Jordanian governments fall into the hands of madmen (a possibility to be discounted but not dismissed), or unless the United States government does so and throws itself unreservedly on Israel's side, it appears unlikely that the Arab-Israel conflict will become fully polarized along cold war lines. However, the question is a relative one, and failure on the part of the Arabs to make any progress toward recovery of lost territories for lack of American assistance may certainly be expected to sway the posture that now passes in Cairo for "nonalignment."

Meanwhile, a word should be said about the impact of the Arab-Israel problem on inter-Arab alignments. Since 1948 the problem of Israel has alternately brought rival Arab factions together and driven them apart; for while all factions have shared a common hostility, the inability of every Arab government to do anything about it has provided its enemies with a convenient stick with which to beat it. This writer is convinced—but others would disagree—that just as the Arab defeat of 1948 gave great impetus to the radicalization of Arab politics, by mobilizing alienated elements, dramatizing some of the weaknesses of existing Arab government and society, and creating a new social problem in the form of the refugees, so also in its turn this political radicalization has rendered the solution of problems with Israel vastly more difficult. The liberation of Palestine has become an integral part of what the radical nationalists portrayed as the long road toward the Arab renaissance. While 'Abd al-Nasir has plainly demonstrated that he has no special ability to liberate Palestine, it has nonetheless by general Arab consensus long been considered his special responsibility to do so. Consequently his non-performance of this duty has repeatedly been noted in public by his enemies of both left and right, but especially the right.

This pattern has now changed as a result of the 1967 defeat which imposed a common adversity on Egypt and Jordan, and the rise of the *fidaiyun* or Palestine guerrilla groups. Egypt and Jordan both face the problem of an immovable Israel occupation; both are dependent on subsidies from the oil monarchies; open inter-Arab antagonisms have been subdued, despite a variety of attitudes on how to deal with Israel.

At the same time, alongside the universal professions of solidarity with Egypt and Jordan there is the universal acclaim for the activities of the Palestine guerrilla groups, which undeniably undermine the efforts of Cairo and 'Amman to secure an Israel withdrawal through diplomacy. Looming in the background, meanwhile, is the hypothetical question of what united or divisive reactions from various Arab states might be expected to follow whatever accommodation with Israel might be negotiated. Given the disruptive role of the guerrillas, it is difficult to imagine that some pattern of antagonism will not arise sooner or later, even if the diplomatic impasse with Israel continues. But it is also hard to see that such antagonism could be one that polarized radical and conservative regimes; for whoever rules in Cairo and whoever rules in 'Amman, whatever their professed ideology, are bound to find the guerrillas constituting a threat to their interest in keeping their countries viable.

IV

Experience elsewhere in the world suggests that the United States and the Soviet Union are most likely to reach accommodations where spheres of influence are already clearly delineated and based on stable local political systems and local arrangements. The superpowers cannot impose stability on their own, not simply because of the difficulty in reaching agreement but more particularly because the dynamics of local instability are beyond their control and even their comprehension. In the Middle East the magnitude of this problem should be obvious. Both Russia and America have substantial commitments that cannot readily be undone, to local parties in deeply rooted conflict with each other, over problems that have no prospect of early resolution.

Nevertheless, there is a more hopeful side to the coin. The local roots of Middle East conflicts, plus the strong resistance of local patterns of attitude and behavior to outside manipulation, place some limits on the ability of outsiders who are drawn into local involvements to pursue their own goals very effectively. The great powers on occasion have almost as exasperating problems with their respective Middle East friends as they do with their opponents. Witness indications of mistrust of the Soviet Union in Egypt and Syria, and of the United States in Turkey and Iran—and even in Israel. In some ways the United States may feel relieved that the difficult Syrians and Egyptians are now Moscow's problem.

The superpowers have found that once they are closely involved, and have built up positions of presumed influence, the consequences are apt to be beyond their powers of prediction and control. With the passage of time and the accumulation of experience, they may become less responsive than before to one another's maneuvers, and less inclined to be alarmed at situations that would seem on the surface to provide preemptive openings, footholds, and opportunities for their rivals. And with the realization that the powers are less responsive, the hope arises that local parties will learn to readjust some of their own more intransigent attitudes. In the Middle East, however, only a fool would bet on it.

Contributors

JOHN S. BADEAU, former United States Ambassador to the UAR and director of the Middle East Institute at Columbia University, is the author of *The American Approach to the Arab World*.

FREDERICK C. BARGHOORN, author of *The Soviet Cultural Offensive* and *Soviet Foreign Propaganda*, is professor of political science at Yale University.

LINCOLN P. BLOOMFIELD, professor of political science at M.I.T. and director of the Arms Control Project at its Center for International Studies, is the coauthor of *Controlling Small Wars: A Strategy for the 1970s*.

JOHN C. CAMPBELL, director of political studies and senior research fellow at the Council on Foreign Relations, is an authority on the Balkans as well as the Middle East, and perhaps best known for his *Defense of the Middle East: Problems of American Policy*.

CHARLES FRANKEL, former Assistant Secretary of State for Educational and Cultural Affairs, and author, among many other works, of *The Neglected Aspect of Foreign Affairs*, is professor of philosophy at Columbia University.

FRANKLYN D. HOLZMAN, a professor of economics in the department of economics and in the Fletcher School of Law and Diplomacy, Tufts University, has written widely on domestic and external affairs of the Soviet Union.

J. C. HUREWITZ, professor of government at Columbia University, is the author, among other works, of *Middle East Politics: The Military Dimension*.

CHARLES ISSAWI, Ragnar Nurkse Professor of Economics at Columbia University, has written many books on the Middle East including *Egypt in Revolution*; he also edited *The Economic History of the Middle East, 1800-1914*.

ELIE KEDOURIE, author of *Nationalism* and *England and the Middle East: The Destruction of the Ottoman Empire, 1914-1921*, and editor of *Middle Eastern Studies*, a quarterly published in London, is professor of political science at the London School of Economics.

GEOFFREY KEMP, formerly a research associate of the Institute for Strategic Studies in London and now on the research staff of the Arms Control Project of the M.I.T. Center for International Studies, is a recognized authority on arms developments in nonindustrial states.

MALCOLM H. KERR, chairman of the department of political science at U.C.L.A. and a member of the university's Near Eastern Center, has written *The Arab Cold War 1958-1967: A Study of Ideology in Politics*.

SYLVIA KOWITT is a graduate student at Columbia University in the department of political science, specializing in the Middle East.

AMELIA C. LEISS, a research associate at the M.I.T Center for International Studies and deputy director of its Arms Control Project, is coauthor of *Controlling Small Wars: A Strategy for the 1970s*.

LAURENCE W. MARTIN, who received his Ph.D. from Yale, is professor of war studies at King's College, University of London. He is an authority on naval diplomacy and author of *The Sea in Modern Strategy*.

PHILIP E. MOSELY, professor of international relations, director of the European Institute, and associate dean of the Faculty of International Affairs at Columbia University, is the author of *The Kremlin and World Politics*.

GARDNER PATTERSON, whose most recent book examined *Discrimination in International Trade*, is now at Princeton, where he is professor of economics and international affairs, after wide-ranging service abroad for the United States government.

J. C. WYLIE, a rear admiral and former deputy commander in chief of the U.S. Naval Forces in Europe, is now commander of the Naval Base at Boston. He is the author of *Military Strategy: A General Theory of Power Control*.

I. WILLIAM ZARTMAN, a former naval officer, is professor of politics at New York University and executive secretary of the Middle East Studies Association. He has written, among other works, *Morocco: Problems of New Power* and *International Relations in the New Africa*.

Selected Bibliography

SYLVIA KOWITT

General

Campbell, John C. *Defense of the Middle East: Problems of American Policy.* Rev. ed. New York, Praeger, 1960.

Fainsod, Merle. "Some Reflections on Soviet-American Relations," *The American Political Science Review,* LXII (December 1968), 1,093-1,103.

Gordon, Kermit, ed. *Agenda for the Nation.* Washington, Brookings Institution, 1968.

Hurewitz, J. C. *Middle East Politics: The Military Dimension.* New York, Praeger, 1969.

Stevens, Georgiana G., ed. *The U.S. and the Middle East.* New York, Columbia University Press, 1964.

Ulam, Adam. *Expansion and Coexistence: The History of Soviet Foreign Policy 1917-1967.* New York, Praeger, 1968.

Williams, Ann. *Britain and France in the Middle East and North Africa.* New York, St. Martin's, 1968.

Wolf, Charles Jr. *United States Policy and the Third World: Problems and Analysis.* Boston, Little, Brown, 1967.

The Struggle for Military Supremacy

Bloomfield, Lincoln C. and Amelia C. Leiss. *Controlling Small Wars: A Strategy for the 1970's.* New York, Knopf, 1969.

Gasteyger, Curt. "Moscow and the Mediterranean," *Foreign Affairs,* XLVI (July 1968), 476-487.

Gilbert, S. P. "Wars of Liberation and Soviet Military Aid Policy," *Orbis,* X (Fall 1966), 839-858.

Herrick, Robert Waring. *Soviet Naval Strategy: Fifty Years of Theory and Practice.* Annapolis, U.S. Naval Institute, 1968.

Hoagland, John H. and John B. Teeple. "Regional Stability and Weapons Transfer: The Middle Eastern Case," *Orbis,* IX (Fall 1965), 714-728.

Hurewitz, J. C. "Russia and the Turkish Straits: A Revaluation of the Origins of the Problem," *World Politics,* XIV (July 1962), 605-632.

Kemp, Geoffrey. "Arms and Security: The Egypt-Israel Case," *Adelphi Paper,* No. 52. London, Institute for Strategic Studies, 1968.

Martin, Laurence W. *The Sea in Modern Strategy*. New York, Praeger, 1967.
————. "Russia's Navy: The Developing Threat," *Spectator*, October 4, 1968.
The Military Balance. Institute for Strategic Studies, London (published yearly).
Safran, Nadav. *From War to War: The Arab-Israeli Confrontation 1948-1967*. New York, Pegasus, 1969.
Schaar, Stuart H. "The Arms Race and Defense Strategy in North Africa," AUFS Report Service, North Africa Series, XIII (December 1967).
"Sources of Conflict in the Middle East," *Adelphi Paper*, No. 26. London, Institute for Strategic Studies, 1966.
Sutton, John L. and Geoffrey Kemp. "Arms to Developing Countries 1945-1965," *Adelphi Paper*, No. 28. London, Institute for Strategic Studies, 1966.
Wolfe, Thomas W. *The Soviet Quest for More Globally Mobile Military Power*. Memo. RM-5554-PR. Santa Monica, RAND, 1967.
Zartman, I. William. "The Mediterranean: Bridge or Barrier?" *U.S. Naval Institute Proceedings*, XCIII (February 1967), 63-71.

Economic Competition

Amuzegar, Jahangir. *Technical Assistance in Theory and Practice: The Case of Iran*. New York, Praeger, 1966.
Berliner, J. *Soviet Economic Aid: The New Aid and Trade Policy in Underdeveloped Countries*. New York, Praeger, 1958.
Bradley, Paul G. *The Economics of Crude Petroleum Production*. Amsterdam, North-Holland, 1967.
Campbell, Robert. *The Economics of Soviet Oil and Gas*. Baltimore, Johns Hopkins, 1968.
"The Financing of Economic Development," in *World Economic Survey, 1965*, Part I. New York, United Nations, 1966.
Cooper, Richard. *The Economics of Interdependence*. New York, McGraw-Hill, 1968.
Goldman, Marshall I. *Soviet Foreign Aid*. New York, Praeger, 1967.
Hansen, B. and G. Marzouk. *Development and Economic Policy in the UAR (Egypt)*. Amsterdam, North-Holland, 1965.
Heiss, Herta. "The Soviet Union in the World Market," *New Directions in the Soviet Economy*, U.S. Congress, Committee Print, Joint Economic Committee (Washington, 1966), 917-934.
Hershlag, Zvi Y. *Introduction to the Modern Economic History of the Middle East*. Leiden, Brill, 1964.
Hirschman, A. O. and Richard M. Bird. *Foreign Aid—A Critique and A Proposal, Essays in International Finance*. Princeton, Princeton University Press, 1968.
Holzman, Franklyn. "Soviet Foreign Trade Pricing and the Question of Discrimination: A 'Customs Union' Approach," *Review of Economics and Statistics*, XLIV (May 1962), 134-147.
Industrial Development in the Arab Countries. New York, United Nations, 1967.
Issawi, Charles. *Egypt in Revolution: An Economic Analysis*. London, Oxford University Press, 1963.
———— and Mohammed Yeganeh. *The Economics of Middle Eastern Oil*. New York, Praeger, 1963.
Kardouche, George K. *The UAR in Development*. New York, Praeger, 1967.

Laufer, Leopold. *Israel and the Developing Countries: New Approaches to Co-operation.* New York, The Twentieth Century Fund, 1967.

Mead, Donald C. *Growth and Structural Change in the Egyptian Economy.* Homewood, Ill., Richard D. Irwin, 1967.

Muller, Kurt. *The Foreign Aid Programs of the Soviet Bloc and Communist China.* New York, Walker, 1967.

O'Brien, Patrick. *The Revolution in Egypt's Economic System: From Private Enterprise to Socialism, 1952-1965.* London, Oxford University Press, 1966.

Pryor, Frederic L. *The Communist Foreign Trade System.* London, Allen & Unwin, 1963.

Ramazani, Rouhallah. *The Middle East and the Common Market.* Charlottesville, University Press of Virginia, 1964.

Sawyer, Carole A. *Communist Trade with Developing Countries: 1955-65.* New York, Praeger, 1966.

Soviet Economic Performance: 1966-67. Washington, U.S. Congress, Joint Economic Committee, 1968.

Studies on Selected Development Problems in Various Countries in the Middle East. New York, United Nations, 1967.

Tansky, Leo. "Soviet Foreign Aid to Less Developed Countries," *New Directions in the Soviet Economy*, U.S. Congress, Committee Print, Joint Economic Committee (Washington, 1966), 947-974.

Tugendhat, Christopher. *The Biggest Business.* New York, Putnam, 1967.

Watt, D. C. "Why There is No Future for the Suez Canal," *The New Middle East*, I (January 1969), 19-23.

Cultural Contest

Barghoorn, Frederick C. *The Soviet Cultural Offensive.* Princeton, Princeton University Press, 1960.

————. *Soviet Foreign Propaganda.* Princeton, Princeton University Press, 1964.

Batatu, John. "Some Preliminary Observations on the Beginnings of Communism in the Arab East," in *Islam and Communism*, ed. by Jaan Pennar. Munich-New York, Institute for the Study of the USSR, 1960.

Bennigsen, Alexandre and Chantal LeMercier-Quelquejay. *Islam in the Soviet Union.* New York, Praeger, 1967.

Berger, Morroe. *The Arab World Today.* New York, Doubleday, 1962.

Gallagher, Charles F. *The United States and North Africa: Morocco, Algeria and Tunisia.* Cambridge, Harvard University Press, 1963.

Harris, George S. *The Origins of Communism in Turkey.* Stanford, Hoover Institution, 1967.

Lewis, Bernard. *The Middle East and the West.* Bloomington, Indiana University Press, 1964.

The Mizan Newsletter: A Review of Soviet Writing on the Middle East. London.

Pennar, Jaan. "The Arabs, Marxism and Moscow: A Historical Survey," *The Middle East Journal*, XXII (Autumn 1968), 433-447.

Polk, William R. and R. L. Chambers. *Beginnings of Modernization in the Middle East: The Nineteenth Century.* Chicago, University of Chicago Press, 1968.

Proctor, J. Harris, ed. *Islam and International Relations.* New York, Praeger, 1965.

Sinai, I. Robert. *The Challenge of Modernization: The West's Impact on the Non-Western World.* New York, Norton, 1965.

Rustow, Dankwart A. and Robert E. Ward. *Political Modernization in Japan and Turkey.* Princeton, Princeton University Press, 1964.

Quest for Stability

Armstrong, John A. "Soviet Relations with the Middle East," in *The Soviet Union: A Half-Century of Communism,* ed. by Kurt L. London. Baltimore, Johns Hopkins, 1968.

Badeau, John S. *The American Approach to the Arab World.* New York, Harper, 1968.

Campbell, John C. "The Middle East," in *Agenda for the Nation,* ed. by Kermit Gordon. Washington, Brookings Institution, 1968.

Cremeans, Charles. *The Arabs and the World. Nasser's Arab Nationalist Policy.* New York, Praeger, 1963.

Draper, Theodore. *Israel and World Politics.* New York, Viking, 1968.

Howard, Michael and Robert Hunter. "Israel and the Arab World: The Crisis of 1967," *Adelphi Paper,* No. 41. London, Institute for Strategic Studies, 1967.

Kerr, Malcolm. *The Arab Cold War 1958-1967. A Study of Ideology in Politics.* 2nd ed. London, Oxford University Press, 1967.

———. "Coming to Terms with Nasser: Attempts and Failures," *International Affairs,* XLIII (January 1967), 65-84.

Khouri, Fred J. *The Arab-Israeli Dilemma.* Syracuse, Syracuse University Press, 1968.

Kissinger, Henry A. "Central Issues of American Foreign Policy," in *Agenda for the Nation,* ed. by Kermit Gordon. Washington, Brookings Institution, 1968.

Laqueur, Walter Z. "Russia Enters the Middle East," *Foreign Affairs,* XLVII (January 1969), 296-308.

Lewis, Bernard. "The Consequences of Defeat," *Foreign Affairs,* XLVI (January 1968), 321-335.

Mosely, Philip E. *The Kremlin and World Politics. Studies in Soviet Policy and Action.* New York, Random House, 1960.

Sayegh, Fayez A., ed. *The Dynamics of Neutralism in the Arab World: A Symposium.* San Francisco, Chandler, 1964.

Seale, Patrick. *The Struggle for Syria: A Study of Post-War Arab Politics, 1945-1958.* New York, Oxford, 1965.

Shulman, Marshall D. "Relations with the Soviet Union," in *Agenda for the Nation,* ed. by Kermit Gordon. Washington, Brookings Institution, 1968.

Stock, Ernest. *Israel on the Road to Sinai: A Small State in a Test of Power.* Ithaca, Cornell University Press, 1967.

Wheeler, Geoffrey. "Soviet and Chinese Policies in the Middle East," *The World Today,* XXII (February 1966), 64-78.

Yost, Charles W. "How It Began," *Foreign Affairs,* XLVI (January 1968), 304-320.

Index